LEST WE FORGET

The Most Outstanding War Memorials

of the First World War

DAVID P HEARN

ELGAR ESTATES PUBLISHING

www.commemorativeplaques.co.uk

First published in 2018 by
Elgar Estates Publishing
Meadow House
Ashington
West Sussex
RH20 3AZ

Design and Origination
MIKE SHORT

A catalogue record for this book is available from the British Library

ISBN 978-1-902269-03-0
Printed and bound by
THOMSON PRESS (INDIA) LTD

CONTENTS

Editor's Notes

In the early 20th century Britain learnt a new form of commemorating the dead – the War Memorial. We were approached by Civic Voice to produce a book which would coincide with the centenary of the end of the First World War, to feature the Grade I and Grade II* memorials that were erected to remember those who had died in the war. Civic Voice helps communities ensure that their local war memorials are protected.

Over 700,000 British soldiers had been killed, and tens of thousands of memorials were erected during and after the war. No one knows the exact figure, so widespread was the nation's grief. There is hardly a town or village across the country without a memorial, many taking the form of a simple cross or an obelisk.

The term the 'Great War' was first used in print in 1920 in The First World War by Charles a Court Repington. He was using it to emphasize the global nature of the war rather than its sequential nature. Different memorials give different years for the end of the war. The Armistice came into force at 11.00am on 11th November 1918, and fighting on the western front finished. However, hostilities continued elsewhere and the peace treaty was not agreed and registered until 21st October 1919. Kaiser Wilhelm had abdicated on 9th November 1918, which allowed the right amount of time for a politically-timed Armistice on the "11th hour, of the 11th day, of the 11th month."

Historic England's Listings are a veritable treasure-trove of Britain's history. They include clock towers and rollercoasters; pie shops and piers; and war memorials. We recognised that this would be an opportunity for Historic England to explain how decisions are made about the selection of such heritage assets, to give them greater protection, ensuring that any proposed changes that affect their appearance or character will require consent.

War Memorials Trust is the charity that provides advice and information for the protection and conservation of war memorials in the UK, and they have written a piece to describe their work.

There are just two memorials to a woman – both are for Edith Cavell. Very few women are depicted on the memorials, and although we cannot re-write history, we examine the key contribution that women made in the war effort, and the vital roles that they played.

Thirty two architects and forty-eight sculptors were involved with the memorials in the book. We have produced brief biographies alongside the memorial with which they were involved, and the most prolific feature with more information in a separate piece.

Three thousand volumes of war poems were published during the war and in the years immediately following. A number of quotations from poets were used on memorials. Amongst a selection of poems, we demonstrate how Rupert Brooke caught the optimism of the opening months of the war, which expressed an idealism about war that contrasts strongly with poetry published later in the conflict. By this stage, the poems articulated the terror of the trenches and the futility of war.

Douglas J Eaton
Editor

Introduction

Memorials to those killed in war was, prior, to the Crimean War of 1853-56 something reserved for officers. The ordinary soldiers and sailors were treated with little or no respect, with their remains being buried in mass and hastily dug graves. For example, visitors to the battle field of Waterloo reported seeing arms and legs protruding from the mass graves so inadequate were the burials that were carried out.

There are some memorials in the UK to those killed in the Crimean War, most remarkably the Grade II listed, Guards Crimean War Memorial in Waterloo Place, Westminster, but it was not until the Second Boer War of 1899-1902 that we see a large scale process of building memorials to the "ordinary serviceman" throughout Britain and the Commonwealth.

It was, however, the First World War that saw the greatest single memorialisation process this country has ever seen, or is ever likely to see, and the stimulus for this came in the decision of the British Government in 1915 that bodies would not be repatriated at the end of the war. Previously, families were able, at their own expense, to have the body of a family member returned to the UK for burial. The catastrophic losses of the First World War, even by 1915, coupled with the difficulties of recovering and identifying bodies meant that repatriation was not going to be logistically possible. It was this decision, coupled with the previously unheard of level of casualties, that was responsible for the surge in creating local and, indeed, national memorials.

When the numbers of those being killed became apparent, as early as 1915 plans had been set in place in a number of towns and by large employers for the creation of memorials to mark the sacrifice of citizens or employees who had been killed in the war.

Whilst the Imperial (later Commonwealth) War Graves Commission (IWGC) was established at the suggestion of Major-General Sir Fabian Ware to consider and design cemeteries and memorials around the world, their influence also extended to the United Kingdom. Ware's attempts to join the Army had initially been rejected as he was deemed to be too old. The IWGC commissioned three of

Tyne Cot Cementry

the most important architects of the day – Sir Herbert Baker, Sir Reginald Blomfield and Sir Edwin Lutyens – to design cemeteries and memorials.

These three architects were also much in demand to design memorials in this country and many by Baker and Lutyens are recorded in this book. Although there are no memorials by Sir Reginald Blomfield in this volume, his work will be familiar to many because he designed the 'Cross of Sacrifice', sometimes referred to as the 'Blomfield Cross', which stands in all cemeteries that contain 40 or more war graves and, as such, is as familiar a sight in the UK as it is in the cemeteries of France and Belgium. Blomfield was also responsible for the design of The Menin Gate at Ypres in Belgium (below).

Rudyard Kipling was also employed by the IWGC to act as a literary advisor for the language to be used on war memorials and, as well as "Lest we Forget", he was responsible for inscriptions to be found on many memorials including: "Their name Liveth for Evermore", "Known unto God" and "The Glorious Dead", which although he did not write, his recommendations did ensure that  these expressions have passed into the psyche of remembrance and memorialisation.

Styles of memorial differ from the triumphant and militaristic, featuring soldiers actually engaged in fighting, through grieving soldiers mourning their fallen comrades, to the almost cold austerity portrayed by, and often copied, Cenotaph in Whitehall, London which was designed by Sir Edwin Lutyens in the matter of a few days. Whilst not totally absent from memorials, 'death' is very rarely portrayed and, indeed, the official guidance on memorials was that dead bodies should not be portrayed. Whilst it is obvious that death is the very reason for the memorial, that death is not the brutal, pointless outcome of the war but, instead, it is a noble thing that was the unfortunate cost of defending King and Empire or families and, especially children who appear surprisingly often in memorials. Equally surprisingly, 'victory' is also comparatively rarely depicted, and where it is depicted it is so allegorically, a foot on an enemy helmet or a creature, often a serpent, being slain by an heroic or classical warrior.

The word cenotaph literally means "empty tomb" – a tomb for someone who is actually buried elsewhere. The national memorial in Whitehall, London which was often replicated by Lutyens in different sizes, in other memorials is, perhaps, the definitive war memorial, as illustrated by the fact that the word cenotaph is often used as a generic description of all war memorials regardless of the actual style.

How can anyone have a "favourite" war memorial? They are all sombre reminders of horrific events and yet, to me, one in particular deserves special mention for a number of reasons. This is not a 'national' memorial in the metropolis, neither was it designed by one of the great architects of the day. Instead it is a Grade I listed memorial, which marks it as being of "exceptional interest", in a small village in Yorkshire.

For a village to have one listed memorial is rare but Sledmere, East Yorkshire has two - the Waggoner's Memorial and the Sledmere Cross, which are within a short distance of each other, and both owe their construction to members of the Sykes family. They had been merchants in Huddersfield and subsequently became substantial landowners with a Baronetcy that dates to 1783.

The 6th Baron, Sir Tatton Benvenuto Mark Sykes, was a soldier, diplomat and Conservative MP in addition to managing his 34,000 acres (120 sq. kilometres) estate. He is probably best known as the co-author of the 1916 Sykes-Picot Agreement, which examined the splitting up of the former Ottoman Empire between Britain, France and Russia at the end of the First World War. Despite having neither architectural nor formal artistic training, Sykes

A soldier of the Great War known unto God

designed bas- relief panels that were added to the Sledmere Cross that is a copy of an Eleanor Cross, that was erected by his father, and then went on to design the Waggoner's Memorial.

The Waggoner's Memorial is not a large, imposing edifice. It is only around 6ft (1.8 m) tall, and yet it is fascinating in its design, which includes an inscription in Yorkshire dialect and carvings of figures telling the story of the Waggoner's Reserve during the war. The style of the memorial is reminiscent, on a much smaller scale, of Trajan's Column in Rome. The Waggoner's Reserve was a territorial unit raised by Sir Mark Sykes in 1912, with the great foresight that if there was to be a war the army would have need for trained waggon drivers. Some 1,100 men, mainly from Yorkshire, signed up and at the outbreak of the war they were posted, with little or no military training, to the Army Service Corps and the Royal Engineers.

Any one of the above facts would single out this memorial as being special, but if you add the fact that the carving was carried out by Carlo Domenico Magnoni, who was an Italian anarchist and, effectively, a refugee in London, the interest just intensifies. Sadly Sir Mark Sykes did not live to see the memorial completed because he died in Paris of Spanish Flu in February 1919 while attending the Paris Peace Conference.

At a time when visiting the graves of family members was a weekly ritual, and cemeteries were almost places of pilgrimage, the importance of war memorials in villages, towns and cities cannot be over emphasised. They were the focal point for families who may never be able to get to visit the graves of their loved ones if, indeed, there was a grave with their name on at all. War Memorials have become so familiar that it is easy for them to be overlooked as we rush through our lives, which are a world away from the horrors of the First World War. The memorials featured in this book were, and still are, reminders of the sacrifice made by many hundreds of thousands of ordinary people caught up in extra-ordinary events, a reminder then and now not of the glory of war but of the sacrifice. So instead of rushing past them, maybe we should linger, even if only for a few minutes, to pay our respects to those who died, and appreciate the efforts of the architects and sculptors who designed such wonderful memorials in their honour.

David P Hearn
Author

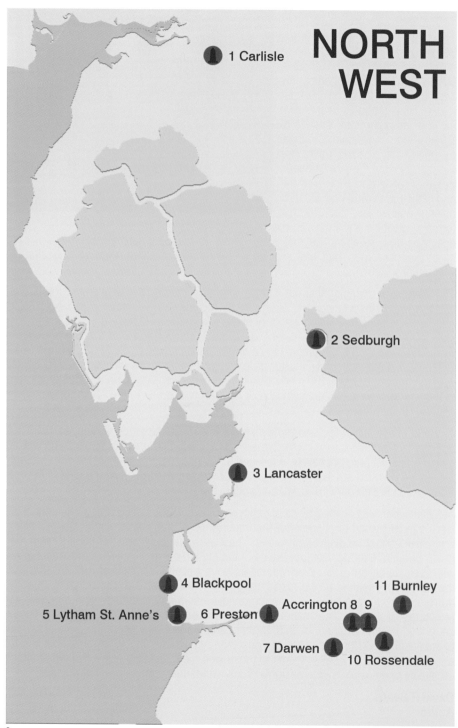

1 Carlisle **NORTH WEST**

2 Sedburgh

3 Lancaster

4 Blackpool

11 Burnley

5 Lytham St. Anne's   6 Preston   Accrington 8 9

7 Darwen

10 Rossendale

CONTENTS

Map reference and Memorial Name · Page

1. Cumberland and Westmorland Joint Counties' War Memorial

Rickerby Park, Carlisle, Cumbria, CA3

Grade II*

Unveiled on 27th May 1922 by Hugh Lowther, the 5th Earl of Lonsdale, Lord Lieutenant of Cumberland. Lowther held a commission in the Westmorland and Cumberland Yeomanry, and during the Second Boer War he was assistant Adjutant-General for the Imperial Yeomanry.

During the First World War he was a recruiting officer for both men and horses, raising his own "Pals" Battalion – the Lonsdales; 11th Battalion the Border Regiment. Lowther helped to found *Our Dumb Friends League* which provided medical care for animals injured during the war. This organisation later became the animal charity, Blue Cross. Henry Williams, Bishop of Carlisle, carried out the dedication and the service was attended by over 5,000 people from across Westmorland and Cumberland.

Design Features:

The memorial is situated at the centre of Rickerby Park, north of the River Eden in Carlisle. It comprises a broad raised platform approximately 29ft (9m) wide, approached by stone steps at the south. The raised platform is constructed of three courses of massive stone blocks; two courses of quarry-faced granite topped by an ashlar parapet with a large terminal block at each angle. It is surrounded by a square enclosure formed of speared cast-iron railings and a cast-iron gate.

The platform supports a cenotaph approximately 39ft (12m) high which is built of Shap granite ashlar and has a tapering rectangular shaft on a chamfered three-tiered base. The shaft rises to a sub-cornice which is enriched by foliage carvings including palm branches, and on the top is a tomb decorated with a laurel wreath. The lower part of the shaft is carved in the front with the crests of Carlisle, Cumberland, the Royal Navy, the Army, the Royal Air Force and medical services. On the back are those of the Border Regiment, the Westmorland and Cumberland Yeomanry Cavalry, and the Cumberland Artillery.

The Story behind The Memorial:

Rickerby Park was laid out in the 1830s as part of the setting for Rickerby House. 68 acres of the park were purchased as a war memorial park by The Carlisle Citizens League and the City Council in 1922. The League had been formed during the first week of the First World War to help ex-servicemen, and it founded the 'Lonsdale Battalion' which looked after soldiers and sailors who were passing through Carlisle.

After the war plans for a memorial were discussed; with initial proposals including a triumphal arch and a new public hall, which were debated at a meeting on 15th November 1918. In June 1919 The League agreed to take an option on Rickerby Park as a suitable site for a memorial, and Carlisle City Council subsequently decided to contribute to a joint scheme that included the acquisition of the park. It was proposed that Rickerby Park itself should also serve as a 'living memorial' and a place of recreation. Near the centre, approached by footpaths, would be a stone cenotaph and, in order to improve access from the city centre, a bridge would be erected across the River Eden.

Ex-servicemen constructed the foundations of both the cenotaph and bridge piers. The cenotaph itself was built by John Laing and Son Ltd while Redpath Brown & Co of Glasgow was appointed to construct the bridge across the River Eden. The total cost of the project was £21,000; comprising, £11,500 for the purchase of the park, £4,500 for the bridge and £5,000 for the cenotaph. A substantial proportion of the cost was raised by public subscription.

The railings were repaired in 2005 at a cost of £2,000 following flood damage and in 2014 conservation work was carried out at a total cost of £14,500. The conservation work involved replacing broken sections of the railings and repainting them; installing a new gate; re-pointing the cenotaph and cleaning the stonework; removing foliage within the enclosure; and planting a new avenue of trees on the approach to the memorial.

The Inscription

On the base is the inscription, which is in raised lettering, and reads: TO THE IMMORTAL MEMORY OF THE MEN AND WOMEN OF CUMBERLAND AND WESTMORLAND WHO GAVE THEIR LIVES DURING THE GREAT WAR AND IN HONOUR OF THE GLORIOUS SERVICES OF THE BORDER REGIMENT WESTMORLAND AND CUMBERLAND YEOMANRY CUMBERLAND BRIGADE ROYAL FIELD ARTILLERY WESTMORLAND DETACHMENT R.A.M.C. Beneath it is a bronze plaque, which is inscribed in raised lettering: ALSO COMMEMORATING THOSE WHO GAVE THEIR LIVES IN WORLD WAR II (1939-1945) AND SUBSEQUENT CONFLICTS.

2. Sedbergh School – War Memorial Cloister

Sedbergh School, Station Road, Sedbergh, Cumbria, LA10

Grade II*

Unveiled on 6th July, 1924 by General Sir Charles Harrington, and the dedication was carried out by Archbishop Henry Lowther Clarke, the first Archbishop of Melbourne, Australia who was a former pupil of Sedbergh School.

General Harrington was a career soldier who served in the Second Boer War and held a number of staff positions during the First World War, including a spell as Deputy Chief of the Imperial General Staff from 1918 to 1920. After this, he assumed command of the Army of the Black Sea that was occupying parts of Turkey. In 1924 Hartington was General Officer Commanding Northern Command.

Designed by Sir John Hubert Worthington, who was born in Alderley Edge, Cheshire and educated at Sedbergh School and Manchester School of Architecture. Having passed his ARIBA (Associate of the Royal Institution of British Architects) exams in 1912, Worthington became an assistant to Sir Edwin Lutyens.

He opened his own practice in Manchester in 1913, and from 1923 to 1928 he was Professor of Architecture at the Royal College of Art, before becoming a lecturer of Architecture at Oxford University in 1929. Worthington received an OBE in 1929 and was knighted in 1949.

Design Features:

Built from sandstone ashlar, the cloisters are built into a slope in the ground in front of a class room block, so that the top of them forms a grassed forecourt to that building. A flight of steps descends from the centre to the centre of the cloister area, which has a wide U-plan to include a 5-bay arcade flanked by short but wide 3-bay arcaded wings; all the arches are round headed. The main arcade has short square piers with a raised square panel on the front of each. Moulded imposts and moulded heads to the arches with keystones run up to a continuous frieze and a plain parapet.

Each wing has a tall central arch flanked by smaller window arches; in the spaces above the arches are lion masks and a raised pane on the parapet has MDCCCCXIV (1914) on the left and MDCCCCXVIII (1918) on the right. Inside the cloisters each bay has a dome-vaulted ceiling, and the rear wall has an archway to the central steps flanked, on each side, by 4 bays of blind arcading. Each blind arch contains a wreathed panel with painted lists of names, the inner four have 248 names from the First World War and the outer four panels have 192 names from the Second World War.

On the forecourt is an hexagonal stone bench with the names of three former pupils who were recipients of the Victoria Cross – Major-General J.S. Campbell, 2nd Lieut. G.W. Gunn and Flg. Off. K Campbell.

The concept of the memorial is that the steps lead downwards into the ground as if in a burial, however, instead of darkness the steps lead to light.

12

The Story behind The Memorial:

The five arches of the memorial represent the five houses of the school. The Cloisters were completely restored in 2005 at a cost of £130,000.

The Inscription

The frieze has the inscription: THEIR NAME LIVETH FOR EVERMORE whilst a raised panel in the centre of the parapet is inscribed: DVRA VIRVM NVTRIX (A stern nurse of men) the school motto.

Back to Rest
Lt. Noel Hodgson MC (Died 1st July 1916. Age 23)

Death whining down from heaven,
Death roaring from the ground,
Death stinking in the nostril,
Death shrill in every sound.
Doubling we charged and conquered –
Hopeless we struck and stood,
Now when the fight is ended,
We know it was good

3. The War Memorial, Westfield War Memorial Village

Storey Avenue, Lancaster, Lancashire, LA1
Grade II*

Unveiled by General Sir Archibald Hunter on 4th August 1926. Although born in London, Hunter had strong ties to the City of Lancaster having joined the King's Own 4th Lancashire Regiment as a nineteen-year-old sub lieutenant straight out of the Royal Military College, Sandhurst in 1875. After serving in the Sudan and distinguishing himself in the Second Boer War, he served as Governor of Gibraltar from 1910 to 1913, after which he was appointed Colonel of the Kings Own (Royal Lancaster Regiment), which was a position he held until 1926. Hunter was considered too old for a field command in 1914 and, instead, served initially as General Officer Commanding Aldershot Training Centre and later as general Officer Commanding Aldershot Command. In the 1918 election, Hunter was elected Coalition Conservative Member of Parliament for Lancaster, although he did not seek re-election in the 1922 General Election.

Sculpted by Jennie Delahunt who was born in 1876, in Hanley, Staffordshire, and trained at the Manchester Municipal School of Art. Little is known of Delahunt's life or career, although in the 1920s she was modelling mistress at Lancaster School of Art. She later went on to teach art at Lancaster Grammar School for Girls.

Landscape Architect: Thomas Mawson (1861-1933) was born in Nether Wyredale, Lancashire and left school at the age of 12. Having worked initially in the building trade in Lancaster, Mawson moved to London to work in a nursery. After becoming proficient in garden design, Mawson and two of his brothers started the Lakeland Nursery in Windermere in the 1880s. The business was a success and this allowed him to concentrate on garden design, his work being a blend of architecture and planting. Mawson was involved in private garden design as well as the construction of municipal parks, not only in Britain but also in Europe and Canada. From 1910 to 1924 Mawson lectured at the School of Civic Design at the University of Liverpool. In 1923 he became President of the Town Planning Institute and in 1929 and was elected as the first President of the Institute of Landscape Architects.

Design Features:

The memorial is set in the centre of a memorial village and comprises a bronze statue of two soldiers. One soldier is standing, wearing his helmet with his rifle across his shoulder: he is supporting the other soldier, who is bare headed, on his knees and appears to be wounded. The standing soldier is offering the wounded soldier a drink from his canteen. Both soldiers are in battle dress and shown as if on a battlefield.

The statue stands on a sandstone, rectangular ashlar plinth, which has re-entrant corners and sits on a base of two steps.

The Story behind The Memorial:

As the First World War was drawing to a close, Mawson started to suggest the construction of a memorial village in Lancaster as a permanent memorial to the men of Lancaster and the surrounding area who had died in the war. The concept was that the village would provide work and accommodation for disable veterans of the war.

The Ministry of Pensions did not support the idea although there was considerable local support, and Herbert Storey, a Lancaster businessman, donated 16 acres of land to the project. Herbert Storey was a director of Storey Bros, a linoleum manufacturer in Lancaster, as well as a number of other businesses and was a notable philanthropist in Lancaster. The full cost of the memorial was paid by Storey.

By 1919 the Westfield War Memorial Village had been planned and it was formally opened by General Haig on 24th November 1924. Following the First World War, Haig was very involved in supporting disabled ex-servicemen. The village was designed as a series of streets which radiate from a central war memorial.

The two soldiers were modelled on veterans of the war: the kneeling soldier is based on Private Henry Allen of Rochdale, while the standing soldier is based on Captain Jack Ward of Walney Island.

The memorial is one of only two in this book where the sculptor was a woman.

[Editors Note: The author's great-grandfather was a regular soldier at the time of the outbreak of the First World War; having served in the Kings Own Royal Lancaster Regiment during the Second Boer War. He was wounded at the Battle of Mons in 1914 and was invalided out of the Army. In 1916 he re-joined the 2nd Battalion Kings Own Royal Lancaster Regiment only to be killed in action in what is now Iraq. His name is on the war memorials in Morecambe and the Basra Memorial in Iraq]

The Inscription

The plinth is inscribed: THE WESTFIELD WAR MEMORIAL VILLAGE FOUNDED IN GRATEFUL REMEMBRANCE OF THE SACRIFICE MADE BY THE KING'S OWN ROYAL LANCASTER REGIMENT THE LANCASTER BATTERIES OF ARTILLERY AND OTHER LANCASTRIANS IN THE GREAT WAR 1914 – 1918 THE CHILDREN OF SIR THOMAS STOREY GAVE THE PROPERTY THE COTTAGES WERE BUILT BY PUBLIC AND INDIVIDUAL SUBSCRIPTION THE VILLAGE WAS DESIGNED BY THOMAS HAYTON MAWSON.

4. Blackpool War Memorial

Princess Parade, Blackpool, FY1

Grade II*

Unveiled on 10th November 1923 by Lt General T.E. Topping with the dedication by Reverend A.W.R. Little in front of a congregation of around 10,000. The two accompanying structures which carry the names of the 907 fallen were unveiled by the mothers of two Victoria Cross winners: Lt Victor Smith and Lt Stanley Boughey, neither of whom survived the war.

Designed by Ernest Prestwich, who studied at Liverpool School of Architecture and the Department of Civic Design. In 1910 he won the competition to complete Port Sunlight Village, the 'model village' built by Lord Leverhulme to house the workforce at his factory. Prestwich was elected as an Associate of the Royal Institute of British Architects in 1918 and a Fellow in 1928.

Sculpted by Gilbert Ledward

Design Features:

The memorial is made from white granite and takes the form of a tall – 100 ft (30.4m) - obelisk on a square pedestal all of which stands on a three-tier plinth and a stepped platform. The base of the obelisk has a raised band of incised Greek key ornament with an overlaid laurel wreath in the centre of each side. Blackpool's coat of arms is incised on the front and back (east and west) sides. The front and rear faces of the pedestal break forward slightly and each has a broad raised panel which is framed in palm branches.

The north and south faces of the pedestal have detailed bronze relief panels in which figures proceed towards a central allegorical female figure. On the south side, which is labelled '1914', the central figure depicts Britannia in the guise of 'Justice'. She is surrounded by young men, some in uniform and others apparently leaving their work to enlist. On the left-hand side, a pregnant woman holding a child looks on. The north side, labelled '1918' depicts 'Peace' holding a dove and a wreath, with her head bowed.

The left side of the plaque depicts war weary soldiers standing in front of an artillery piece, and over the body of a dead German soldier. The right side shows a grieving woman and man, a grieving nurse, a girl and her cat and a bare-chested youth in a martial pose, with a rifle over his shoulder. The reliefs, which wrap around the returns of the front and rear faces of the pedestal, depict figures "guarding" and they flank the inscribed panels. On the front there are a pair of soldiers, and to the rear, an airman and a seaman.

There are projections to the north and south sides of the platform which carry a pair of free-standing granite structures that are based on Sir Edwin Lutyens Stone of Remembrance. These structures have shallow-pitched lids of cast bronze. Each slope is divided into 16 panels with bead and reel frames and carries the names of the dead from the First World War.

At the front of the plinth is a third granite structure with a single sloping lid in bronze, with the names of the 616 dead of the Second World War together with those from subsequent conflicts.

To the east is a semi-circular singers' platform known as the 'choir loft', which was installed in 2008, and is dedicated to those who struggle for freedom in all conflicts. It is built in white granite with a contrasting band of blue granite inscribed: SING SOFTLY. BE STILL. CEASE.

This forms an integral part of the listing ensemble.

The memorial is enclosed by granite kerbs with a series of low, tapering granite posts and chain links.

The entrance to the south is flanked by squat cruciform piers with a bronze lion mask roundel to the front face, surmounted by a fluted bronze column with acanthus leaf ornament and a globe lamp.

The Story behind The Memorial:

The memorial was built in an existing sunken garden on Blackpool's north promenade. The cost of the memorial was £17,000, which was paid by the Blackpool County Borough Council from its wartime munition profits.

The memorial is one of comparatively few that includes women from the home front and is very rare in its portrayal of a dead German. Depicting dead bodies, in general, was not encouraged and it was more usual that a German helmet, or some sort of allegorical creature, was used to depict the defeat of Germany.

The builders were H A Clegg and Sons and the stonemasons were Kirkpatrick Stonemasons.

A permanent projection and illumination project has been installed to the memorial in which still photography and moving images are projected onto the upper 70ft of the memorial with a changing programme each year.

The memorial was cleaned and repaired in 2009 with the assistance of grants from War Memorials Trust, English Heritage and the Wolfson Foundation.

The Inscription

The main inscription is in panels to the front and back of the memorial and is incised, it reads: IN MEMORY OF OUR GLORIOUS DEAD 1914 -1918 1939 - 1945.
To the north and south sides of the platform, on the outward faces of the free-standing granite structures are the inscriptions: THEIR NAME LIVETH FOR EVERMORE and LEST WE FORGET

5. Lytham St Anne's War Memorial

Ashton Gardens, St George's Road, Lytham St Anne's, Lancashire, FY8

Grade II*

Unveiled on 12th October 1924 by Alderman Charles Critchley, whose son Burton 'Plum' Critchley had been killed whilst serving with the Royal Air Force in 1918. Also present at the unveiling were the Rt. Hon. Stephen Walsh, Secretary of State for War in the Labour Government – Walsh had lost a son in the war; Major General Sir Cecil Lothian Nicholson whose only son was killed at the Battle of Arras; and Lt General Sir Richard Butler, General Officer Commanding-in-Chief for Western Command.

Also in attendance were 1,000 ex-servicemen, together with 9 children of fallen servicemen who each received a gold medal inscribed with the coat of arms of the borough.

Designed by Thomas Smith Tait who was born in Paisley and, following education at the John Neilson Institution, he entered into an apprenticeship with an architect in his home town. Following further studies at the Glasgow School of Art, Tait travelled in Europe in 1904 and 1905 after which he joined the architectural practice of Sir John Burnet.

Tait was a leading exponent of the Art Deco and Streamline Moderne styles and worked a number of important private and institutional commissions, including the Daily Telegraph building in Fleet Street, Unilever House and the Pylons for the Sydney Harbour Bridge.

Sculpted by Walter Marsden, who was born near Accrington in Lancashire where his father was a blacksmith. As an apprentice at the Accrington Brick and Tile Company the owners, the McAlpine family, recognised his potential and encouraged him to study at the Accrington Technical School from where he went on to study at the Manchester Municipal College of Art.

During the First World War Marsden served as an officer in the Loyal North Lancashire Regiment and was awarded the Military Cross. After the war Marsden continued his studies at the Royal College of Art and was a member of the Art Workers Guild and the Royal Society of British Sculptors.

Design Features:

At the head of the memorial is a bronze figure of a woman in a classical robe with both arms raised. She stands on a hemisphere on a white granite pylon which is on a stepped pedestal and plinth. The pylon has slightly raised panels on each face. There are projections on the two sides of the plinth which support over-life size bronze statues. On the left is the seated figure of an infantryman, who is holding his rifle by the muzzle, with his head turned sideways and his left fist is clenched.

To the right side is a seated woman representing a wife who has been told of her husband's death. She gazes ahead and appears not to notice the pleadings of a naked child on her lap.

Panels wrap around the left and right returns of the pedestal depicting, respectively, a nurse bandaging a soldier's hand, and a departing soldier who is embracing his wife, whilst their small daughter is tugging her mother's shawl. The rear face of the pedestal has a bronze panel, which also wraps around the sides. This panel depicts a procession of soldiers returning from the battlefield, including stretcher-bearers, men carrying their wounded comrades, and a line of men blinded by gas.

The Story behind The Memorial:

The construction of the memorial was enabled by a donation of £10,000 from businessman and Liberal politician Lord Ashton. James Williamson, 1st Baron Ashton, who ran a highly successful coated fabrics business in Lancaster which produced oilcloth and linoleum.

The memorial is rare for its depiction of both a dead soldier and some gassed soldiers in the 'story' that is portrayed on the reliefs. The inclusion of dead and wounded soldiers on memorials was discouraged by the authorities.

There was a booklet produced for the unveiling ceremony which gives the thoughts of the sculptor on his work. It is important to remember that the sculptor served as an infantry officer on the Western Front during the war. The booklet described the mother and child sculpture on the monument as showing "the agony of mind caused to womanhood by the tragedies of war. [The mother] sits in anguish and sorrowful reverie, quite unconscious that her babe is looking to her for a mother's love. She looks, as it were, into the unknown future, realising what her sacrifice means, and wondering why". In a similar way, the sculpture of the soldier was described as depicting: "The constant nervous strain of continuous trench warfare, brought about the ever-present feeling that danger was lurking near, a state of tension which, in the opinion of the artist, was the cause of more mental agony than any other phase of the War". Contemporary newspaper reports describe the memorial as "a monument which arouses deep emotion", and "a vivid and impressive expression of the sorrows of war time".

The Inscription

The front (west) face of the pedestal has a rectangular bronze panel with raised lettering inscribed: 1914: NAMES OF THE FALLEN: 1918, and has 170 names beneath, flanked on the left by relief figures of an airman and a seaman, and on the right by two infantrymen.
The front and rear faces of the pylon have a plaque inscribed: IN MEMORY OF THOSE WHO FELL 1939 – 1945, each with 64 names. A further plaque commemorates the dead of later conflicts.

6. Preston War Memorial

Market Place, Preston PR1
Grade I

Unveiled on 13th June 1926 by Admiral of the Fleet Earl Jellicoe of Scapa. Jellico was a career sailor and had seen service in the Anglo-Egyptian War and the Boxer Rebellion before commanding the Grand Fleet at the Battle of Jutland in 1916. In 1926 he was in retirement, having served as Governor General of New Zealand from 1920 to 1924. Canon Morris, the Mayor's Chaplain read the dedicatory prayer.

Sculpted by Henry Pegram who was born in London and attended the West London School of Art. In 1881 he entered the Royal Academy schools, after which he went to work as an assistant to Hamo Thornycroft. Pegram became a member of the Art Workers Guild in 1890 and became an Associate of the Royal Academy in 1904, becoming a Royal Academician in 1922. His war memorial work also includes 'Victory' on the memorial at the Cunard Building in Liverpool, and the Edith Cavell monument in Norwich.

Design Features:

Market Place, Preston, is the biggest open space in central Preston and contains, as well as the War Memorial, a number of Grade I and Grade II listed buildings. The memorial is almost 69ft (21m) tall and comprises a tapering Portland Stone pylon with panelled faces that are reminiscent of the Boer War obelisk that previously stood on the site. On the top of the pylon there is a large sepulchral block with shallow pediments, above which is a large block decorated with swags to each side and held by cherubs at the corners.

At the base, the pylon stands on a large slab with a block, supported on brackets, projecting to the front to represent the sarcophagus. On the front of the sarcophagus is a bronze cross within a wreath. To the front face of the pylon is an opening like a doorway, with a pediment supported by columns within which is a helmeted figure representing Sorrowing Victory.

Victory holds wreaths and is flanked by two pairs of naked figures of the dead who are "pleading for acceptance of their sacrifice" – as if victory is welcoming those who made the supreme sacrifice into the realms of glory. Above Victory is a frieze of five cherubs with linked hands and above them the pediment contains the arms of Preston.

The Story behind The Memorial:

Fundraising began after the Armistice in 1918 to replace a temporary shrine that had been established in 1917. There was considerable debate about both the nature and the site of a memorial with a strong lobby suggesting the building of a new children's hospital.

For many years a large, temporary, wooden cross was used as focus for the Remembrance Sunday ceremony. In 1920 the War Memorial Committee arranged for a large temporary memorial to be constructed in the Flag Market in order to gauge public opinion. However, in July 1924 a decision was made to move the Boer War memorial from Market Place to Avenham Park.

Scott produced three designs for the memorial with the style becoming more austere and the emphasis changing from Victory carrying a sword, to a grieving Victory, and the representation of a closed tomb to symbolise a soldier buried abroad.

The memorial was constructed by George Longden and Sons of Sheffield.

The unveiling ceremony was attended by some 40,000 people and the proceedings were broadcast around the town by loud speakers.

Although not part of the memorial as such, the names of 1,956 men from Preston who died in the First World War are listed on plaques, also designed by Sir Giles Gilbert Scott in the adjacent Harris Museum.

These plaques were unveiled and dedicated on 2nd November, 1927. Whilst the inscription of the memorial was changed to include the Second World War, no additional plaques were added to those in the Harris Museum to record the names of those killed in that conflict.

In 1927 bronze railings were installed to protect the flower beds although these were not part of Scott's design and they have now been removed.

In 2012 the memorial was restored at a cost of £835,600 and was re-dedicated on 13th June 2014, exactly 88 years after its original dedication.

The Inscription

To the front of the memorial, below the sarcophagus, is the incised and gilded inscription: BE EVER MINDFUL OF THE MEN OF PRESTON/ WHO FELL IN THE GREAT WARS/ 1914 – 1918 1939 – 1945/ THIS LAND INVIOLATE YOUR MONUMENT.
The memorial stands on a two-stepped cruciform plinth and is flanked by two flagpoles which have bronze bases and stand on stone blocks decorated with swags. The outer face of the west wall had the following inscription add in 2013: BE EVER PROUD OF THE PEOPLE OF PRESTON WHO/ HAVE GIVEN THEIR LIVES IN CONFLICTS SINCE 1945.

7. Darwen War Memorial

Bold Venture Park, Darwen, Lancashire, BB3

Grade II*

Unveiled on 27th September 1921 by Mrs Chadwick, a bereaved mother from Darwen, who had lost three sons in the war.

Sculpted by Louis Ferderic Roslyn

Design Features:

The principal element of the memorial is a bronze statue of winged Victory standing on a globe. She holds a laurel wreath aloft in her left hand, whilst in her right she holds an olive branch. The statue stands on a tall, square sandstone ashlar pedestal. This pedestal has a deep cornice and a torus and cavetto moulding above the plinth. On the west, north and east faces of the plinth there are detailed bronze reliefs of, respectively, an infantryman, a nurse and a sailor. Each panel has a bronze laurel wreath above it.

The plinth stands on a three-stepped base which, in turn, is on a platform which is enclosed by several short tapering posts, four to each side and two to the rear. The two posts nearest the front of the platform are topped with carved lions. These posts used to be joined with chains although these have now been removed. The platform is approached from the front by five steps one to represent each year from 1914 to 1919.

Bold Venture Park where the memorial stands is, itself, a Grade II listed landscape.

The Story behind The Memorial:

The memorial was, like many others throughout the country, built by public subscription. The decision that bodies would not be returned was taken early in the war due to the logistics involved, and the cost of visits to the cemeteries in France and Belgium would have been beyond the reach of many working-class people, so the local war memorial would have been the only place where many could "pay their respects" to loved ones who had died.

The memorial was damaged by vandals pushing over some of the posts in 2014 although the damage was quickly repaired, with the work being paid for, in part, by money from War Memorials Trust.

The Inscription

The front (south) face of the pedestal is inscribed: IN GRATEFUL MEMORY AND TO THE HONOUR OF OVER 1200 CITIZENS OF THIS TOWN WHO GAVE THEIR LIVES IN THE GREAT WAR 1914 – 1918 AND THOSE WHO DIED IN THE WAR OF 1939 – 1945. Above this is a carved relief of the Darwen Borough arms flanked by inverted torches. The three bronze reliefs have inscriptions below them; the soldier represents HONOUR, the nurse HUMANITY and the sailor FREEDOM.
There are further linked inscriptions: the front face of the plinth is inscribed: LEST WE FORGET; the west: IS IT NOTHING TO YOU ALL YE WHO PASS BY this is taken from Lamentations 1:12; the north: THEY DIED NOT IN VAIN; and the east: THEIR NAME LIVETH FOR EVERMORE.

Darwen War Memorial (left) previous page

Oswaldtwistle War Memorial (below) on next page

Anthem for Doomed Youth
Lt. Wilfred Owen MC (Died 4th November 1918. Age 25)

What passing bells for these who die as cattle?
Only the monstrous anger of the guns.
Only the stuttering rifles' rapid rattle
Can patter out their hasty orisons.
No mockeries now for them, no prayers nor bells,
Nor any voice of mourning save the choirs.
The shrill, demented choirs of waiting shells;
And bugles calling for for them from sad shires.
What candles may be held to speed them all?
Not in the hands of boys, but in their eyes
Shall shine the holy glimmers of good byes.
The pallor of girls' brows shall be their pall;
Their flowers the tenderness of patient minds,
And each slow dusk a drawing down of blinds.

8. Oswaldtwistle War Memorial

Union Road, Oswaldtwistle, Accrington, Lancashire, BB5   Grade II*

Unveiled on 14th January 1922 by Major General Herbert Shoubridge, a career soldier who had been commissioned into the Dorset Regiment in 1893. He took part in the Tirah expedition on the North West Frontier of India and in the Second Boer War. At the start of the First World War, he was Assistant Adjutant and Quartermaster General of the 2nd Army Corps and finished the war as General Officer Commanding 7th Infantry Division. From 1919, Shoubridge was General Officer Commanding 42nd (East Lancashire) Infantry Division, a command he still held at the time of the unveiling of this memorial.

Sculpted by Louis Frederick Roslyn

Design Features:

The memorial is made from polished granite and is made up of a tall obelisk, supported by a pedestal on a three-tier stone platform, the lowest step of which is surrounded by a rake of granite setts. The obelisk has a deep cornice and is topped by a bronze figure of winged Victory standing on a globe and holding a laurel wreath in her hands.

On top of the second plinth is a bronze figure of an infantryman defending a wounded colleague who is lying at his feet. The infantryman has his bayonet fixed and his uniform and equipment are depicted in great detail. To the north and south sides of the memorial carved ships prows emerge from the base of the obelisk, each of them with a small, seated figure of Victory. To one side the figure holds a laurel wreath which encircles the Royal Navy insignia and, to the other side, a winged laurel wreath like an Air Force pilot's "wings". The ships prows are derived from Roman rostal columns which were erected to commemorate naval victories. Although not unknown on war memorials, this type of symbolism is very rare.

The Story behind The Memorial:

The number of men from Oswaldtwistle who died in the First World War is, as in other locations, disputed although it is estimated that over 400 men from the town died. The names of the dead are inscribed on a series of bronze plaques which are mounted on a freestanding granite wall built near the memorial at a later date. The wall and the plaques are not included in the listing. The cost of the memorial, £3,500, was met by public subscription. The memorial was re-dedicated on 27th June 2009 following a restoration programme at a cost of £30,000.

The Inscription

The main inscription is to be found on a second plinth supported on the base and reads: GREATER LOVE HATH NO MAN THAN THIS THAT A MAN LAY DOWN HIS LIFE FOR HIS FRIENDS. S.JOHN XV.13. The front face of the pedestal is inscribed: ERECTED BY PUBLIC SUBSCRIPTION TO THE HONOURED MEMORY OF THE MEN OF THIS TOWN WHO GAVE THEIR LIVES IN THE GREAT WAR 1914-1918. The south face is inscribed 1939-1945 TO THE MEMORY OF THOSE WHO GAVE THEIR LIVES IN THE WORLD WAR ALSO THOSE WHO DIED IN THE KOREAN WAR 1950-1953. The east face carries the following inscription: ALSO IN MEMORY OF THOSE WHO DIED IN NORTHERN IRELAND.

9. Accrington War Memorial

Oak Hill Park, Hollins Lane, Accrington, Lancashire, BB5

Grade II*

Unveiled on 1st July 1922, the sixth anniversary of the start of the Battle of the Somme. The memorial was unveiled by a local industrialist, H.H. Bolton, who had lost three sons during the First World War. The first of many wreaths and floral tributes that were laid was by Captain Harwood, who had raised the Accrington Pals Battalion during his year as Mayor.

Designed by Sir Charles Reilly, who was born in London and educated at a preparatory school in Hove, Merchant Taylors School in London and Queens College, Cambridge ,where he received a 'first' in mechanical science. In 1898 Reilly became an Associate of the Royal Institute of British Architects and in 1900 he applied for the position of Chair of Architecture at Kings College London without much hope of success, so he was surprised to reach the final shortlist of three and be offered a part-time lectureship position.

In 1904 Reilly was invited to become the Roscoe Professor of Architecture at the University of Liverpool. Reilly was to hold the post for the next 29 years making dramatic changes in the teaching of architecture. Reilly was awarded the Royal Gold Medal for Architecture in 1943 and knighted in 1944.

Sculpted by George Herbert Tyson-Smith

Design Features:

This large, impressive, memorial built of sandstone ashlar is at the highest point in Oak Hill Park and overlooks Accrington and the area around the town. The memorial comprises of a wide podium with a projecting, pedimented centre, from which rises a tall square, tapering obelisk.

The obelisk is flanked to both left and right by embedded fluted half columns with Ionic capitals that support alters of sacrifice from which burn eternal flames. To the front of the memorial, overlooking the park, is a tall free-standing female figure, who represents Compassion and Piety, she holds a wreath and palm leaf.

Steps on each side in front of the plinth lead to a retaining wall, on which are mounted thirteen Westmoreland slate tablets which carry the names of the 865 men from Accrington who died in the First World War. There is a separate pedimented stone wall in front which reflects the form of the original memorial bearing four more panels with 173 names from the Second World War, one from Northern Ireland and two from the Falklands Campaign.

The Story behind The Memorial:

The 11th Battalion of the East Lancashire Regiment was raised in September 1914 and was one of the early "Pals Battalions", whose volunteers joined up on the basis that they would serve together with friends and workmates rather than being allotted arbitrarily to other battalions. Whilst serving alongside men that you knew might have been good for morale it could also spell "disaster" for an area in a fierce battle.

25

The battalion had started by guarding the Suez Canal but, fatefully, they were moved in France in the spring of 1916 to participate in the forthcoming Battle of the Somme.

1st July 1916, the first day of the Battle of the Somme, was to be the first day that the men had been in action. At 7:20 am the battalion went "over the top" and within half an hour out of 720 men, 235 had been killed and 350 wounded – the remnants of the battalion were withdrawn from the front line at 1am the next morning. The brother of one of those killed said that there was scarcely a street in Accrington that did not have its blinds drawn and that the bell at Christ Church tolled all day. In total Accrington lost 865 men killed in the First World War.

The cost of the memorial was £6,885.

The Inscription

To the rear of the podium there is a rectangular cartouche which contains the following inscription: THIS LAND INVIOLATE, THEIRS THE GLORY. To the front of the podium, in a similar cartouche, is the principal inscription, in raised letters, which reads: TO THE HONOURED MEMORY OF THE MEN OF ACCRINGTON WHO GAVE THEIR LIVES IN THE GREAT WAR 1914-1919. Below this is carved: THEIR NAME LIVETH FOR EVER MORE.

On the front of the separate wall is inscribed: IN MEMORIUM 1939-45 whilst to the rear is the following inscription: LETS US REMEMBER THOSE WHO IN THEIR LIVES FOUGHT AND DIED FOR US.

10. Rawtenstall Cenotaph

Library Gardens, St Marys Way, Rawtenstall, Greater Manchester

Grade II*

Unveiled on 29th June 1929 by Miss Carrie Whitehead, a former suffragette, who was a town Councillor and later Mayor of Rawtenstall.

Designed and Sculpted by Louis Fredrick Roslyn

Design Features:

The memorial is built from Shap granite with bronze figures and plaques. The Cenotaph takes the form of a broad needle which sits on a base of three square steps of granite and a square plinth, which has two further steps.

Above the plinth is a substantial and detailed bas relief, which depicts a member of the armed forces at each corner and civilian works on the faces in-between. The four soldiers represent an infantryman, an airman a sailor and a member of the Royal Army Medical Corps. The other figures represent a cross section of workers and civilians.

On the south side there is a member of the Women's Land Army, the Women's Forestry Service, the Women's Royal Naval Service and a woman with a child. On the west face there is a Voluntary Aid Detachment nurse, a munitions worker and a member of the Women's Army Auxiliary Corps. The north face has labourers, a fisherman and a Special Constable. On the east face can be found a miner, a postman, a railwayman and a mechanic On the south face of the top of the obelisk, which is twice stepped, is a bronze palm leaf with a garland to symbolise both victory and commemoration.

The Story behind The Memorial:

This is one of only very few memorials which pays considerable acknowledgement not only to male civilian workers but also to women who served both at home and abroad, as well as a woman and child waiting for the return of a loved one or mourning their loss. The inclusive nature of the memorial extends to the inscriptions and the invitation to a local champion of women's rights rather than an army officer to unveil the memorial.

The Inscription

Two faces of the plinth are carved with a wreath and a garland whilst the south face has a bronze plaque with the inscription – A TRIBUTE OF HONOUR TO THE MEN WHO MADE THE SUPREME SACRIFICE TO THE MEN WHO CAME BACK AND TO THOSE WHO WORKED AT HOME TO WIN SAFETY FOR THE EMPIRE 1914-1915. On the north face there is a plaque with the inscription TO THE MEMORY OF ALL WHO GAVE THEIR LIVES IN THE SERVICE OF THEIR COUNTRY DURING THE SECOND WORLD WAR 1939-1945 ALL WHO SERVED ON SEA, LAND OR IN THE AIR AND ALL WHO WORKED AND SERVED AT HOME 1939-1945 (This plaque was replaced in 2009 following the theft of the original plaque).

11. Burnley War Memorial

Near Towneley Hall, Towneley Park, Burnley, Lancashire BB11
Grade II*

Unveiled by Edward Stanley, 17th Earl of Derby. Lord Derby had served as Secretary of State for War from 1916 to 1918, and again from 1922 to 1924, and was British Ambassador to France during the time of the Versailles peace talks. Lord Derby had been responsible for the creation of what were known as "Pals" Battalions where friends, neighbours and workmates served together. During the Second Boer War, Lord Derby was Honorary Colonel of the volunteer battalion of the Loyal North Lancashire Regiment and later the Manchester Regiment. The unveiling was watched by a crowd of 20,000 to 30,000 people.

Designed by Walter Gilbert and Louis Weingarten. Gilbert was born in Rugby and studied at the Birmingham Municipal School of Art and the National Art Training School, which is now the Royal College of Art. In 1898, he was the co-founder of the Bromsgrove Guild of Applied Arts which enjoyed an international reputation.

Little is known about Louis Weingartner except that he was from Lucerne in Switzerland and was a jeweller at the School of Art in Birmingham before starting to work with Gilbert in the early1900s.

Together Gilbert and Weingartner were responsible for some nationally important work including the gates at Buckingham Palace, the Victoria Monument in the Mall and various works at Liverpool Cathedral.

Design Features:

The memorial stands in a small triangular Garden of Remembrance enclose by hedges and trees. The memorial comprises a plain Portland stone wall, the top of which is transformed gradually into three figures. A soldier in the centre who is wearing a great coat and carries a telescope; to the soldier's left is a sailor, stripped to the waist with a coat over his arm; and to the soldier's right is an airman with helmet, scarf and goggles. On each side of the wall there is a bronze figure of a woman standing on a low stub wall. To the left is a depiction of an older woman, a mother perhaps, who is stooping to lay a wreath. By her side is a rosemary branch together with a cricket bat and ball. The woman portrayed to the right of the wall is a younger woman, a sister or wife maybe, she is wearing a flowing gown and is looking up towards the group. She is carrying a large floral garland and has a palm leaf at her feet.

The memorial stands on a shallow stone platform within a circular paved enclosure bisected by a pathway, surrounded by low walls with terminal posts. Within the front section of the enclosure is a hemispherical pond.

The Story behind The Memorial:

The principal cost of the memorial was covered by a bequest of £5,000 Caleb Thornber, who was a cotton manufacturer and former Mayor of Burnley. To this was added £900 which was raised by public subscription.

A letter from the sculptor is reported in contemporary newspapers which describes the monument as intending 'to express the emotion felt in the human heart at the ideals

of those who have fallen in the Great War. The mother, overwhelmed in this emotion, places a wreath in memory of her son at the foot of the Cenotaph and, as she stoops, the Cenotaph shapes itself in her heart into the features of her son ... The sculptor has endeavoured to conceive a memorial that shall breathe nothing of slaughter, but only of duty fulfilled and by fulfilment of duty, the comfort and thankfulness brought to those who remain'.

H H Martyn & Co of Cheltenham built the memorial and founded the bronze figures.

The memorial was cleaned and re-pointed in 2007 with the works being funded by Historic England, the Wolfson Foundation and War Memorials Trust.

The Inscription

The wall is inscribed at the foot: THIS MONUMENT WAS ERECTED IN MEMORY OF THE MEN OF BURNLEY WHO GAVE THEIR LIVES FOR THEIR FELLOW COUNTRYMEN IN THE GREAT WAR 1914-1918 Make them to be numbered with Thy Saints in Glory everlasting (a quotation from the Te Deum). Beneath is a further inscription: THIS MONUMENT STANDS ALSO IN HONOUR OF THOSE WHO DIED FOR OUR FREEDOM 1939-1945. The rear is inscribed: THE SUM NECESSARY FOR THE ERECTION OF THIS MEMORIAL WAS BEQUEATHED BY CALEB THORNBER, J.P., A FORMER MAYOR AND ALDERMAN OF THIS BOROUGH, TO ENSURE THAT THE SACRIFICE COMMEMORATED SHOULD EVER BE HELD IN GRATEFUL REMEMBRANCE. THE GARDEN OF REMEMBRANCE WAS PROVIDED BY THE TOWNSPEOPLE OF BURNLEY.

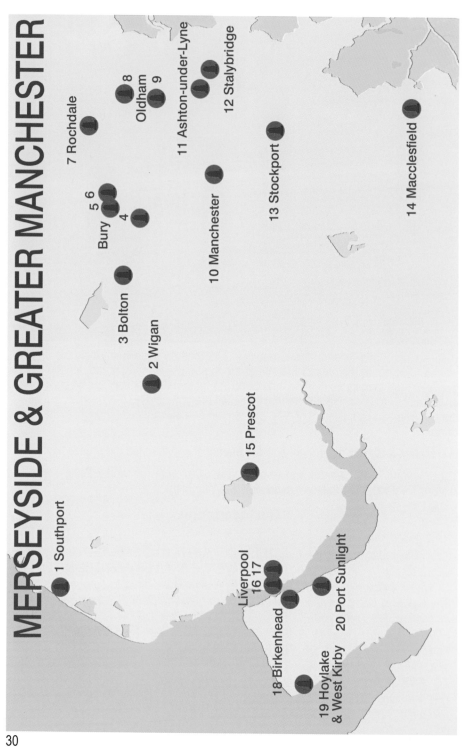

MERSEYSIDE & GREATER MANCHESTER

1 Southport
2 Wigan
3 Bolton
Bury
5
6
4
7 Rochdale
8
Oldham
9
11 Ashton-under-Lyne
12 Stalybridge
10 Manchester
13 Stockport
14 Macclesfield
15 Prescot
Liverpool
16 17
18 Birkenhead
19 Hoylake
& West Kirby
20 Port Sunlight

CONTENTS

Map reference and Memorial Name   **Page**

1. Southport War Memorial Obelisk, Colonnades, Pools of Remembrance and Memorial Gardens

London Square, Southport, PR8

Grade II*

Unveiled by The Earl of Derby on 18th November 1923. Edward George Villiers Stanley, 17th Earl of Derby, had served as Secretary of State for War from 1916 to 1918 and held the same position from October 1922 to January 1924. He had served in the Army and saw active service during the Second Boer War.

Designed by Liverpool architects Grayson and Barnish, who were selected following a competition assessed by Sir Reginald Blonfield.

Sculpted by Herbert Tyson Smith.

Design Features:

This large and complex memorial consists of a number of elements; a tall central obelisk is flanked by two separate colonnades which are further flanked by pools and memorial gardens. The obelisk, which is made from Portland Stone, is 67'6" (20.6m) high on a square pedestal and stepped base.

The two colonnades, built in the style of Greek temples, are similar to each other in as much as they have a rectangular plan, are single storey and have flat roofs, although they have different carvings, inscriptions and contents. On each side of both of the colonnades are four pairs of fluted Doric columns which form five bays. At each end of the two colonnades are enclosed cenotaphs with entablatures with inscriptions and two open windows over which are carved panels.

There are also carved panels and inscriptions on each end of both of the colonnades. At the entrances to the cenotaphs are fluted Ionic columns and at the centre of each cenotaph there is a pedestal alter, whilst, on the walls, there are marble tablets with the names of engagements during the First World War, regimental badges and the names of the dead, together with their rank, regiment or unit.

Adjacent to the colonnades and around the obelisk are cast iron lamp standards which have fluted columns, and bases decorated with acanthus leaves.

The Story behind The Memorial:

In August 1914 Lord Derby, who unveiled the memorial, had organised one of the most successful recruiting campaigns of the First World War, over two days in Liverpool 1,500 recruits joined the Army and in the days following another three battalions were raised in Liverpool.

Speaking to the first recruits Lord Derby said: "This should be a battalion of pals, a battalion in which friends from the same office will fight shoulder to shoulder for the honour of Britain and the credit of Liverpool". It was these comments that inspired the raising of the "Pals Battalions" in which workmates and neighbours served together.

The Inscription

Roundels are incised into three side of the obelisk and the side that faces northwest bears a carved wreath and the inscription: LOOK UPWARD STANDING MUTE. SALUTE. These are the last two lines of the poem The Army of the Dead, Barry Pain's Armistice Day poem. On the base below this inscription are the dates MCMXIV-MCMXVII (1914-1918). On the southeast face, are the arms of the town of Southport and the inscription: SALUS POPULI (The welfare of the people) the town's motto. On the southwest face is an inscription which was added in 1956 in respect of the Second World War: TO THE MEN AND WOMEN OF THIS COUNTY BOROUGH WHO GAVE THEIR LIVES FOR THE LIBERTY OF THE WORLD AND THE SECURITY OF THS REALM IN THE WORLD WAR 1939-1945. THEIR NAMES ARE RECORDED IN THE BOOK OF REMEMBRANCE WHICH LIES NEARBY IN THE KEEPING OF CHRIST CHURCH. THE FOUNTAINS ADDED TO THE MEMORIAL POOLS ARE DEDICATED TO THEIR HONOURED MEMORY.

On the northeast colonnade, the entablature on the side facing the obelisk is inscribed: TELL BRITAIN YE WHO MARK THIS MONUMENT whilst on the side facing the garden is inscribed: THEIR PORTION IS WITH THE ETERNAL – from the poet Laurence Binyon. On the northwest face of this colonnade is a carved panel of Britannia holding a statuette of Victory. Facing the garden is a platform with the following inscription: THEY DIED THAT WE MIGHT LIVE/WE LIVE ONLY AS WE SAFEGUARD THE IDEALS FOR WHICH THEY DIEDFREEDOM JUSTICE MERCY SO LET US LIVE THAT WE MAY SHARE WITH THEM THE LIFE ETERNAL – written by Frederick Riley, . The altar in the northwest cenotaph has carved representations of Achilles and Patroclus, his beloved brother in arms and a tablet inscribed: FOR THE SACRED CAUSE OF JUSTICE.

On the southeast colonnade; upon the side of the entablature facing the obelisk is the inscription: FAITHFULL TO HER WE FELL AND REST CONTENT – an adaptation of the epitaph of Simonides on the Spartans who fell at Thermopylae. On the face fronting the garden is: TO FAMOUS MEN ALL EARTH IS SEPULCHRE – this is a translation by Thucydides in his book of the funeral oration of Pericles, in respect of the Athenians who fell in the first year of the Peloponnesian War. The panel to the northwest side of the colonnade depicts Britannia offering a tribute to the dead which represents 'mourning'. On the northeast side is a panel inscribed: REMEMBER THAT THE MEN WHOSE NAMES LIVE ON THESE WALLS DIED IN YOUTH OR PRIME THAT FUTURE GENERATIONS MIGHT INHERIT A HAPPIER WORLD AND A HUMAN SOCIETY MORE RIGHTEOUS AND MORE LOVING THAN THOSE BRAVE MEN AND THEIR GENERATION KNEW. The altar in the southwest cenotaph is carved with a representation of "Death and the Soldier". There are also two inscribed tablets; one which reads: ALL THAT THY HAD THEY GAVE – by Rudyard Kipling from his poem The Kings Pilgrim, and the other: THEIR NAME LIVETH.

Outside each colonnade is a memorial garden laid to lawns. In the middle of each garden is a Pool of Remembrance surrounded by flat copings in Portland Stone. At the colonnade end of the pool is a low curved parapet with a spout in the form of a lion's head. The garden areas are surrounded with balustrades in Portland Stone. In each of the Pools of Remembrance are three fountains which were added in 1956 to extend the provisions of the memorial to include those killed in the Second World War.

Southport War Memorial (above) and Obelisk, (left) details previous pages

Wigan War Memorial (right) details page opposite

2. Wigan War Memorial

Outside All Saints Church, Wallgate, Wigan, WN1

Grade II*

Unveiled in 1925 by General Sir Herbert Alexander Lawrence, the son of a former Viceroy of India. He was a career soldier who left the Army in 1903 with the rank of major to build a career in Glyn Mills Bank. He re-joined the Army in 1914 and, within eleven months he had risen to the rank of Brigadier-General after serving in Egypt and Gallipoli. Lawrence returned to Glyn Mills in 1919 and saw it become Britain's largest private bank. Both of Lawrence's sons were killed on the Western Front.

Designed by by Sir Giles Gilbert Scott and built by Messrs Edward Owen Griffith & Co

Design Features:

The memorial is an elaborate Eleanor cross made from Portland Stone on a high octagonal pillar with panelled sides atop a three stage plinth. The centre and upper stages are surrounded by rectangular bronze plaques carrying the names of the fallen in raised lettering. The memorial is set within a curved triangular memorial garden surrounded by dwarf walls with chamfered coping stones and dwarf iron railings. There are entrances at the corners of the garden which are flanked by lamp standards on octagonal plinths.

The Story behind The Memorial:

David Lindsay, 27th Earl of Crawford, was supposed to carry out the unveiling. However, due to bad health he was unable and, instead, sent a letter which was read out at the unveiling. In many ways Lindsay was better placed to unveil the memorial than Lawrence because Lindsay's family seat was at Haigh Hall in Wigan, and he had extensive interests in the Lancashire coal field, owning a number of mines. Lindsay had attended Eton and Oxford and, at the outbreak of the First World War, he was offered the position of Viceroy of India which he declined. Instead he joined the Royal Army Medical Corps as a private soldier, which meant that he would have understood well the sufferings of the ordinary infantryman during the war.

The Wigan war memorial is unusual in as much as it carries the name of a woman – Janet Johnson – who lost her life in the First World War whilst serving with the Royal Navy.

By 1935 the incised lettering on the memorial was showing signs of serious weathering and it was decided to install bronze plaques with the names of those killed instead of re-cutting the stone. These plaques were stolen by metal thieves in 2006 and replaced by the Local Authority in 2007. The adjacent All Saints Church is also listed Grade II*

The Inscription

. On the south side there is inscribed REMEMBER THE MEN OF WIGAN WHO GAVE THEIR LIVES TO THE GREAT WAR 1914-1918 AND THE SECOND WORLD WAR 1939-1945 whilst on the north side is the inscription A GOOD LIFE HATH BUT A FEW DAYS BUT A GOOD NAME LIVETH FOR EVER.

3. Bolton Cenotaph

Victoria Square, Bolton, BL1
Grade II*

Unveiled on 4th July 1928, together with a Hall of Memory in the Town Hall, by the Earl of Derby. He had been Secretary of State for War from1916 to 1918, and again between 1922 and 1924. From 1918 to 1920 he was Ambassador to France, which means that he was there during the peace talks which culminated in the Treaty of Versailles. The 17th Earl of Derby certainly received a better welcome in Bolton than his ancestor the 7th Earl, who was beheaded in the town following his unsuccessful defence of it on behalf of the King during the Civil Wars.

The Bolton Cenotaph is unique in this book by way of having two separate unveilings. The second was necessary because the finishing of the bronze sculptures was badly delayed and they were not installed on the memorial until 1932. The second unveiling was carried out by Lt Colonel C K Potter of the Kings Liverpool Regiment on Armistice Day 1932.

Designed by A J Hope (1875-1960), who was born in Atherton, Lancashire and attended Wigan Grammar School before studying civil engineering at the Bolton School of Science and Art. Joining the Bolton firm of Bradshaw & Gass as a pupil 1892, Hope was made a partner in 1902 and in 1911 he was admitted as a licentiate of the Royal Institute of British Architects. Universally known as "AJ", Hope was a poor draughtsman and needed assistants to interpret his ideas. Notable among Hope's work is the extension to Bolton Town Hall together with the Civic Centre behind it.

Sculpted by Walter Marsden (1882-1969), who was born near Accrington in Lancashire and joined the Accrington Brick and Tile Company as an apprentice. He studied at the Accrington Technical School from where he went on to the Manchester Municipal College of Art. During the First World War Marsden served as an officer in the Loyal North Lancashire Regiment and was awarded the Military Cross. After the war, Marsden continued his studies at the Royal College of Art and became a member of the Art Workers Guild and the Royal Society of British Sculptors.

Design Features:

The memorial, which is made from Kemnay granite with bronze sculptures, stands in Victoria Square in front of the portico of Bolton Town Hall. The style of the memorial is neo-classical with Graeco-Roman detailing. The centre of the memorial is a tall pylon on a moulded base and platform with inset steps. There are pedestals to each side, parallel with the Town Hall that support bronze figures. The pylon has an arch in the centre which contains a bronze cross overlaid with an inverted sword.

The open sides of the memorial each have an architectural frame of columns with palm-frond capitals and a dentilled cornice, above which are carvings of the arms of Bolton. The sculpture on the north side, 'Struggle', is a seated female figure who portrays 'Peace'; she is restraining a vigorous, loin-clothed male 'Youth' who is eager for combat. On the south side is a Pietà-like composition, 'Sacrifice', 'Peace' now has the prostrate body of the dead 'Youth' across her lap, her hands raised in anguish.

The Story behind The Memorial:

The town of Bolton lost over 3,500 in the First World War including Alice Thomasson, of the Queen Mary's Army Auxiliary Corps; whilst far from unknown, the death of women during the war was not common.

Both the nature and the site of a war memorial was the subject of some debate in the town until a site directly in front of the Town Hall was decided upon in 1925.

The Hall of Memory, in which the Book of Remembrance is displayed, is at first floor level in the Town Hall directly facing the memorial.

A competition to find the designer for the sculpture was launched in 1927, with the brief that the figures should be symbolic of struggle, sacrifice and victory, and Victory as the crowning figure. Although his design did not incorporate 'Victory', Walter Marsden's submission won the competition.

The bronze sculptures were cast by A B Burton of Thames Ditton and the £7,600 cost of the memorial was raised by public subscription.

The Inscription

On the east face, there is a carved panel above the arch which is inscribed: TELL YE YOUR CHILDREN. The base is inscribed: OUR BROTHERS DIED TO WIN A BETTER WORLD OUR PART MUST BE TO STRIVE FOR TRUTH GOODWILL AND PEACE THAT THEIR SELF-SACRIFICE BE NOT IN VAIN. A panel on the west face is inscribed LEST WE FORGET and the base: IN UNDYING MEMORY OF THE MEN AND WOMEN OF BOLTON WHO GAVE THEIR LIVES IN THE GREAT WAR 1914-1919.

4. Radcliffe War Memorial

Blackburn Street, Radcliffe, Bury, Greater Manchester M26

Grade II*

Unveiled on 26th November 1922.

Designed by by A. Baines Barker of London

Sculpted by Sydney March (1876-1968) who was born in Hull, the second of nine children, eight of whom became artists.

He was apprenticed to a monumental sculptor, attended the Royal Academy Schools, and exhibited thirteen times at the Royal Academy of Arts. In 1901, March produced the coronation bust of Edward VII and a bust of Cecil Rhodes, which are now in the National Portrait Gallery. His other works included two equestrian statues of Lord Kitchener and, most famously, the National War Memorial of Canada in Ottawa.

Design Features:

The memorial stands outside Radcliffe Town Hall, and comprises an obelisk in Darley Dale sandstone, set on a square raised terrace with surrounding walls and steps. It consists of a square base of seven steps with a cruciform pedestal and a 35ft (11m) obelisk. The four faces of the pedestal have square bronze panels, which bear the names of the 642 killed in the First World War and the 146 killed in the Second World War. On the front of the obelisk is a large sword with a laurel wreath around its hilt. Around the front and two sides of the obelisk where it meets the pedestal, are three allegorical winged female figures representing Liberty, Victory and Peace. Liberty stands at the front holding Liberty in one hand and a laurel wreath in the other hand. Victory to the left of the obelisk is raising a flaming torch, whilst Peace to the right reclines on one leg, with roses of remembrance on her lap, whilst listening to a message delivered by a dove on her shoulder.

The Inscription

To the rear of the obelisk there is a bronze cartouche with the inscription in raised lettering – TO OUR GLORIOUS DEAD 1914-1918, and the Radcliffe Coat of Arms

5. War Memorial to the Lancashire Fusiliers, Gallipoli Gardens

Gallipoli Gardens, Silver Street, Bury, BL9   **Grade II***

Unveiled on 25th April 1922 – the 7th anniversary of the Cape Helles, Gallipoli landings – by Lt General Sir Henry de Beauvoir De Lisle, General Officer Commander-in-Chief Western Command. He was a career soldier who had been wounded and mentioned in despatches three times during the Second Boer War, and had commanded the 29th Division during the Gallipoli Campaign.

Designed by Sir Edwin Lutyens, who declined to take a fee for his services because both his father and grandfather had served with the Lancashire Fusiliers.

Design Features:

The memorial is constructed of Portland Stone and consists of a tapered obelisk 13ft (4m) tall on a square base incorporating a moulded cornice. The overall height of the memorial is 22ft 6ins (6.9m). The obelisk stands on a rectangular pedestal, which has convex east and west ends and incorporates a carved frieze and moulded cornice to the upper part, all set on a rectangular plinth, the whole standing on two shallow circular steps.

The Story behind The Memorial:

Sufficient money was raised through public subscription, not only to build the memorial, but also to buy new drums and bugles for the regiment, as well as making a donation to the Fusiliers Compassionate Fund. 13,642 Lancashire Fusiliers were killed during the First World War, taking especially heavy casualties at the Cape Helles landings on 25th April 1915 during the Gallipoli landings, where six men of the regiment earned the Victoria Cross in one morning – "six VC's before breakfast".

The Lancashire Fusiliers were amalgamated, with other fusilier regiments, to form the Royal Regiment of Fusiliers in 1968, and the memorial was adopted by the new regiment to commemorate all fusiliers killed in the line of duty.

This memorial has been moved twice, having been originally erected outside Wellington Barracks in Bury which were the regimental headquarters; however the barracks closed in 1968 and were mostly demolished during the 1970s. During 2009 Sparrow Park was redeveloped as Gallipoli Gardens and the Fusilier Museum was moved there from the former regimental headquarters; the memorial was later re-installed next to the regimental museum.

The Inscription

On the front and rear faces of the obelisk are carvings of the regimental badge, together with a gilded inscription XX (the Lancashire Fusiliers were formerly the 20th Regiment of Foot) circled by a wreath. Beneath the wreath on the front of the memorial is the inscription: OMNIA AUDAX (all valiant). To the sides of the obelisk are life sized stone and painted regimental flags, a feature used by Lutyens on many of the memorials he designed. To the left of the obelisk, viewed from the front, is the King's Colour whilst on the opposite side the colour of the 1st Battalion Lancashire Fusiliers.

There are further inscriptions on the lower part of the front face, again in gilded lettering: MCMXIV + MCMXIX on the base of the obelisk and TO THE LANCASHIRE FUSILIERS THEIR DEEDS AND SACRIFICES FOR KING AND COUNTRY on the upper part of the pedestal. On the lower part of the pedestal is inscribed MCMXXXIX+MCMXLV and, on the plinth: AND ALL FUSILIERS WHO DIED IN SUBSEQUENT CAMPAIGNS.

War Memorial to the Lancashire Fusiliers, Gallipoli Gardens (left) details previous page

Bury War Memorial (below) details next page

6. Bury War Memorial

The Rock, Bury, Lancashire BL9

Grade II*

Unveiled on 11th November 1924 by Mrs Peachment of Bury, the mother of Rifleman George Peachment VC, who was posthumously awarded the Victoria Cross at the age of 18 years and 4 months, which made him the youngest recipient in the First World War.

Sculpted by by Joseph Hermon Cawthra, who was born in Baildon, Yorkshire and studied at Salts Art School in Shipley, the Leeds School of Art, the Royal College of Art and the Royal Academy Schools.

Cawthra worked on six First World War and one Second World War memorials, along with work at Sadler's Wells Theatre, Selfridges Store, Manchester Town Hall Extension and Braintree Town Hall. His bas reliefs for the Bury War Memorial were exhibited at the Royal Academy and he was elected to the Royal British Society of Sculptors.

Design Features:

The main feature of the memorial is a tall Cornish granite cross of the style designed by Sir Reginald Blomfield for the Imperial War Graves Commission. Crosses like this are commonly called a "Cross of Sacrifice" or a "Blomfield Cross". The cross stands on an octagonal base with curved flanking walls which have bronze bas reliefs. The two bas relief bronze panels are of very high quality.

The panel on the left depicts representatives of the three armed forces moving from right to left: the panel also portrays a nurse and a wounded soldier being carried on a stretcher: the right-hand panel depicts a coal miner, engineer, munitions worker and a boy scout, indicating the involvement of the whole community in the war effort.

The Story behind The Memorial:

Discussions about providing some sort of memorial to those from Bury killed in the war started soon after the end of the war, although the main debate centred around building a children's wing for the Bury Infirmary, which would cost £50,000. Although there was less support for a physical memorial, the situation was decided when an anonymous donation of £1,000 was made to pay for a memorial on the condition that it be sited in the Market Place. The grounds of St Mary's Church faced the Market Place and the church donated the land for the memorial.

The statue was built by William Kirkpatrick Ltd, Manchester Granite and Marble Works, of Trafford Park, Manchester.

The Inscription

The simple inscription is below a small bronze wreath on the pedestal and reads: TO THE MEMORY OF THE MEN OF BURY WHO GAVE THEIR LIVES IN THE GREAT WAR 1914 1918. A later inscription was added above the wreath which reads simply: 1939 1945. The ends of the flanking walls bear shields – on the left the arms of Bury and on the right the arms of Lancashire – with the inscriptions PRO REGE [For King] and PRO PATRIA [For country] respectively.

7. Rochdale Cenotaph
Memorial Gardens, The Esplanade, Rochdale, OL1
Grade I

Unveiled by the Earl of Derby on Sunday 26th November 1922. During the war Lord Derby, a former regular soldier, had been Director-General of Recruiting and later Secretary of State for War.

The consecration of the memorial was by Rev. Thomas Sale, the Archdeacon of Rochdale.

Designed by by Sir Edwin Lutyens and built by Hobson Limited of Nottingham.

Design Features:

The memorial is constructed of Cornish granite and comprises a 33ft (10 m) tall Stone of Remembrance based on Lutyen's design for larger Imperial (later Commonwealth) War Graves Commission cemeteries. The cenotaph sits on a three stepped platform with a further six steps leading to the base. A rectangular pier recedes as it rises to a tall, narrower, pier with semi-pillars to the north east and south east sides.

On the plain first tier are four carved and painted flags representing the Union Flag

and White Ensign on one side, and the Royal Air Force Ensign and Red Ensign on the other face. Above these flags are carved wreaths surrounding the arms of Rochdale. The top of the memorial comprises a bier with a draped human figure.

The cenotaph was not Lutyen's first design, which took the form of a memorial bridge over the River Roch. At the time the river ran through the town although it has now been culverted.

The change in designed followed the purchase by Alderman William Cunliffe, a former Mayor, of a property known as The Manor House or The Orchard, which had been a recruiting centre during the war. Alderman Cunliffe donated the land and property for the creation of a memorial park.

The property was in a very poor condition and was demolished to make way for the cenotaph

The Story behind The Memorial:

. In February 1919, the Mayor of Rochdale, Cllr W Davidson called a public meeting to discuss how best to remember the 2,000 local men who were killed in the First World War. It was agreed that whilst there should be a permanent memorial in the town there should also be a fund to provide assistance to wounded soldiers and their families as well as the families of those killed. A public subscription raised £29,443 10s, out of which the cost of the memorial was £12, 611.

The Inscription

The semi-pillars and longer sides of the middle tiers bear the inscription – 1914-1919 1939-1945 TO THE MEMORY OF THE MEN OF ROCHDALE WHO GAVE THEIR LIVES IN THE GREAT WAR MCMXIV MCMXIX ET MCMXXXIX MCMXLV THEY WERE A WALL UNTO US BOTH BY NIGHT AND DAY.

There is a further small stone of remembrance separate from the cenotaph, although on the same base, which is inscribed THEIR NAME LIVETH FOR EVER MORE. A bronze plaque was added at a later date with the inscription TO ALL THOSE WHO DIED IN THE SERVICE OF THEIR COUNTRY.

The memorial gardens are dedicated to the men of the local regiment, the Lancashire Fusiliers and the Royal Regiment of Fusiliers. In 2015 a rough stone memorial was erected in the gardens in memory of the service of the Lancashire Fusiliers at Gallipoli in 1915. This memorial bears a circular plaque inscribed with the words THIS STONE COMMEMORATES THE SERVICE OF THE 6th BATTALION THE LANCASHIRE FUSILIERS AND THE SACRIFICE OF THE PEOPLE AT HOME. GALLIPOLI 1915 LEST WE FORGET. Two smaller plaques show the cap badge of the Lancashire Fusiliers and the arms of Rochdale. In the initial landings at Gallipoli six men of the Lancashire Fusiliers won the Victoria Cross.

DID YOU KNOW THAT?

It wasn't until 2015 that the final payment of £1.9bn was made to America to repay loans that were incurred to fight the First World War.

During the war, UK government propaganda was used to encourage the public to make a patriotic investment

8. Crompton War Memorial
High Street, Shaw and Crompton, Oldham, OL2
Grade II*

Unveiled on 29th April 1923 by General Sir Ian Hamilton. He was a career soldier having attended the Royal Military College, Sandhurst in 1870, which was the first year that entrance to the Army was by examination, rather than buying a commission. Hamilton served in Egypt, Burma and India, and was wounded in his left wrist during the First Boer War, which left it almost useless, and he used to "hide" it in subsequent photographs. During the Second Boer War he was close to the action, and twice recommended to receive the Victoria Cross, the United Kingdom's highest award for gallantry.

However, it was considered inappropriate because he was a Major-General at the time. Kitchener appointed him Commander of the Mediterranean Expeditionary Force in the First World War, which was tasked with taking control of the Dardanelles and capturing Constantinople, but was unsuccessful, although largely for reasons outside his control. Hamilton was recalled to London in October 1915 and was not given any further field commands during the war. Following the war, Hamilton became very involved in the Royal British Legion and held the position of Scottish President.

The dedication of the memorial was carried out by Rev. A.R. Mackintosh; Vicar of Shaw. Also present were Mr Ormerod, Chairman of the District Council and Mrs Hopley Chair of the Council. All of Mrs Hopley's eight sons had served during the war and three were killed – their names are included on the memorial.

Designed by Richard Reginald Goulden.

Design Features:

The memorial is in public gardens in Shaw and Crompton High Street, and comprises a large bronze sculpture in the style of other Goulden memorials. An athletic warrior, naked other than for a loin cloth and a cape that billows out behind him, is leaning forward and plunging a sword into one of two beasts at his feet. It is not apparent what type of animal the beasts are although the closest similarity is to dogs. The warrior is defending a group of children, naked apart from loin clothes, two are on his right side, three to his left and one behind; with his empty left hand, he is holding the hand of one of the children.

The sculpture stands on top of a four-stepped pedestal of Aberdeen granite which, in turn, stands on a two-stepped granite plinth.

On each of the two sides of the pedestal there are tall rectangular bronze panels which carry the names of 346 local men who fell in the First World War. There are wreaths at the tops of these panels, together with relief profiles of servicemen – on the east side a soldier and airman are depicted, and on the west side a sailor and a soldier. On the rear face of the pedestal is a further bronze plaque with 76 people from the town who died in the Second World War.

The Story behind The Memorial:

In common with many other towns and cities, Crompton set up a War Memorial Committee to consider a suitable way to commemorate the men of the area who had died in the First World War.

The committee were not in favour of realism preferring, instead, to seek symbolic or allegorical designs, and the proposal submitted by Goulden was one of a strong and athletic man defending the weak, as portrayed by children, a theme which he used in other memorials.

There is a time capsule, in the form of a lead casket, built into the memorial which contains coins, a local newspaper, cotton and woven fustian produced locally, reports of the local Disabled Sailors and Soldiers Association, the Urban District Council and details of the war memorial project. In 1926 Goulden provided Crompton with a fountain in memory of the women of the district, although this was stolen in 1968.

The memorial cost £4,000 plus £2,067 for the landscaping of the site. The sculpture and bronze plaques were produced by A B Burton of Thames Ditton, who also made other works for Goulden.

The Inscription

The main inscription, which is in raised bronze letters, and on the front face of the pedestal, reads: IN MEMORY OF MEN OF CROMPTON WHO FOUGHT AND GAVE THEIR LIVES TO FREE MANKIND FROM OPRESSION AND BRUTAL TYRANNY OF WAR 1914-1919 1939-1945. Above the panels on the sides of the pedestal are the words PRO PATRIA. The inscription on the rear face reads: TO THE HONOUR AND GLORY OF THE MEN WHO LOST THEIR LIVES 1939 – 1945.

9. Oldham War Memorial

Church Street, Oldham, Greater Manchester, OL1
Grade II*

Unveiled on 28th April 1923 by General Sir Ian Hamilton, and his biographical details are included in the Crompton War Memorial on page 44, which he also unveiled. The dedication was carried out by William Temple, Bishop of Manchester. A crowd of approximately 10,000 people attended the unveiling.

Designed by Thomas Taylor of Messrs Taylor and Simister of Oldham

Sculpted by Albert Toft

Design Features:

The memorial stands on a raised stone paved area above the High Street, south of the Church of St Mary and St Pete, which is the highest point in the town. The memorial comprises of a large rectangular granite pedestal 9ft 9in (3m) tall, which is on a shallow stepped base and represents a mausoleum containing a chamber access via a pair of bronze coffered doors on the north side.

The doors are decorated with wreaths and cartouches. There was a matching set of doors to the south side, although these were replaced in 1955 by a window which displays a mechanised Roll of Honour of those from the town who died during the war.

On the top of the pedestal is a large and dynamic bronze sculpture of five, life-sized, infantrymen in the process of 'going over the top': two soldiers are depicted moving along the trench, while two more climb the parapet and a fifth stands on top of the parapet. The composition is extremely detailed and shows a high degree of action by the soldiers.

The forecourt surrounding the memorial is enclosed to the south and the west by sandstone ashlar walls, which incorporate a flight of steps from High Street to the south and a shorter flight from the west. There is a cast iron balustrade with a Greek-key pattern frieze on these walls. The adjoining stone walls to the west enclose a small memorial garden, although these were added later.

The surrounding wall, piers, gates and steps into St Mary's churchyard, as well as the forecourt walls, steps and balustrade, together with the railings to the churchyard are all included in the listing.

The Story behind The Memorial:

For a town of its size Oldham suffered heavily during the First World War with approximately 2,688 men from the town dying and in 1919 it was resolved that the town should have a war memorial. A campaign was started by the Oldham War Memorial Committee to raise £20,000, not only to pay for the memorial, but also to provide educational scholarships to children who had lost a father, with any surplus funds going to the Oldham Royal Infirmary.

There was considerable local debate about where to site the memorial. Although the obvious location was the highest point of the town, being close to both the parish church and the old Town Hall.

46

It was also adjacent to the Greaves Arms Public House, which was thought by many to be inappropriate.

In the absence of a better position the site was eventually agreed, even though it also meant the rebuilding of the south-western section of the retaining wall of St Mary's churchyard in order to provide the wall that would carry the plaques with the names of those who died.

The memorial was cleaned and restored in 2012-13 and was rededicated on 10th November 2013.

The Inscription

The main inscription is on the south side pedestal and reads: DEATH IS THE GATE OF LIFE 1914-1918, whilst on the north side it simply reads: TO GOD BE THE PRAISE. On the flanking walls of the memorial there are a series of continuous bronze panels, two to the left of the gate and five to the right, with the names of the fallen in relief and shields above the joints. The shields depict, the Royal Arms, the arms of the Duchy of Lancaster, the arms of the County Borough of Oldham, the RAF badge and the White Ensign. On the frieze running across the top of the panels there is the following inscription: THESE TABLETS WERE ERECTED BY THE CITIZENS OF OLDHAM AS A LASTING MEMORIAL TO THEIR FELLOW TOWNSMEN WHO GAVE THEIR LIVES IN THE GREAT WAR ANNO DOMINI 1914-1918. The lower section of the war has a further series of bronze panels with the names of those who died in the Second World War.

10. Manchester War Memorial

St Peter's Square, Manchester M2   Grade II*

Unveiled by Lord Derby on 12th July 1924. He had served with the Grenadier Guards during the Second Boer War, and was Secretary of State for War, a post he had also held from December 1916 to April 1918 (further biographical details can be found on page 28). Lord Derby was assisted by Mrs Dingle from Ancoats, Manchester, who had lost all three of her sons during the First World War. The Dean of Manchester, Rev Gough McCormick and the Baptist minister Rev John Edward Roberts led the service of dedication.

Designed by by Sir Edwin Lutyens and built by the Nine Elms Stone Masonry Works of London.

Design Features:

The cenotaph is made of Portland stone and is flanked by two obelisks and a war stone on a slightly raised coved platform. The memorial is essentially the same design as Lutyen's cenotaph in Whitehall, London, with a pylon in diminishing stages, which supports a bier with the figure of a soldier partially covered by a greatcoat. A wreath sits beneath and to either side of the pylon, which contains Manchester's coat of arms: to the front and rear there is a sword and imperial crown.

The Story behind The Memorial:

Manchester City Council did not make any efforts towards a First World War memorial until 1922, when it was faced by pressure from the local branch of the Royal British Legion. Sites in Piccadilly Gardens and Albert Square were rejected and a site chosen in St Peter's Gardens, although it was thought that it was too close to the stone cross that marked the site of the church that had been demolished in 1907. In his speech at the unveiling of the memorial Lord Derby said that the memorial was not only a tribute to the dead but a warning as to the cost of war.

Rev John Edwards, the Baptist minister of Union Chapel in Oxford Road said that Mrs Dingle, who had lost her three sons in fighting in 1918, represented 'the mothers and wives of Manchester who had made sacrifices greater than life itself.' In 2011 Manchester City Council began a consultation about moving the memorial to allow for an expansion of the city's Metrolink tram system. Although there was some opposition, veteran, church and heritage groups supported the move and the memorial was cleaned and rebuilt in a memorial garden near the south entrance of the Town Hall.

The Inscription

The north-west side of the cenotaph carries the inscription TO THE HONOURED MEMORY OF THOSE WHO GAVE THEIR LIVES FOR THEIR COUNTRY. On the south-east side the words O LORD GOD OF OUR FATHERS KEEP THIS FOREVER IN THE IMAGINATION OF THE THOUGHTS OF THE HEART OF THY PEOPLE are inscribed and THEIR NAME LIVETH FOREVER MORE on the war stone.

A marble plaque was placed near to the memorial inscribed OUR ITALIAN COMRADES 1915-1918. This plaque was removed during the Second World War and returned in 1949 when the dates of the war were added to the memorial. A further plaque was added to commemorate the Korean War.

Everyone Sang

*Siegfried Sassoon MC (1886-1967) commissioned in the Royal Welsh
Fusiliers and posted to France in 1915: nicknamed "Mad Jack".*

Everyone suddenly burst out singing:
And I was filled with such delight
As prisoned birds must find in freedom,
Winging wildly across the white
Orchards and dark-green fields; on – on – and out of sight

Everyone's voice was suddenly lifted;
And beauty came like the setting sun:
My heart was shaken with tears and horror
Drifted away...O, but Everyone
Was a bird and the song was wordless: the singing will never be done.

11. Ashton-under-Lyne and District War Memorial

War Memorial Gardens, Ashton-under-Lyne, Lancashire, OL6

Grade II*

Unveiled on 16th September 1922 by General Sir Ian Hamilton. Hamilton was a career soldier and his biographical details are included in the Crompton War Memorial on page 44, which he also unveiled. The dedication was carried out by Rev W A Parry.

Designed by Percy Howard, a local architect.

Sculpted by John Ashton Floyd, who studied at the Municipal School of Art in Manchester and worked predominately around the city. He worked on war memorials in Ashton-under-Lyne, Royton near Oldham and the Manchester Post Office peace memorial. Lutyens commissioned him to produce the sculptural decoration for the Midland Bank office in Manchester which is Grade II* listed.

Design Features:

The memorial is situated at the centre of a dedicated memorial garden and comprises a bronze group with a winged Victory, who is offering comfort to a collapsed and wounded soldier with her right arm around his shoulder and holding his wrist by way of support. The soldier, who is in battledress, holds a laurel wreath in his left hand and an inverted sword in his right. Victory is on top of a mass of military equipment that represents all of the armed forces. There is an aircraft propeller, rope, sails and an anchor, a tank gear wheel, guns, rifles and steel helmets.

The sculpture stands on a tall square shaft made of Portland stone, which is supported on a pedestal with a moulded plinth and stands on a three-stepped platform. The main pedestal is flanked by rectangular set-back 'wings' whose ends break forward slightly. The faces of the shaft have broad pedimented pilasters with stylised palm leaf friezes. The pedestals and top of the shaft have fluted friezes. Each wing has a life-sized bronze lion, whose heads face outwards: the lion to the left is fighting a writhing serpent, while the one to the right has crushed the serpent under its feet.

The wings carry 38 bronze panels, with the names of those killed in the First World War in relief lettering. The east and west return walls each have a bronze panel and on these are recorded the names of 301 people killed in the Second World War.

The Story behind The Memorial:

Ashton-under-Lyne suffered losses in excess of 1,500 in the First World War, a large number for a small town. An original plan for a memorial was put forward by a local art teacher in 1919: it was a grandiose design and had to be abandoned due to cost. Howard, and Ashton Floyd, who had been responsible for the memorial in the Waterloo and Taunton district of the town, were asked to submit a design. The £8000 cost of the memorial was raised by public subscription.

At the opening ceremony, a temporary wooden viewing platform collapsed and 40 people were injured.

The panels commemorating those killed in the Second World War were unveiled on 11th November 1950 by Alderman E. Clark, Mayor of Ashton.

The Inscription

On both the front and rear of the pedestal are bronze plaques in the form of Roman Army standards adorned with wreaths and bands that give the various theatres of war.

The plaque on the front reads: *BELGIUM FRANCE GALLIPOLI EGYPT ITALY*, whilst the one on the rear reads: *MESOPOTAMIA AFRICA TURKEY MACEDONIA.*

The main inscription which is carried on a bronze panel which has a border and relief lettering reads: *ERECTED IN HONOUR OF THE MEN OF ASHTON-UNDER-LYNE AND DISTRICT WHO FOUGHT FOR KING AND EMPIRE IN THE GREAT WAR, ESPECIALLY THOSE WHO SACRIFICED THEIR LIVES, AND WHOSE NAMES ARE RECORDED HEREON 1914-1919* there are coats of arms to either side of the panel. A similar, narrow panel has been added below which simply reads: *1939-1945.*

12. Stalybridge War Memorial

Junction of Trinity Street and Market Street, Stalybridge, Tameside SK15

Grade II*

Unveiled on 6th November 1921 by the Mayor of Stalybridge, Councillor Mrs Ada Summers. She unveiled the army pedestal and Alderman James Bottomley, who had been mayor of Stalybridge during the war, unveiled the navy pedestal. A wreath was laid on behalf of Stalybridge Royal British Legion of ex-servicemen by former Private Ernest Sykes V.C. who - although from Mossley - his family lived in Stalybridge. The memorial was dedicated by Canon T.H. Sheriff, the Rural Dean of Mottram.

Designed and Sculpted by Ferdinand Victor Blundstone and built by Messrs William Kirkpatrick Ltd.

Design Features:

The memorial takes the form of a large bridgehead in the shape of an ellipse, with the River Tame flowing behind it. In total it is a 110 feet (34m) long wall which is 5ft (1.5m) high, with a pedestal at each end and secondary pedestals, originally topped by crouching lions, although one of these has now been removed. These pedestals are topped with larger than life-size bronze figures. The navy pedestal is topped with a figure of a dying sailor being ministered to by an angel, whilst the army pedestal shows a similar composition with a dying soldier. The cap of the sailor on the navy pedestal bears the name Good Hope.

The Story behind The Memorial:

When the memorial was unveiled in 1921 the ceremony was attended by 24,000 people, which was virtually the whole population of the town, whereas the congregation for the unveiling of the extension for the Second World War on St George's Day 1950 was only in the region of 3,000 to 4,000. The Second World War extension was unveiled by Mrs Gertrude Monday, who had lost her husband in the First World War and her son in the Second World War.

The Inscription

From the left of the memorial, the minor pedestal with a lion and the town coat of arms has the inscription FRANCE PALESTINE MESOPOTAMIA EGYPT EAST AFRICA. The wall then leads to the navy pedestal which also has the coat of arms and the inscription 1914 1918 JUTLAND ZEEBRUGGE THE FALKLAND ISLES – REMEMBER THE LOVE OF THEM WHO CAME NOT HOME FROM THE WAR. SEE YOU TO IT THAT THEY SHALL NOT HAVE DIED IN VAIN. The army pedestal also has the coat of arms and the inscription – 1914 1918. THE MARNE, YPRES, THE SOMME. ALL YOU WHO PASS BY REMEMBER WITH GRATITUDE THE MEN OF STALYBRIDGE WHO DIED FOR YOU. The pedestal on the far right of the memorial, from which the lion has been removed, has an inscription taken from Katherine Tynan's poem Flower of Youth and reads – NOW HEAVEN IS BY THE YOUNG INVADED. THEIR LAUGHTER'S IN THE HOUSE OF GOD. The tablets of Polish granite are engraved with 628 names of those who fell in the First World War.
Bronze railings and a flower garden were added after the Second World War. The railings again bear the coat of arms of the town and a tablet which says – 1939 – 1945 ON LAND, ON SEA, AND IN THE AIR AT HOME AND ABROAD.

Stalybridge War Memorial (left) details previous page

Stockport War Memorial Art Gallery (below) details next page

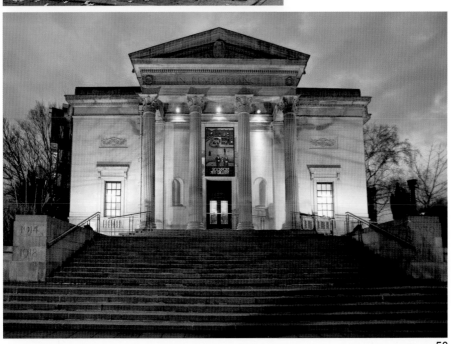

13. Stockport War Memorial Art Gallery

Wellington Road South, Stockport, Greater Manchester SK3   Grade II*

Inaugurated on 15th October 1925 by Prince Henry, the third son of King George V and Queen Mary. Prince Henry left Eton in 1919 and joined the Army as a career soldier He took a commission in the Kings Royal Rifle Corps, by which time he had been given the title Duke of Gloucester.

Designed by James Theodore Halliday (1882-1932), senior partner in Halliday, Paterson and Agate, who worked with Giles Gilbert Scott on Battersea Power Station.

Sculpted by Gilbert Ledward

Design Features:

The war memorial is the whole art gallery, which is designed in the neoclassical Greek revival style with a central portico. The building is on a prominent corner site above street level with a broad flight of 23 steps rising from the street. The low flanking walls are constructed of Portland Stone, with cast-iron lamp standards, and the dates 1914-1918 on one side and 1939-1945 on the other. There is a deep frieze carved with the words – IN REMEMBRANCE – flanked with laurel wreaths, and the pediment has the arms of Stockport in the tympanum. The large double doors have brass paterae and glazed lights protected by brass balusters, with niches and windows to each side of the doors.

The entrance leads into a marble paved hall, to each side of which is a gallery and ahead, the memorial hall itself. There is an open staircase with a brass hand rail and iron balusters leading to the first floor. The Memorial Hall itself has a glass dome and a marble paved floor. The walls are lined with white marble plaques bearing the names of 2,200 men killed in the First World War and further plaques added later with the names of those who died in World War Two and subsequent wars.

In the Memorial Hall is an apse, which contains a statue of a life-sized figure of Britannia, draped in a flag, holding a sword of honour in her right hand, with a laurel wreath signifying victory in her left hand. There is a figure of a kneeling man at Britannia's feet. Underneath the man is a shield which is crushing a serpent, symbolic of the victory of good over evil, and a broken sword to signify the cost of victory.

The Story behind The Memorial:

Stockport Council had already decided to build an art gallery by 1912, although work was not started by the beginning of the First World War with its restrictions on building materials and labour shortages, which brought the plan to a temporary halt. In 1919 it was decided that the gallery should include a commemorative sculpture and that the whole building should be a war memorial. The land was donated by the trustees of the late Samuel Kay and the cost of the building was £24,000, out of which £2,100 represented the cost of the sculpture. The total cost was raised by public subscription and the foundation stone was laid in 15th September 1923.

The Inscription

Around the wall behind the statue are the inscriptions – LET THOSE WHO COME AFTER SEE THAT THEIR NAME BE NOT FORGOTTEN and THEY DIED FOR FREEDOM AND HONOUR. On the staircase to the first floor is the inscription THIS MEMORIAL WAS ERECTED BY VOLUNTARY SUBSCRIPTION TO PERPETUATE THE MEMORY OF THE MEN OF STOCKPORT WHO FELL IN THE GREAT WAR, 1914-1918.

14. Macclesfield War Memorial
Park Green, Macclesfield, Cheshire, SK11 7NE
Grade II*

Unveiled by the Mayor of Macclesfield unveiled the memorial on 21st September 1921, in front of a crowd of 20,000 with the Bishop of Chester performing the dedication.

Designed by John Millard (1862-1948), who was born in Wigan, attended art schools in Warrington and Manchester where he won a scholarship to study in Paris, before teaching at the Dover School of Art. From 1905 he was Principal Master of the Modelling School at the Manchester School of Art where, by 1919, he had become Professor of Sculpture and by 1934 Head of Modelling and Sculpture. Millard also taught at Manchester Grammar School and he taught anatomy and dissection at Manchester University Medical School.

Design Features:

A tall - 23ft (7m) - tapering ashlar pillar rises from a three-stage base. To the front of this base is an engaged column which bears the principal inscription and supports two bronze sculptures. The base is flanked by low curved walls, which end in tapering capped piers to create a semi-circular forecourt.

The front of the pillar has a Latin cross, carved in low relief and the other three sides together with the wall piers have bronze wreaths. Four similar piers, which are freestanding, are placed separately in a square pattern and have the names of the dead from the First World War on them.

There are three bronze figures on the memorial: on top of the pillar is a hooded female mourner with her head bowed and her draped gown partly gathered in her right hand, while in her left hand she holds a wreath by her side.

On the base, a gassed soldier lies on his back as Britannia leans over him offering him a laurel wreath; in her hand she holds a furled flag.

The Story behind The Memorial:

The idea of a war memorial for Macclesfield was first mooted by Mayor J. G. Frost in December 1918, and he suggested that it would be better if the town had a single point of remembrance rather that a series of church based memorials.

A War Memorial Committee had its first meeting in February 1919 and immediately set itself the very ambitious goal of raising £10,000. By May, £2,000 had been raised and it was agreed that two thirds of the funds should go to widows and orphans of those killed with the remaining third to be spent on a memorial, which would be sited in either the Market Place or Park Green. By June donations had reached £3,500.

Millard submitted a model of his proposed design to the War Memorial Committee along with an estimate of the total cost which was a little over £4,000. There was concern over the portrayal of a dead soldier on the memorial, especially because it showed a soldier who had been gassed and had died because of a mistake on his part. Dead bodies on First World War memorials are very rare because the official view was that they should not be included on memorials, and where they do feature it usually involves an heroic death so the proposal was controversial. The vicar of Macclesfield also wanted some Christian iconography, so a cross was added. Although Millard produced an alternative model, it was his first design that was eventually agreed.

There was a further debate in the town over which names were to be included on the memorial. The widow and brother of William Knight of the Royal Engineers asked that his name be included on the memorial although he had committed suicide. The committee was sympathetic but took the decision that the names of only those killed in action should be included.

Following the Second World War two curved bronze relief panels were added to the flanking walls to bear the names of those who died in the Second World War.

The Inscription

THIS MEMORIAL WAS ERECTED IN HONOUR OF MACCLESFIELD MEN WHO GAVE THEIR LIVES FOR THEIR KING AND EMPIRE IN THE GREAT WAR 1914-1918 UNVEILED BY THE MAYOR OF MACCLESFIELD ALDERMAN J.G. FROST J.P. SEPTEMBER 21ST 1921.

There is a bronze wreath to the right side of the pillar, below which is inscribed: FRANCE/ BELGIUM/EGYPT, whilst in a similar position to the rear is inscribed PALESTINE/ MESOPOTAMIA/RUSSIA, and to the left side, ITALY/MACEDONIA/DARDENELLES. There are bronze plaques on the flanking walls which have the names of the dead of the Second World War, above which is the inscription: IN MEMORY OF THOSE WHO GAVE THEIR LIVES IN THE WAR 1939-1945.

West Derby War memorial (above) see next page

15. West Derby War Memorial

Junction of St Helens Road and Burrow's Lane, Eccleston Lane Ends, Prescot, Liverpool, L34   Grade II*

Unveiled on 23rd July, 1922 by Francis Chavasse, Bishop of Liverpool. His son, Captain Noel Chavasse, was the most decorated British officer of the First World War, and the only person in the war to be awarded the Victoria Cross twice, the second time posthumously.

Designed by Walter Gilbert and Louis Weingartner. Gilbert was born in Rugby and studied at the Birmingham Municipal School of Art and the National Art Training School, which is now the Royal College of Art. Little is known about Louis Weingartner except that he was from Lucerne in Switzerland and was a jeweller at the School of Art in Birmingham before starting to work with Gilbert in the early 1900s.

Together Gilbert and Weingartner were responsible for some nationally important work including the gates at Buckingham Palace, the Victoria Monument in the Mall and various works at Liverpool Cathedral. They were also responsible for the Liverpool Exchange Newsroom Memorial and the memorial in Burnley, Lancashire.

Design Features:

The memorial is in a paved area enclosed by brick walls, gates and railings on a busy road junction. It comprises a life-sized bronze statue of a young army officer who is raising his field glasses to his eyes with his left hand whilst holding a revolver in his right. The officer's left foot is resting on a German Pickelhaube helmet. The sculpture stands on a square Portland stone pedestal on a three-tier plinth. A life-size figure of a young woman, dressed in the style of the day, is climbing the steps of the plinth and she is stretching upwards offering a laurel branch to the soldier. To symbolise the fact that the officer did not survive the war, the young woman is just out of reach of the officer.

There is a bronze panel that encircles all four faces of the pedestal on which bas-relief figures represent marching soldiers, airmen, soldiers with camels and seamen loading a naval gun.

The Story behind The Memorial:

Although geographically the memorial is in Prescot rather than West Derby in Liverpool, West Derby was the principal manor of the six ancient divisions of the County of Lancashire which were known as Hundreds. The memorial was commissioned by Dr Frederick Dixon-Nutall, a glass manufacturer whose son, Lieutenant J F Dixon-Nutall, served with the West Lancashire Divisional Royal Engineers and was killed in action. The figures in the memorial are modelled on Lt. Dixon-Nutall's wife and brother.

The Inscription

Around the bronze panel on the pedestal there is the following inscription in relief: THE LAURELS OF THE SONS ARE WATERED FROM THE HEARTS OF MOTHERS.
The main inscription which is on the front face of the pedestal reads: TO THE GLORIOUS MEMORY OF ALL THOSE FROM THE WEST DERBY HUNDRED OF THE COUNTY PALATINE OF LANCASTER WHO FOUGHT & GAVE THEIR LIVES FOR THEIR KING AND COUNTRY IN THE GREAT WAR 1914-1918.

16. Liverpool Cenotaph

St George's Plateau, Lime Street, Liverpool L1

Grade I

Unveiled at 11am on 11th November 1930 by Edward George Villiers Stanley, 17th Earl of Derby, Lord Lieutenant of Lancashire, a former regular army office. He was Secretary of State for War from 1916 to 1918, and again from 1922 to 1924, and Ambassador to France 1918 to 1920. The Stanley's family seat was Knowsley Hall on the outskirts of Liverpool. In August 1914 Lord Derby had been instrumental in a campaign that saw 1,500 men joining the Kings Liverpool Regiment in two days with a further three more battalions raised within a week.

Designed by Lionel Budden (1877-1956) who was born in Liverpool, and attended Merchant Taylors School. He graduated from the University of Liverpool with an MA in 1910, before starting to teach there from 1911. Budden became an Associate Professor and was later appointed Roscoe Professor in Architecture, before retiring in 1952. He also designed the Grade II* Birkenhead War Memorial.

Sculpted by by Herbert Tyson Smith

Design Features:

The Cenotaph is in a prominent position in front of the neo-classical St George's Hall. Described in Pevsner Architectural Guides as "one of the most remarkable war memorials in the country" the large scale of St George's Hall with its colonnaded front demanded a grand and horizontal memorial and the resulting design is an altar that is 35 feet (10.7m) long and 11 feet (3.4M) high sitting on a platform that is 61 feet (18.6m) long and 15 feet (4.6m) deep. On the two faces of the cenotaph are large bronze panels measuring 31 feet (9.4m). On the ends of the cenotaph are circular bronze shields are the arms of Liverpool and the years of the two world wars.

It is, undoubtedly, the bronze low relief sculptures that give the memorial its dramatic appearance. The panels are neither allegorical nor heroic as seen on other First World War memorials but, instead, it is in a modern and realistic style. The face that is towards St George's Hall has serried ranks of servicemen representing in a change from the usual order the Navy, Air Force and Army with officers and enlisted men included n each of the arms of service. The panel facing Liverpool Lime Street Station shows mourners of all ages and social classes placing flowers and wreaths on a Stone of Remembrance behind which are ranks of Commonwealth War Graves Commission graves fading into the far distance.

The Story behind The Memorial:

The Cenotaph is on a site occupied by a temporary wooden memorial, which had been in situ since the end of the war, and was among the later of the permanent First World War memorials to be unveiled. A plan had been put forward to have a memorial paid for my public subscription as had been common with other memorials in Liverpool although this was abandoned in 1920 due to the high levels of social depravation being suffered in the city. In 1926 an alternative proposal was adopted using public funds and a competition to be judged by Charles Reilly, Professor of Architecture at the University of Liverpool.

Over 250 entries were received, anonymously, and the competition was won by Lionel Budden who was Reilly's assistant. It was chosen because of its "dignity, simplicity and reserve" that represented an "idea of permanence and immovability". There were dissenters about the shape of the Cenotaph and its location, but Professor Reilly said that "it will be seen that Liverpool has placed in front her finest building, as the Greeks placed in front of their temples, a grand altar".

The sculptor of the panels was Liverpool born Herbert Tyson Smith and it is, perhaps, due to his service in the Royal Flying Corps during the First World War that led to him portraying airmen immediately behind men of the Royal Navy rather than after the Army as military precedence would normally dictate. The ranks of marching men have been likened to automatons although every face is different and the expressions are of determination rather than unthinking obedience. The panels on both sides of the memorial are wonderfully detailed with finger nails, knuckles and boot laces being clearly distinguishable. The mourners depicted include children together with men and women of different ages and social classes "all the people" reflecting the inscription. The front rank of the graves depicted show all arms of service together with the badges of local regiments and Irish regiments together with a Star of David to illustrate the background of Liverpool's population.

The Inscription

Three of the four inscriptions on the memorial are of biblical origin: on the side facing St George's Hall – AS UNKNOWN AND YET WELL KNOWN AS DYING AND BEHOLD WE LIVE – 2 Corinthians 6:9 above the bronze plaque and OUT OF THE NORTH PARTS A GREAT COMPANY AND A MIGHTY ARMY – Ezekiel 38:15. Below the panel on the other face – AND THE VICTORY THAT DAY WAS TURNED INTO MOURNING UNTO ALL THE PEOPLE – 2 Samuel 19:2 above the panel is inscribed TO THE MEN OF LIVERPOOL WHO FELL IN THE GREAT WAR to which was subsequently added AND ALL WHO HAVE FALLEN IN CONFLICT SINCE.

17. Heroes of the Marine Engine Room
St Nicholas Place, Liverpool, L3
Grade II*

Unveiled on 6th May 1916, one year after the sinking of RMS Lusitania by a German U-Boat.

Designed by by Sir William Goscombe John.

Design Features:
A banded granite obelisk 47ft 5ins (14.5m) tall rises from a pedestal which sits on a tall squared champhered plinth. The east and west faces of this plinth each have two life-sized faces – those on the east representing stokers whilst those on the west are of engineers. The corners at the foot of the obelisk, over the level of the heads of the figures, are carved representations of the "elements": Earth on the north east corner, Water on the north west, Fire on the south east, and Air on the south west. On each face there are stylised waves with a rising or setting sun above them, which are carved in low relief in the same modernistic-style in which the whole memorial is carved. At the top of the obelisk, on each face, is a female form, draped and representing the sea. Between these figures are breech buoys and above them a gilded torch flame crowns the memorial.

The Story behind The Memorial:
The Heroes of the Marine Engine Room is an unusual memorial in several respects. Firstly, it was not designed as, or intended to be, a war memorial. Although not paid for by the White Star Line, they commissioned it to commemorate the 32 engineers of RMS Titanic who stayed at their posts as the ship sank, to ensure that the electric telegraph and the lights remained in operation as long as possible – all 32 sacrificed their lives. By the time the memorial was ready, losses among engine room crews during the First World War were already mounting, and it was decided to extend the scope of the memorial to encompass all maritime engine room fatalities. Secondly, as it was unveiled in May 1916, this memorial is probably the first memorial to those killed in the First World War. Thirdly, and perhaps, most importantly, at the time of its construction, it was the first memorial in the United Kingdom to represent "ordinary" men or women rather than members of the social or military elite. The design, style and depiction of "ordinary" people had considerable influence on memorials built after 1919.

The Inscription

There are two inscriptions on the pedestal. On the south face it reads: THE BRAVE DO NOT DIE THEIR DEEDS LIVE ON FOREVER AND CALL UPON US TO EMMULATE THEIR COURAGE AND DEVOTION TO DUTY. On the north face it reads: ALL HEROES OF THE MARINE ENGINE ROOM THIS MEMORIAL WAS ERECTED BY INTERNATIONAL SUBSCRIPTION MCMXVI.

Into Battle: A Prayer for Those on the Staff

Capt. The Hon. Julian Grenfell DSO (Died 26th May 1915. Age 27) – known as "the happy warrior" "I adore war. It is like a big picnic without the objectlessness of a picnic. I've never been so well or so happy"

The naked earth is warm with spring,
And with green grass and bursting trees
Leans to the sun's gaze glorying,
And quivers in the sunny breeze;
And life is colour and warmth and light,
And a striving evermore or these;
And he is dead who will not fight;
And who dies fighting has increase.

The fighting man shall from the sun
Take warmth, and life from the glowing earth;
Speed with the light-foot winds to run,
And with the trees to newer birth;
And find, when fighting shall be done,
Great rest, and fullness after death.

All the bright company of Heaven
Hold him in their high comradeship,
The Dog-Star, and the Sisters Seven,
Orion's Belt and sworded hip.

The woodland trees that stand together,
They stand to him each one a friend;
They gently speak in the windy weather;
They guide to valley and ridge's end.

Bid him be swift and keen as they,
As keen of ear, as swift of sight.

The blackbird sings to him, "Brother, brother,
If this be the last song you shall sing,
Sing well, for you may not sing another; Brother, sing"

In dreary, doubtful, waiting hours,
Before the brazen frenzy starts,
The horses show him nobler powers;
O patient eyes, courageous hearts!

And when the burning moment breaks,
And all things else are out of mind,
And only joy of battle takes
Him by the throat, and makes him blind,

Through joy and blindness he shall know,
Not caring much to know, that still
Nor lead nor steel shall reach him, so
That it be not the Destined Will.

The thundering line of battle stands,
And in the air death moans and sings;
But Day shall clap him with strong hands,
And Night shall hold him in their wings.

18. Birkenhead War Memorial
Hamilton Square, Birkenhead, Merseyside CH41
Grade II*

Unveiled on 1st July 1925 by Lt General Sir Richard H.K. Butler, a career soldier who fought with distinction, and was wounded during the Second Boer War. During the First World War, Butler rose to the rank of Lt General and commanded III Corps. By 1925 Butler was General Officer Commanding-in-Chief Western Command. Around 20,000 people attended the unveiling.

Designed by Lionel Budden

Sculpted by Herbert Tyson Smith.

Design Features:

The cenotaph is rectangular in plan, made from Portland Stone and stands 25ft (7m) high. The longer sides of the rectangle face east and west. Set on three steps on a paved area there are flag poles flanking the memorial which are part of the listing. On the longer sides of the memorial are Westmorland stone panels bearing the names of those men of Birkenhead who fell in the war, whilst on the shorter sides in smaller panels are the names of those killed in the Second World War; above these panels are carvings of female figures, one holding a wreath and the other a medallion; above them are the arms of Birkenhead.

Above the figures and panels there is a frieze of festoons of laurel. Below the panels on the two longer sides are circular plaques carved with crests of the forces involved in the war. The top of the memorial is a sarcophagus.

The Story behind The Memorial:

Birkenhead's War Memorial Executive Committee organised a competition in 1922 in order to find a design for the town's war memorial. Twenty-one proposals were submitted and these were exhibited in Birkenhead in February 1923, where they were assessed by Charles Reilly, who was a Professor at the Liverpool School of Architecture. A number of designs were put forward, to be judged by Major Gilbert Fraser, President of the Liverpool Architectural Society. including one by Lionel Budden, a former student of Charles Reilly and senior lecturer at the School of Architecture in Liverpool. Budden's design was chosen and he, in turn, appointed Herbert Tyson Smith as sculptor.

The memorial was always intended to be situated in Hamilton Square in Birkenhead, and the original choice was on the vacant north side of the square. However public opinion favoured a more prominent position on the east side of the square in front of the Town Hall. The site in front of the Town Hall already had a statue of John Laird, a former MP for Birkenhead and Chairman of Camel Lairds Shipbuilders. It was agreed that the war memorial should take precedence and Laird's statue was moved to the west side of the square.

The memorial cost £3,932 and was built by Joseph Davies of Birkenhead and H.A. Clegg and Sons of Chester.

In anticipation of the First World War centenary commemorations the memorial was cleaned and restored in 2013.

The Inscription

There are the following inscriptions on the memorial: on the east side which faces the Town Hall: IN MEMORY OF THE MEN OF BIRKENHEAD WHO GAVE THEIR LIVES IN THE GREAT WAR; whilst, on the west side: ALL THESE WERE HONOURED IN THEIR GENERATIONS AND WERE THE GLORY OF THEIR TIMES. On the medallion held in one of the carvings are the words: HE DIED FOR FREEDOM AND HONOUR – the words on the Memorial Plaque or 'Dead Man's Penny' which were issued to the next-of-kin of all British and Empire personnel who were killed as a result of the First World War. Above the front seat ledge a later addition states: 1939-45 THE BOOK OF REMEMBRANCE MAY BE INSPECTED IN THE TOWN HALL. The dates 1914-1919 are inscribed below the figures on the short sides whilst above them 1939-1945 WAR is inscribed.

19. Hoylake and West Kirby War Memorial

Grange Hill, West Kirby, Wirral CH48
Grade II*

Unveiled on 16th December 1922 by the local dignatory F.E. Smith, the first Earl of Birkenhead, a barrister and Conservative politician. He had recently held the office of Lord Chancellor and was a future Secretary of State for India. During the First World War, Smith had served in France, as Solicitor-General and then Attorney-General

Designed by local architects Hall & Glover.

Sculpted by Charles Sargent Jagger (1885-1935), who had been recommended by Sir George Frampton, was the son of a Sheffield colliery manager, and educated at Sheffield Grammar School, before taking an apprenticeship with the jewellers, Mappin & Webb. After attending Sheffield School of Art, from 1908 to 1911 he continued his studies at the Royal College of Art in London. Jagger was in Rome when the First World War broke out and immediately returned to England, where he enlisted into the Artists' Rifles, before being commissioned into the Worcestershire Regiment. He served in Gallipoli and on the Western Front, was wounded three times and awarded the Military Cross. Jagger designed or contributed to 18b war memorials in Britain, Europe, Egypt, India and Australia. His style, especially when portraying soldiers, went for realism against the idealism and modernism of some of his contemporaries.

Design Features:

The memorial is situated on Grange Hill, near the north west corner of the Wirral Peninsular, from where there are views to both Liverpool and North Wales, as well as across Liverpool Bay. The monument is surrounded by black metal railings and is over 47ft (15m) tall and built from granite, with two larger than life-size bronze figures. The four-sided shouldered obelisk with a curved top stands on a granite plinth and T-shaped pedestal. On the front of the memorial, facing west, is a bronze figure of a woman who represents Humanity.

She is standing on a globe, which is itself standing on a squat cross-shaped granite plinth and a square pedestal. The dates 1914-1919 are inscribed on the pedestal. Hanging from the woman's wrist are, broken chains to signify that humanity is again free. She is holding a wreath of twigs and poppies whilst her head rests against a pillow of lilies, and on her chest is an oval form containing a baby. On the curved shoulders of the obelisk, which flank the figure, are the names of those killed in the First World War. There are also names inscribed on the north and south faces of the obelisk.

On the opposite face of the obelisk to the sculptor of 'Humanity' is the figure of a soldier – 'Soldier on Defence, who represents redemption and sacrifice. The soldier is dressed in full campaign kit with his rifle held in both hands across his body in a gesture of defence. A German helmet lies at his feet, symbolic of the defeat of an enemy. The soldier's helmet is pushed back in a realistic manner, rather than square on his head as it should be.

The Story behind The Memorial:

The 'Soldier on Defence' figure was exhibited at the Royal Academy in 1921 and it earned Jagger a number of commissions.

64

The Inscription

The granite plaque below the figure of the woman is inscribed – AT THE CALL OF
KING AND COUNTRY THEY LEFT ALL THAT WAS DEAR TO THEM, ENDUING
HARDNESS, FACED DANGER, AND FINALLY PASSED OUT OF THE SIGHT OF
MEN BY THE PATH OF DUTY AND SELF SACRIFICE, GIVING UP THEIR OWN
LIVES THAT OTHERS MIGHT LIVE IN FREEDOM. LET THOSE WHO COME
AFTER SEE TO IT THAT THEIR NAMES BE NOT FORGOTTEN. A small plaque
under this inscription bears the dates 1939-1945, whilst larger plaques are inscribed
with the names of those killed during the Second World War. A further plaque records
the names of those killed in conflicts after the Second World War.

Below the 'Soldier on Defence' sculpture is the inscription – IN GRATITUDE TO GOD
AND TO THE MEN AND WOMEN FROM THESE PARTS WHO LAID DOWN THEIR
LIVES IN THE GREAT WAR 1914 - 1919 – 1939 – 1945 THEY WERE A WALL UNTO
US BOTH BY NIGHT AND DAY. Starting on the east face of the obelisk and in an
anti-clockwise direction is the inscription – WHO STANDS IF FREEDOM FALL WHO
DIES IN ENGLAND LIVE.

The names of thirty-seven men are not included on the memorial but are recorded in
the parish church.

20. Port Sunlight War Memorial

Junction of the Causeway and the Diamond, Port Sunlight, Wirral, CH62

Grade I

Unveiled on 3rd December 1921 by two Lever Brothers Limited employees – Sergeant E G Eames of Port Sunlight, who had been blinded on the Somme, and Private R E Cruikshank from the London office, who had been awarded the Victoria Cross in Palestine. These two employees were chosen by a ballot conducted among staff who had served during the First World War.

Designed and Sculpted by Sir W Goscombe John R.A.

Design Features:

The memorial comprises a runic granite cross with a chamfered shaft on an octagonal podium. Around the podium is a parapet broken by four flights of steps between which, at road level, are seating areas and flower beds. Around the base of the cross are figures representing three soldiers, one of whom is wounded and is being tended by a nurse and the other two are in a defensive posture facing an unseen enemy. The soldiers are defending a seated woman and three children.

Children also feature on plaques that flank the top of the steps, these children are holding wreathes. Around the parapet there are a further four reliefs depicting the Royal Navy, the Army, an Anti-Aircraft gun section and Red Cross Services. The overall theme of the memorial is "Defence of the Realm". The whole memorial stands 38ft (12m) high and is 73ft (22m) in diameter.

The Story behind The Memorial:

This dramatic memorial was conceived by William Hesketh Lever of Lever Brothers, the cleaning materials company, most famous at the time for Sunlight Soap. It is situated at the cross road of the two widest boulevards of Port Sunlight Village, the model village built by Lever for his employees. Lever, later 1st Viscount Leverhulme, was Chairman of the

Empire War Memorial League and realised that sculptors would be busy at the end of the war, so he commissioned Goscombe John in 1916 to design a memorial to those of his workers who were killed in the war.

Goscombe John exhibited figures he created for the memorial at the Royal Academy exhibitions in 1919 and 1920. It was Lever's wish that the figures were not only servicemen but he wanted to express the social cohesion of his workers and their family in a war that affected the whole population. From the various figures designed, Lever and his committee chose the ones that were to be cast. The casting was carried out by A.B. Burton of Kings Ditton with the stonework and construction by William Kirkpatrick Limited in Manchester.

The Inscription

There are 511 names on the memorial including 117 from the Second World War. There are substantial inscriptions on the memorial:
THEIR NAMES SHALL LIVE FOR EVER AND THEIR GLORY SHALL NOT BE BLOTTED OUT.
South panel: THESE ARE NOT DEAD SUCH SPIRITS NEVER DIE; ON THE ADJOINING PANELS ARE INSCRIBED THE NAMES OF THOSE FROM THE OFFICES AND WORKS OF LEVER BROTHERS LIMITED AND THEIR ASSOCIATED COMPANIES OVERSEAS AND ALSO FROM PORT SUNLIGHT WHO LAID DOWN THEIR LIVES IN THE GREAT WAR 1914 1919.

North panel THIS MEMORIAL ERECTED BY LEVERS BROTHERS LIMITED AND THE COMPANY'S EMPLOYEES IN ALL PARTS OF THE BRITISH EMPIRE AND I ALLIED COUNTRIES WAS UNVEILED ON DECEMBER 3RD 1921 BY SERGEANT E.G. EAMES OF PORT SUNLIGHT WHO LOST HIS SIGHT AT THE FIRST BATTLE OF THE SOMME IN FRANCE 1916 AND BY PRIVATE R.E. CRUICKSHANK OF THE LONDON BRANCH OFFICE WHO WAS AWARDED THE VICTORIA CROSS IN 1918 FOR CONSPICUOUS BRAVERY AND DEVOTION TO DUTY IN PALESTINE.
Base of the plinth south side – THE NAMES OF ALL WHO SERVED NUMBERING OVER FOUR THOUSAND AND RECORDED IN A BOOK DEPOSITED BENEATH THIS STONE AND ALSO IN SIMILAR BOOKS IN CHRIST CHURCH AND THE LADY LEVER ART GALLERY.
Wall surrounding the central platform – DULCE ET DECORUM EST PRO PATRIA MORI THEIR NAME SHAL LIVE FOR EVER AND THEIR GLORY SHALL NOT BE BLOTTED OUT.
Reverse of wall – TO OUR GLORIOUS DEAD.

How War Memorials are selected to be Grade I and Grade II*

War memorials form a poignant and integral part of our cultural heritage. They stand as eloquent witnesses to the tragic impact of world events on local communities and the sacrifices they made.

Although the war memorial tradition as we know it today began in England in the 19th century, the vast majority (97%) of those listed were constructed in the period following the First World War.

The scale of loss following the First World War was, and remains, incomprehensible, and the outpouring of grief that followed this tragic conflict sparked the first widespread construction of war memorials in England. Historic England has always cared deeply about the nation's war memorial heritage and the first war memorial listing took place in 1948. Yet, in the lead up to the centenary of the First World War it was recognised that many war memorials across the country were not getting the level of protection they deserve.

As a result, in 2014 Historic England embarked upon a five-year project to add 2,500 war memorials to the National Heritage List for England (known as The List). Listing war memorials is not a preservation order but it is intended to ensure that a memorial's essential character and interest is maintained and listed building consent via the planning system is needed for changes that might affect its special interest.

War Memorials can be added to the National Heritage List for England because of their architectural, historical or special interest and can be listed at either Grade II, Grade II* or Grade I. As most war memorials erected by communities are conventional in terms of their architectural design they are mainly listed at Grade II.

However, some war memorials are of such high visual or historical interest that they are listed at Grade II* or even Grade I.

Grade II* status will be awarded to memorials with an above- average level of special interest. They may be highly unusual in form or symbolism, or demonstrate a high level of artistic accomplishment. In some cases they may be the works of celebrated designers and sculptors, such as the Hoylake and West Kirby memorial obelisk (image right)by C.S. Jagger at Hoylake, in Merseyside of 1922, but the designers, masons or artists do not need to be famous for this level to be achieved.

Those that are of exceptional interest and rarity can be listed at Grade I.

These will possess outstanding levels of design interest, in terms of architectural or sculptural conception, and will be of the greatest historic interest.

For example the Hall of Memory in Birmingham, West Midlands designed by S. N. Cooke and W. N. Twist,  with exterior sculptures by renowned sculptor Albert Toft. If further research brings up new information relating to the significance of a memorial it is possible for its listing to be upgraded to either Grade II* or Grade I.

Anyone can put forward a war memorial for listing, whether it is an exceptional example, such as those listed in this book, or a more standard example that nonetheless stands as a poignant testament to the grief and suffering caused by conflict.

Why not visit the National Heritage List for England and search for your local memorial to see if it is already listed. If it is a freestanding memorial and does not already appear on the list you can apply for it to be listed. In this way you can ensure that your local memorial is protected and that it can continue to commemorate those who lost their lives through conflict for generations to come.

Dr. Emma Login
First World War Memorials Programme Manager

 Historic England

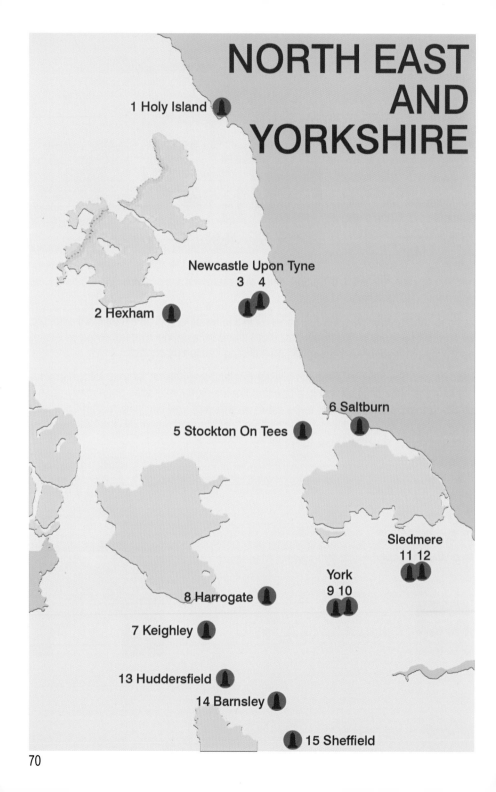

NORTH EAST AND YORKSHIRE

1 Holy Island

Newcastle Upon Tyne
3 4

2 Hexham

6 Saltburn

5 Stockton On Tees

Sledmere
11 12

York
9 10

8 Harrogate

7 Keighley

13 Huddersfield

14 Barnsley

15 Sheffield

CONTENTS

Map reference and Memorial Name   **Page**

1. Holy Island War Memorial (also known as the Lindisfarne War Memorial)

The Heugh, Holy Island, Northumberland, TD15
Grade II*

Unveiled on 4th June 1922 by Major M. Crossman: the Crossman family were Lords of Lindisfarne. The dedication of the memorial was made by Rev. W.B. Hall.

Designed by Sir Edwin Lutyens.

Design Features:
Lutyens designed 15 War Crosses which were essentially the same: the earliest was at Miserden in Gloucestershire in 1920. This example is made of Doddington Stone and is a slender tapering cross 16ft (5m) tall, lozenge in section and the short cross arms are linked to the base by stop chamfers and cyma moulding. The shaft rises from a three stage base which stands on a low, circular step.

The memorial is to the south of the ruins of Lindisfarne Priory and overlooks Lindisfarne Castle and harbour.

The Story behind The Memorial:
Lutyens had carried out the conversion of Lindisfarne Castle into a house for Edward Hudson in 1902, and it is doubtless through this connection that Lutyens came to be commissioned to design the island's war memorial. Lutyens donated his fee for his work to the War Memorial Committee.

During the winter of 1983/4 the top of the shaft of the cross was so badly damaged in storms that it was necessary to replace it.

The Inscription

On the east face of the middle section of the base is inscribed: TO THE GLORY OF GOD AND IN GRATEFUL MEMORY OF OUR GLORIOUS DEAD 1914-1918. On the west face the inscription reads: TO THE GLORY OF GOD AND IN GRATEFUL MEMORY OF OUR GLORIOUS DEAD 1939-1945. The names of the dead are incised below the faces of the lower stage.

2. Northumberland Fusiliers War Memorial Gateway

**Beaumont Street entrance to Abbey Gardens,
Hexham, Northumberland NE46   Grade II***

Unveiled on 2th October 1919 by Major-General Sir Percy S Wilkinson. General Wilkinson was a career soldier who commanded the 9th (Secunderabad) Division during the First World War and had been Colonel of the Northumberland Fusiliers since 1915. The memorial was dedicated by Rev. J.E. McVitie (also shown as being spelled McVittee and McVittie).

Design Features:
The memorial was an existing structure and the name of the builder is no longer known. It was a late eighteenth or early nineteenth century arch that was moved from its original site and placed at the entrance to the Abbey Gardens, where plaques were added so that it could serve as a memorial to the men of the 4th Battalion Northumberland Fusiliers who were killed in the First World War. The plaques on the memorial were restored in 1998.

The Story behind The Memorial:
The memorial was created at the personal expense of James T. Robb JP of Hexham, who was the owner of Robb's Department Store.The store was built on the site of the White Hart Inn in Fore Street Hexham, and the arch which serves as the memorial was the entrance to the inn.

Mr Robb gave the arch to the town "...in order to commemorate the splendid services of the 4th Battalion of the Northumberland Fusiliers (TF) throughout the war, and as a personal thank offering for the return of my three sons." Robb's three sons had all served as Captains in the 4th Battalion Northumberland Fusiliers and all returned safely from the war.

The Inscription

The left hand plaque is headed by an image of St George slaying a dragon and reads – THIS ARCH WAS PRESENTED TO THE TOWN TO COMMEMORATE THE SERVICES OF THE 4th NORTHUMBERLAND FUSILIERS (T.F.) IN FRANCE AND BELGIUM DURING THE WAR 1915-1918. THE COMPANIES WERE FROM THE FOLLOWING PLACES - A HEXHAM; B BELLINGHAM; C HAYDON BRIDGE; D PRUDHOE; E CORBRIDGE; F HALTWHISTLE; G NEWBURN; H PRUDHOE; HEADQUARTERS HEXHAM (Editor's note - the letters refer to the title of the Company, for example C Company was based at Haydon Bridge) THE GIFT OF J.T.R. 1919.

The right hand plaque is also headed by an image of St George and carries the inscription – THE BATTALION WAS MOBILISED AT HEXHAM ON AUGUST 4th 1914 & PROCEEDED TO FRANCE ON APRIL 20th 1915 IT TOOK PART IN THE FIGHTING AT THE FOLLOWING PLACES 1915 APRIL-MAY YPRES (St JULIEN) MAY-JULY HOOGE SANCTUARY WOOD-WULVERCHEM AUG-NOV ARMENTIERS 1915-6 DEC-MARCH (HILL 60 (YPRES) 1916 APRIL-JULY WYTSCHAETE-KEMMEL 1916-7 AUG-JAN THE SOMME (HIGH WOOD EAUCOURT L'ABBAYE BUTTE DE WARLENCOURT) 1917 FEB-MARCH THE SOMME (BELLOY) APRIL-MAY ARRAS (WANCOURT CROSSILLES) MAY-SEPT ARRAS (CHERISY FONTAINE LES GROSEILLES 1917-8 OCT-FEB YPRES (HOUTHULST FOREST PASSCHENDALE) 1918 MARCH St QUENTIN APRIL THE LYS MAY CRAONNE HILL CHEMIN DES DAMES JUNE THE AISNE THE GIFT OF J.T.R. 1919

DID YOU KNOW THAT?

There is no known Memorial to the 20,000 Chinese who died in the First World War in France.

China declared neutrality in April 1914, but 140,000 Chinese volunteered to join the 'Chinese Labour Corps', to help free British and French troops for front-line duty, by undertaking manual labour.

3. The Response
In the public gardens north of St Thomas Church, Barras Bridge
Newcastle upon Tyne NE1   Grade I

Unveiled on 5th July 1923 by Edward, Prince of Wales, the future Edward VIII. He had been in the Grenadier Guards during the First World War, and although never directly involved in fighting, because the War Office were worried that he may be captured, he did visit the front line as often as possible, which made him popular with former soldiers after the war. Following a substantial restoration the memorial was rededicated on 25th October 2007 in the presence of the Duke of Edinburgh.

Designed by Sir William Goscombe John.

Design Features:
The memorial is a substantial granite screen wall with a raised and curved centrepiece that is set on a rusticated plinth. The plinth supports a large and very impressive bronze group of dozens of soldiers and civilians. In the centre there is a sloping apron which gives the impression of an altar from a distance. The bronze sculptures are predominately soldiers marching behind two drummer boys. Children and wives are attempting to catch a final touch or embrace as the men march away. One shipyard worker marches with the soldiers to symbolise the importance of such workers is equal to that of the soldiers themselves.
On the back of the screen, the ends are broken forwards to create stubby pylons, and relieved by three sculptures – in the centre is St George who is bare headed and standing on a bracket formed by two seahorses: seahorses are the supporters of the arms of Newcastle-upon-Tyne. On the flank walls are two figures of Northumberland Fusiliers: one in the uniform of 1674, the year in which the regiment was first raised: and the other in the uniform of First World War service dress.

The Story behind The Memorial:
The memorial has the appearance and style of a memorial built to remember those of a whole city who made the ultimate sacrifice. However, it represents the raising of the Territorial Battalions of the Northumberland Fusiliers by the Chamber of Commerce. These battalions were known in Newcastle as "The Commercials", in much the same way as "The Pals" battalions.
The memorial was paid for by Sir George Renwick Bt who was a local ship owner and MP for Morpeth. The whole tone of the memorial is celebratory more than sombre, because it also commemorates Sir George Renwick's fifty years in business in Newcastle but also, perhaps most importantly from his point of view, the safe return of all of his five sons from the war which, given the losses among young officers, was something to celebrate.

The Inscription

The front slab reads NON SIBI SED PATRIE – [For country not for themselves] THE RESPONSE 1914 and the inscription on the rear is QUO FATA VOCANT [where fate calls] and TO COMMEMORATE THE RAISING OF THE B COMPANY/9th BATTALION and the 16th, 17th, 18th and 19th SERVICE BATTALIONS NOTYHUMBERLAND FUSILIERS, BY THE NEWCASTLE AND GATESHEAD CHAMBER OF COMMERCE AUGUST – OCTOBER THE GIFT OF SIR GEORGE RENWICK Bt DL and LADY RENWICK MCMXXIII.

The Resonse (left) from previous page

Newcastle and District War Memorial and its inscription (below) next page

The Inscription

The south facing, front, of the pedestal has a relief carving of a lion with the inscription: 1914-1918   1939-1945, whilst the rear face is inscribed: MEMORY LINGERS HERE above a bronze laurel wreath. The base of the memorial carries the inscription: A TRIBUTE OF AFFECTION TO THE MEN OF NEWCASTLE AND DISTRICT WHO GAVE THEIR LIVES IN THE CAUSE OF FREEDOM THEIR NAME LIVETH FOR EVERMORE.

4. Newcastle and District War Memorial

Eldon Square, Blackett Street, Newcastle upon Tyne, NE1

Grade II*

Unveiled on 26th September by Field Marshal Earl Haig, with the dedication carried out by the Bishop of Newcastle. Haig was a career soldier who had seen action in the Sudan War and the Second Boer War and commanded the British Expeditionary Force on the Western Front from late 1915 until the end of the First World War. During his time in command, the British Expeditionary Force suffered some two million casualties.

Following his retirement from the Army in 1920, Haig devoted himself to the welfare of ex-servicemen and was President of the Royal British Legion from its formation until his death in 1928.

Designed by the Newcastle architects Cackett and Burns Dick, although Cackett had retired from the practice before it received the commission to design the memorial.

Sculpted by Charles Leonard Hartwell (1875-1951) was born in London and attended the City and Guilds School in Kennington, where he won a silver medal for sculpture. From 1806 he attended the Royal Academy Schools where he won silver and bronze medals. Hartwell was elected an Associate of the Royal Academy in 1915 and a member in 1925. In 1929 he won the Royal British Society of Sculptors' silver medal.

Design Features:

The memorial consists of a tall Portland stone pedestal that has a deep moulded base and plinth and stands on a shallow stepped platform. On top of the pedestal sits an impressive bronze St George on a rearing horse as he thrusts his lance into the throat of a dragon.

There are minor, one word, inscriptions on two of the faces accompanying bronze relief panels. On the east face there is a bronze panel entitled JUSTICE. The figure of Justice carrying her scales is in relief with another female figure, and both of them looking at a kneeling, abject, semi-nude figure. On the west face, a bronze panel with the single word PEACE shows a mother and child in relief watched over by the winged figure of Peace who is holding a palm leaf.

The Story behind The Memorial:

There were various plans for a memorial in Eldon Square, Newcastle including a statue of Lord Kitchener. The celebrated London sculptor, Alfred Drury, was commissioned although, for some unrecorded reason, he never completed even a model and Charles Hartwell was engaged instead. The memorial, which cost £13,260, was paid for by public subscription, with slightly over £3,000 being left over which was donated to the Royal Victoria Infirmary in Newcastle.

After he had unveiled the memorial, Field Marshal Haig was taken to see Goscombe John's nearby memorial "The Response – 1914" – see page 75 – a more realistic portrayal of war which Haig, apparently, preferred.

A plan to redesign Eldon Square in the 1970s proposed moving the memorial, with the architects and city planners on one side, and the Royal British Legion on the other. The Royal British Legion emerged triumphant and the statue remained, although the rest of the square was altered. The memorial was refurbished in 1991 after some vandalism and was completely renovated in 2007.

5. Stockton on Tees War Memorial

**Outside the parish church of St Thomas, High Street,
Stockton on Tees, Durham TS18** Grade II*

Unveiled on 13th May 1923 by John Frederick Lambton, later 5th Earl of Durham, who had served as a Captain in the 3rd/7th Northumberland Fusiliers during the First World War.

Designed by Henry Vaughan Lanchester (1863-1953) who was born in London, the son of an architect. After being articled to his father, Lanchester studied at the Royal Academy between 1886 and 1889, before establishing his own practice in 1894 and designing a number of important buildings in the United Kingdom, including Cardiff City Hall and Law Courts and the Methodist Central Hall, Westminster, and in India, Egypt and Africa. From 1910 to 1912 he was the editor of The Builder magazine, before being appointed Professor of Architecture at University College London, and was awarded the Royal Gold Medal of the Royal Institute of British Architects in 1934.

Design Features:

The memorial is in the south west corner of the churchyard of the parish church of St Thomas. Taking the form of a cenotaph, the memorial is made from Portland Stone with bronze panels; it is rectangular with large niches to north and south faces, both of which are colonnaded over which the cornice is returned.

The memorial is set on a tall base with framing pilasters which have three lion masks above them. It is topped with a sarcophagus which has fluted sides with trophies and wreaths on each side. The sarcophagus is topped with a bronze torch and stone pedestal. The memorial bears the arms of the borough of Stockton on Tees and the Durham Light Infantry.

The Inscription

The memorial bears the inscription – TO THE LASTING MEMORY OF THE MEN OF STOCKTON-ON-TEES WHO FELL IN THE GREAT WAR 1914 – 1919 AND IN WORLD WAR 1939 – 1945 THEY DIED THE NOBLEST DEATH A MAN MAY DIE, FIGHTING FOR GOD, AND RIGHT, AND LIBERTY – AND SUCH A DEATH IS IMMORTALITY. SEE YE TO IT THAT THESE SHALL NOT HAVE DIED IN VAIN

6. Saltburn War Memorial

Glenside, Saltburn by the Sea, Langbaurgh, Cleveland TS12

Grade II*

Unveiled on 14th November 1920 by Major General Sir Percy S Wilkinson, who was a career soldier and commanded the 9th (Secunderabad) Division during the First World War, and had been Colonel of the Northumberland Fusiliers since 1915.

Designed and Sculpted by by Sir William Reynolds-Stephens (1862-1943) who was born in Detroit, America of English parents. He studied at Blackheath School of Art and the Royal Academy: his father wanted him to be an engineer, but as soon as he able to choose for himself, Reynolds-Stephens chose art as his subject. He described himself as a craftsman rather than an artist, and his work can be seen at St Paul's Cathedral, Lambeth Palace and Southwell Minster.

Design Features:

The elaborate memorial stands in gardens just off the Promenade. It comprises an Arts and Crafts style polished pink granite cross on a wide stepped plinth, which stands on a grey granite base. A bronze relief sculpture is set across the shaft and arms of the cross, which shows a figure of Christ in the tomb. Stooping angels with outstretched wings are at the head and foot of Christ. There are bronze wreaths on the east and west faces of the cross which encircle the dates 1914 and 1918.

The Story behind The Memorial:

The memorial was commissioned by Mr and Mrs Letherby, whose son Wilfred was killed at Ypres.

The Inscription

The names of all sixty-four Saltburn residents who died are inscribed on the front and the sides of the base. An inscription on the lower section reads – TO THE MEMORY OF THOSE FROM SALTBURN WHO GAVE THEIR LIVES FOR ENGLAND IN THE GREAT WAR – WE HAVE NO GLORY GREAT ENOUGH FOR YOU.

7. Keighley War Memorial

Town Hall Square, North Street, Keighley, Bradford, West Yorkshire, SK11

Grade II*

Unveiled on 7th December 1924 by Lieutenant General Sir Charles Harrington, a career soldier who had fought during the Second Boer War and held various staff posts during the First World War, including Deputy Chief of the Imperial General Staff before becoming Commander-in-Chief Allied Occupation Forces in Turkey. By 1924 Harrington was General Officer Commanding Northern Command. The dedication was carried out by the Rev. S. Howard-Hall, Chaplain of 6th Battalion Duke of Wellington's (West Riding) Regiment. The band of the Duke of Wellington's Regiment played and the ceremony was attended by approximately 25,000 people.

Designed by Henry C. Fehr.

Design Features:

The memorial is built from locally quarried sandstone and comprises a tall obelisk on a two-tier pedestal and a three-stepped base. The whole memorial stands in a paved area that is enclosed by low stone walls and is accessed by four steps. The paved area is now surrounded by metal railings, which were added in 2010 when the memorial was cleaned and four flag poles were also installed.

On the top of the obelisk is a bronze female figure of Victory with one hand outstretched, holding a laurel wreath, whilst the other hand holds a palm branch to represent peace. There are curved projections to the east and west sides pedestal. On the projection to the east side there is a sailor holding a telescope to his eye, whilst on the west projection is a soldier in full battle dress standing at ease. Both of these figures are sculpted and cast in great detail.

On the north pedestal, beneath the inscription, is a tablet which commemorates the Royal Flying Corps and the Royal Air Force. The bronze panel on the south pedestal depicts the Keighley coat of arms in relief, and on the pedestal beneath there is a stone tablet which was put in place in 2000 by the Royal British Legion and the Keighley branch of the Duke of Wellington's Regimental Association, commemorating those who gave their lives in the service of their country.

The Story behind The Memorial:

Keighley Municipal Borough commissioned the memorial to commemorate the 900 men of the Borough who died in the First World War. The £5,000 cost of the memorial was met by public subscription.

The Mayor of the French town of Poix-du-Nord, which had been adopted by Keighley in 1922 under the British League of Help scheme, attended the unveiling. The scheme had been established in 1920 to provide aid to towns in northern France that had been devastated during the war. This visit was the first recorded example of "town twinning". Although there are no names on the memorial, since 2010 a Book of Remembrance containing the names of the fallen has been on display in Keighley Town Hall.

The Inscription

The inscriptions are on heavily wreathed bronze panels, which are within a projecting stone frame to the north and south sides of the memorial. The panel on the north side reads: 1914-1919 / 1939-1945 IN PROUD AND GRATEFUL MEMORY OF THOSE MEN OF KEIGHLEY WHO GAVE THEIR LIVES IN THE GREAT WAR AND THE WORLD WAR IN DEFENCE OF FREEDOM AND JUSTICE THEIR NAME LIVETH FOR EVERMORE.

Harrogate War Memorial (left) see next page

8. Harrogate War Memorial

Prospect Square, Harrogate, North Yorkshire HG1   Grade II*

Unveiled by Henry Lascelles, 6th Earl of Harewood, a career soldier who commanded the 3rd Battalion Grenadier Guards during the First World War. He was accompanied by his wife, Princess Mary, only daughter of King George V and Queen Mary, and their infant child Viscount Lascelles. The dedication was performed by Thomas Strong, Bishop of Ripon with a crowd of 9,000 people attending the unveiling.

Designed by Ernest Prestwich (1889-1977). Not much is known about Prestwich's early life, although he studied at Liverpool School of Architecture and the Department of Civic Design. He won a competition in 1918 to complete Port Sunlight, the 'model village' built by Lord Leverhulme to house the workforce at his factory. Prestwich practiced in Leigh, Lancashire, and was admitted as an Associate of the Royal Institute of British Architecture in 1918 and a Fellow in 1928.

Sculpted by Gilbert Ledward.

Design Features:

The memorial is a tall Portland stone obelisk on a square plinth, standing on a shallow platform, which has stepped entrances on the east and west side. At the top of each face there is a relief carving of a laurel wreath. At the bottom of the north and south faces there are the cost of arms of Harrogate in relief, and on the east and west faces there is a carved long sword pointed down.

On the plinth there are a number of bronze plaques, and the Roll of Honour is on the east and west faces. On the north face there is a bronze relief of a soldier standing in front of a field gun: the soldier is in a dramatic pose, bare headed, holding a large flag and looking backwards. He is about to blow a bugle: the image depicts the call to arms. The relief on the south face shows a woman who depicts Peace, and her arms are outstretched, holding a long sword, pointing down, and a laurel wreath. Curled around her feet is a serpent impaled by a bayonet depicting the defeated enemy. The heads and rifles of soldiers are depicted at the feet of the woman, although their heads are bowed in mourning, with one rifle held aloft in victory. A dove of peace flies over the whole scene.

The Story behind The Memorial:

The memorial is located in the garden of a former hotel which was bought specifically for the purpose. The original estimate for the cost of the memorial was £10,000 although the final cost was £12,000.

The Inscription

The east face of the monument is inscribed OUR GLORIOUS DEAD 1914 – 1918 1939 – 1945 PRO PATRIA 1914 – 1918. The west face is inscribed PRO PATRIA 1914 – 1918   1939 – 1945.   A small plaque below the sculpture of Peace on the south face is inscribed TO ALL MEN AND WOMEN WHO HAVE GIVEN THEIR LIVES IN THE SERVICE OF THEIR COUNTRY IN VARIOUS HOSTILITIES SINCE THE SECOND WORLD WAR WE WILL REMEMBER THEM.

Two small plaques between the bollards on the south side of the monument are inscribed HARROGATE BORN RECIPIENTS THIS PLAQUE IS DEDICATED TO THE MEMORY OF THE MEN WHOSE SERVICE TO THEIR COUNTRY EARNED THEM THE HIGHEST MILITARY HONOUR THE VICTORIA CROSS REMEMBER

9. York City War Memorial

Leeman Road, York, YO1   **Grade II***

Unveiled Prince Albert, Duke of York, on 25th June 1925. The Duke of York was the future George VI and had served in both the Royal Navy and the Royal Air Force during the First World War. The dedication was by Cosmo Gordon Lang, Archbishop of York and later Archbishop of Canterbury. Earlier in the day, the Duchess of York had unveiled the Five Sisters Window in York Minster, a memorial to 1,450 "Women of the Empire" who had died in the First World War.

Designed by Sir Edwin Lutyens.

Design Features:
The memorial is built from Portland stone and stands in the War Memorial Gardens which overlooks the River Ouse and, to the north, St Mary's Abbey. The memorial is Sir Edwin Lutyens' 33ft (10m) tall slender tapering War Cross. The shaft is lozenge shaped in section with short cross arms, and linked to the base by stop chamfers and torus moulding. The base comprises four stepped rectangular blocks of unequal heights standing on a square, undercut platform which, in its turn stands on tow further square blocks and two square shallow steps. The surrounding War Memorial Garden is included in the listing.

The Story behind The Memorial:

A war memorial fund was started in York in August 1919 to commemorate the 1,162 men from York who had died in the war, but it would not be until June 1925 that the memorial was unveiled. It was at a meeting in January 1920 that it was decided that the City's dead should be commemorated by a memorial rather than a new City Hall, a nursing home or another of a number of alternative suggestions. The City Engineer prepared a plan for a Memorial Garden with an archway and memorial and it was agreed to appoint Lutyens to design a suitable memorial with a budget of £2,000. Lutyens was already designing a memorial for the North Eastern Railway Company near the station in York.

Nine potential sites were visited by Lutyens with a view to erecting a Stone of Remembrance, which he had designed for the Imperial War Graves Commission. The site preferred by Lutyens, close to the city walls, was rejected because it was close to the proposed North Eastern Railway Company memorial which had a budget, paid for by the company, of £20,000 – ten times the budget for the city memorial - and it was thought that it might over shadow the city memorial. The Leeman Road site, which was owned by the North Eastern Railway, was chosen as an alternative. The lowest tender that came in for building the memorial was almost £2,500, more than twice the £1,100 that the War Memorial Committee had collected even with the North Eastern Railway Company donating the land. It was decided to build a War Cross instead of the Stone of Remembrance and that the City staff would carry out the work instead of an outside contractor, all of which meant that there was £400 remaining in the fund when the memorial had been built, so Lutyens was asked to design pillars and entrance gates for the Memorial Park.

The Inscription

The inscription on the south face of the largest block of the base reads: TO THE CITIZENS OF YORK 1914-1918 1939-1945, whilst on the opposite face there is the inscription: THEIR NAME LIVETH FOR EVERMORE.

York City War Memorial (above) previous page

North Eastern Railway War Memorial (below) next page

10. North Eastern Railway War Memorial
Station Approach, York, YO1
Grade II*

Unveiled on 14th June 1924 by Field Marshal Lord Plumer, who was a career soldier having joined the army in 1876. He was one of two corps commanders in the British Expeditionary Force in 1914 and was offered the job of Chief of the Imperial General Staff in 1918: he turned it down and, instead, commanded the Second Army. By 1924 Plumer had retired from the Army, although in 1925 he accepted the position as the first High Commissioner of the British Mandate for Palestine.

Approximately 6,000 people attended the unveiling of the memorial and the dedication was by the Archbishop of York, Cosmo Gordon Lang. In attendance was Edward Grey, 1st Viscount Grey of Fallodon, a director of the North Eastern Railway and former Foreign Secretary. He is best remembered for his comment "the lamps are going out all over Europe" at the start of the First World War

Designed by Sir Edwin Lutyens.

Design Features:

The memorial is built of Portland stone and comprises an obelisk mounted on slightly canted walls which screen three sides of a shallow stepped podium. A Stone of Remembrance stands on the podium. On the pedestal to the obelisk there is a laurel wreath carved in relief, within which are the arms of the North Eastern Railway Company.

The Story behind The Memorial:

Before railway nationalisation in 1947, the country was served by various railway companies, largely organised geographically, with the North Eastern Railway (NER) covering Yorkshire, County Durham and Northumberland, with workshops in Darlington and its Head Office in York. In 1920 the company voted £20,000 to construct a memorial within the city walls to the members of staff who had died in the First World War.

Controversy followed when York City Council decided to erect their own memorial just 100 yards from the NER's, and local hostility to the NER memorial was vented as it was thought that it was too close to the city walls, and would be the first memorial that visitors arriving in York by train would see, rather than the city's own memorial. By way of compromise, the NER's memorial was moved away from the city walls to the head of Station Road, and the city council re-sited theirs to a plot just outside the walls, ironically on a piece of land owned by the railway company, who donated it to the city council.

The Inscription

On the screen wall there is a central panel bearing the dedication – IN ABIDING REMEMBRANCE OF THE 2236 MEN OF THE NORTH EASTERN RAILWAY WHO GAVE THEIR LIVES FOR THIER COUNTRY IN THE GREAT WAR THE COMPANY PLACES THIS MONUMENT. This panel is flanked by laurel garlands. The screen wall is carved with the names of the men of the company who lost their lives in the First World War, whilst those who lost their lives in the Second World War are recorded on fifteen slate panels behind the Stone of Remembrance, which carries the inscription THEIR NAME LIVETH FOR EVERMORE.

11. Waggoners' Memorial
Main Street, Sledmere, East Yorkshire, YO25
Grade I

Unveiled by Sir Ivor Maxse KGB, General Officer Commanding-in-Chief, Northern Command on 5th September 1920. A guard of honour was provided by a detachment of 5th Battalion, The Green Howards (Territorial Army), of which Sir Mark Sykes had been Colonel at the outbreak of the First World War. and over 2,000 members of the public attended the ceremony.

Designed by Sir Mark Sykes Bt. 'The Story behind the Memorial' that follows includes brief biographical details of this talented amateur sketch artist, who had no architectural or design experience.

Sculpted by Carlo Domenico Magnoni, an Italian anarchist, while the mason was Alfred Barr.

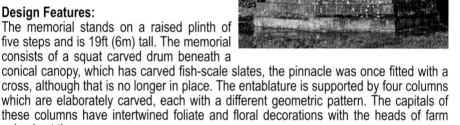

Design Features:
The memorial stands on a raised plinth of five steps and is 19ft (6m) tall. The memorial consists of a squat carved drum beneath a conical canopy, which has carved fish-scale slates, the pinnacle was once fitted with a cross, although that is no longer in place. The entablature is supported by four columns which are elaborately carved, each with a different geometric pattern. The capitals of these columns have intertwined foliate and floral decorations with the heads of farm animals at the corners.

There is a square patterned cornice with octagonal finials each crowned by a coronet.

The carved central drum is decorated somewhat in the style of Trajan's Column in Rome although it is in a naive style that shows nothing of triumphalism, but rather a simple depiction that would be familiar to those that served. The drum is divided into three separate sections divided by stone bands. The "story" begins with enlisting volunteers, including the inscription: CAPTAIN SYKES OF THE A.S.C. ATTESTED ONE THOU. AND FARM HANDS BETWEEN MARTIMAS.

The carvings continue to show a waggoner driving a load of sacks and a depiction of the course of the annual wagon-driving completion. The inscription continues: THIS WAS THE COURSE OF THE ANNUAL COMPETITION HELD IN FIMBER FIELD. The carvings then depict the outbreak of the war with the reservists who are working in the fields receiving their call-up papers; saying farewell to family; walking to join the colours; joining the colours and being kitted-out; taking troop transport ships to cross a mined English Channel; disembarkation in France; German soldiers committing atrocities; a British Tommy confronting German infantrymen; and the waggoners loading artillery ammunition and rifle bullets, while under bombardment on the road to Amiens and the Battle of the Marne.

The Story behind The Memorial:

Mark Sykes was the heir to a considerable fortune and a substantial Yorkshire land owner, whose family seat was in the small Yorkshire village of Sledmere. He could have occupied himself by helping to run the family estate, but how he chose to have a full and exciting life. As a boy, Sykes travelled extensively in the Middle East with his father and became an expert on the people and the area. While he was at Cambridge University, where he did not actually complete his degree, Sykes wrote four books and was commissioned into the 3rd (Militia) Battalion of The Green Howards, serving during the Second Boer War in South Africa with the 5th Battalion. From 1905 to 1906 he was honorary attaché to the British Embassy in Constantinople. In 1911 Sykes was elected to Parliament as the Unionist member for Hull Central and in 1913 he succeeded to the Baronetcy.

At the outbreak of war, Sykes was a Lieutenant-Colonel and Commanding Officer of 5th Battalion The Green Howards, although instead of accompanying them to France, he was asked to work for Lord Kitchener in the Intelligence Department at the War Office, and joined the committee that advised the Cabinet on Middle East affairs. It was Sykes who designed the flag for the Arab Revolt in 1916, and variations on his design were subsequently used as the national flag of a number of Arab nations. He is probably best known for his diplomatic work in the Middle East during the First World War, when he was partly responsible for drawing-up the Asia-Minor Agreement of 1916, which is commonly known as the Sykes-Picot Agreement.

In November 1912 Sykes started to form the Waggoners' Reserve from men working on farms in Yorkshire, on the basis that if there was to be a war the Army would require people who were used to dealing with horses and wagons. By the outbreak of the First World War, 1,127 men were in the Waggoners Reserve Corps and they were immediately called up and posted to the Army Service Corps and the Royal Engineers. Around 80 men of the Waggoner's Reserve were killed in the war.

Sykes took great pride in the unit that he had raised, and in 1918 he designed a memorial to record their service and sacrifice. His design incorporated words and carvings that would be understandable to the Waggoneers and their families, and although the memorial is ornate, its decoration would be familiar to country people. Sykes paid the full cost of the memorial but, sadly died of Spanish Flu in Paris, aged 39, whilst attending the Versailles Peace Conference.

He never saw the Waggoners' Memorial completed.

The Inscription

The inscription of the frieze reads: LT. COL: SIR MARK SYKES. BART: M.P. DESIGNED THIS MONUMENT AND SET IT UP AS A REMEMBRANCE OF THE GALLANT SERVICES RENDERED IN THE GREAT WAR 1914-1919 / BY THE WAGGONER'S RESERVE A CORPS OF 1000 DRIVERS RAISED BY HIM ON THE YORKSHIRE WOLD FARMS IN THE YEAR 1912 / THOMAS SCOTT FOREMAN. CARLO MAGNONI SCULPTOR. ALFRED BARR MASON

The drum also includes a poem in five verses, written by Sir Mark Sykes in the local dialect:

THESE STEANS A NOBLE TALE DO TELL ON WHAT MEN DID WHEN WAR BEFELL AND IN THAT 'FOURTEEN' HARVEST TIDE THE CALL FOR LADS WENT FAR AND WIDE TO HELP TO SAVE THE WORLD FRO' WRONG TO SHIELD THE WEAK AND BIND THE STRONG
WHEN FROM THESE WOLDS XII HUNDRED MEN CAME FORTH FRO FIELD AND FOLD AND PEN TO STAND AGAINST THE LAW OF MIGHT TO LABOUR AND TO DEE FOR RIGHT AND TO SAVE THE WORLD FRO' WRONG TO SHIELD THE WEAK AND BIND THE STRONG

THESE SIMPLE LADS KNEW NOWT OF WAR GOD'S OWN LAW WHICH SATAN'S WILL CONTROLS MUST FALL UNLESS MEN THEN DID HEED THE CALL TO GAN TO SAVE THE WORLD FRO' WRONG TO SHIELD THE WEAK TO BIND THE STRONG

ERE BRITAIN'S HOSTS WERE RAISED OR PLANNED THE LADS WHAE JOINED THIS HOMELY BAND TO NORMANDY HAD PASSED O'ER SEA WHERE SOME WERE MAIMED AND SOME DID DEE AND ALL TO SAVE THE WORLD FRO' WRONG TO SHIELD THE WEAK AND BIND THE STRONG

GOOD LADS AND GAME OUR RIDING'S PRIDE THESE STEANS ARE SET BY THIS ROADSIDE THIS TALE YOUR CHILDREN'S BAIRNS TO TELL ON WHAT YE DID WHEN WAR BEFELL TO HELP TO SAVE THEIR WORLD FROM WRONG TO SHIELD THE WEAK AND BIND THE STRONG

From a Base Hospital in France

Lt.Col. J H M Hardyman DSO MC (Died 24th August 1918. Age 23)

Christ! I am blind!
God give me strength to bear
That which I must have dreaded all my days:
The palsied shuffling, grasping air,
The moving prison five foot square,
The haunting step that isn't there –
These pictures dance before my sightless gaze........

12. Eleanor Cross

Main Street, Sledmere, East Yorkshire, YO25

Grade I

The unveiling of this memorial was unusual, in as much as it was an existing structure to which effigies were added, and these were unveiled one by one as they were completed and installed. Perhaps the most poignant unveiling was on 3rd April 1921 when the two final panels were unveiled. A guard of honour was provided by the Driffield Company 5th Battalion The Green Howards, who lined a rope enclosure around the cross. Within the ropes stood fifty veterans of the 5th Battalion Yorkshire Regiment, together with Lady Sykes, widow of Sir Mark Sykes, and other members of the Sykes family along with Mrs J A Raymond Thompson, the widow of Lieutenant Colonel Thompson. An effigy of Sir Mark Sykes was unveiled by the Rev J Smith, Abbot of Ampleforth Abbey and the effigy of Lieutenant Colonel Thompson by Colonel Commandant B G Price DSO.

Design Features:

The original Eleanor Cross is constructed of ashlar limestone: it is octagonal in plan and has a base of eight steps. The cross has four distinct stages and is a close copy of the 1291 Eleanor Cross to be found at Hardingstone, Northampton. The first stage comprises a plain plinth, which is inscribed with the words of the Lord's Prayer, from which rises a moulded base. There is an arcade of eight paired blind tracery panels with ogee transoms and blind hoods beneath an engaged crocheted canopy, separated by perpendicular-style staged square pillars with pinnacles. Between the ogee transoms there are sixteen carved and painted heraldic shields suspended from oak branches. These heraldic shields relate to the brass plaques that were added in the conversion of the cross into a war memorial and represent, England, the Borough of Kingston upon Hull, the Borough of Beverly, the Holy Trinity, the See of York, Archbishop Maclagan, a Gallic Cock, and the crests of the Sykes, Harcourt, Mortimer, Woodcock, Robson and Matthew families. The source of the coat of arms on the final shield has never been identified.

The twenty-two brass panels situated below the shields represent fallen officers and men of the 5th Battalion Yorkshire Regiment; one commemorates a soldier of the 1st Battalion Cheshire Regiment, another depicts a soldier from Princess Patricia's Canadian Light Infantry and the final one depicts Lieutenant Colonel Sir Mark Sykes. The plaques, which were drawn by Sir Mark Sykes, with the exception of his own, are not uniform in design nor are the figures to a common scale. One panel illustrates six officers in pairs, whilst another shows three soldiers, and a further one has two full length figures, with a third figure standing behind. The panels depicting officers show them in knightly clothing or have chivalric references including gothic canopies, scrolls, a supporting angel, St George slaying the dragon and an image and quotation from Joan of Arc. The image of Lieutenant Colonel Sir James Thompson depicts him standing on the chained and prostrate figure of Wotan, whilst that of Captain Edward Bagshaw is an adaptation of the brass of Sir Robert de Septvans in the Church of St Mary, Chatham, Kent. The effigies were originally gilded and elements such as awards and stained glass were coloured.

The non-commissioned officers and soldiers are shown in the style of crusaders with hands together in prayer. All of the effigies are illustrated wearing British Army uniforms

89

and equipment of the First World War, although some are also wearing medieval equipment, including chain mail gloves and hoods. Most of the soldiers have at their feet the tools of their civilian trades before the war: these include a salver, a bill-hook and a plane. The figure of Sir Mark Sykes depicts him as a knight carrying a shield, which bears the arms of the Sykes family and, underneath, a scroll inscribed LAETARE JERUSALEM (Jerusalem Rejoice) with a depiction of Jerusalem in the background.

The first stage is topped by a band, which is decorated with flowers and beasts and which forms the base to the second stage. The second stage contains four statues of Queen Eleanor in open niches underneath carved canopies with foliate hoods and a crocheted pinnacle, supported by square profile corner pillars with small crocheted pinnacles. The third stage, which rises out of the second stage, comprises four blind tracery panels beneath engaged foliate carved hoods and pinnacles. The fourth stage has four statues of the Virgin Mary, which are in open niches beneath elaborately carved canopies with foliate hoods and a crocheted pinnacle supported by square-profile corner pillars with small crocheted pinnacles and foliate finials. The central crocheted pinnacle terminates in a jewelled bronze crucifix with drop pendants and Christ crucified on its north-eastern side.

The Story behind The Memorial:

Twelve Eleanor Crosses were built in the 13th century to mark the route taken by the funeral procession of Eleanor of Castile's body from Lincoln to London, with the final cross being erected at Charing Cross. Sledmere's 'Eleanor Cross' was not originally built as a War Memorial, but a reproduction constructed in 1896-98 to a design by the architect, Temple Lushington Moore (1856-1920).

Moore was born in Ireland and educated at Glasgow High School, then privately in Yorkshire. In 1872 he became articled to architect George Gilbert Scott before setting up his own practice in London at the age of 22, although he continued to work with Scott. Moore continued his involvement with Scott by accepting into articles his son, Giles, who would go on to design Liverpool Cathedral. He worked almost exclusively in the gothic revival style, and his major area of design was in churches, totalling forty, of which thirty-four are listed. He was elected into fellowship of the Royal Institute of British Architects in 1905. It was expected that Moore's son would follow him into the practice; however, he was killed in the sinking of RMS Leinster in 1918

In 1918, Moore's Eleanor Cross was converted to create a War Memorial, with the design for the conversion being carried out by Sir Mark Sykes, the celebrated soldier, politician and expert on the Middle East. (More biographical details of Sykes are noted in the Waggoners' Memorial on page 78). The brass effigies were gilded and engraved by Gowthorpe and Sons of London. Although he had no formal architectural or artistic training, Sykes was a talented sketcher and he designed the panels that would convert the existing Eleanor Cross into a War Memorial. He worked with relatives of those memorialized in order to achieve a good likeness, and it was his proposal that the tools of their trade be included, to remind people that those killed had a trade rather than being career soldiers. As with the *Waggoners Memorial*, sadly Sir Mark died and never saw the completed memorial. It was he who paid for the conversion work to the Eleanor Cross, and after his death, the tenants and villagers from the Sledmere Estate raised funds in order to add an effigy of him to the memorial, even though, technically, he was not a victim of the First World War.

Eleanor Cross (left) from
previous pages

Huddersfield War Memorial
(below) next page

13. Huddersfield War Memorial
Greenhead Park, Huddersfield, HD1
Grade II*

Unveiled by General Sir Charles Harington on 26th April 1924 (of whom more information is available on page 80.)

Design Features:

The Belvedere is at the end of the main avenue in the park which leads from the main entrance. The terrace which encloses the mound to the front and to the north side is made up of two long perpendicular retaining walls, which have circular projections as viewing platforms. The walls are made from rock faced sandstone and mirror those of the nearby bandstand which is listed Grade II; with ashlar balustrades which are pierced with square and circular openings, piers which have ball finials and heavy moulded copings. The terraced is approached by flights of stone steps bordered by low balustrade walls and squat piers, with a second flight of stairs leading to the memorial itself. The principle stairs, which rise from the main path, have flanking curved viewing platforms and piers topped with cast iron vases.

The memorial is built from sandstone ashlar and stands on a circular platform on top of the Belvedere. It consists of a tall free-standing column in front of a semi-circular Tuscan colonnade. The column has pilasters to the front and rear and half-columns to each side, supported on a cruciform pedestal that stands on a two-stepped square base. The top of the column has a deep cornice and a large gilded cross with raised diamond and cabochon ornament. The colonnade is two columns deep with a walkway between them with entablature, which terminates in paired compound piers with pilasters. The rear of the colonnade is enclosed by a wall to the lower part. Modern iron railings enclose the platform.

The Story behind The Memorial:

Standing on an existing mound known as the Belvedere created in Greenhead Park as a viewing area during the 1880s, this memorial has a commanding position over Huddersfield

This large and impressive memorial which has fine views of Huddersfield was paid for by public subscription which raised the huge sum, at the time, of £40,000 against the construction costs of £14,000, with the balance of the funds being placed in trust for Huddersfield Royal Infirmary.

The Inscription

The front of the pedestal bears the inscription:1914-1918 IN MEMORIUM 1939-1945. There are no names recorded on this memorial as these are noted, instead, on other memorials. Huddersfield lost 3,439 inhabitants during the First World War and the size and position of the memorial is intended to reflect the scale of this sacrifice.

14. Barnsley War Memorial
Church Street, Barnsley, S70
Grade II*

Unveiled by Lt General Sir Charles Harrington, General Officer Commanding Northern Command on 11th October 1925. He unveiled a number of memorials in Yorkshire, and brief biographical details feature on page 80 The dedication was performed by the Dean of York – Reverend Dr Foxley Norris.

Designed by William Thomas Curtis about whom few biographical details are available, other than that he practiced in London, became an Associate of the Royal Institute of British Architects in 1926 and a fellow in 1933.

Sculpted by John Tweed (1869-1933), who was born in Glasgow, where he attended the Glasgow School of Art before moving to London in 1890, and studied part time at the South London Technical Art School and the Royal Academy Schools. Having undertaken work for Lutyens and Herbert Baker, Tweed was commissioned in 1901 to complete the portrait of the First Duke of Wellington in St Paul's Cathedral after the death of Alfred Stevens. He produced a number of war memorials after the First World War, including the Rifle Brigade Memorial and the statue of Kitchener on Horse Guards.

Design Features:

A massive sandstone pylon, with a large square capstone and recessed angles, a heavy rectangular base and moulded plinth, raised on three steps on the forecourt of Barnsley Town Hall, is topped by a large than life bronze statue of a soldier. The soldier is wearing his greatcoat, a steel helmet and is standing "at ease".

To the rear of the plinth, facing the Town Hall, is a large bronze plaque in Art Nouveau style, which depicts a winged victory who carries a wreathed standard in her left hand, and a shield with the town's arms in her right hand.

The Story behind The Memorial:

There is no Roll of Honour in Barnsley and so the memorial represents all those from the town killed in the First and Second World Wars. When Harrington was unveiling the memorial he said, referring to the recent introduction of white road markings "What I would like to see is a white line drawn each side of every war memorial with the message – 'Slow, War Memorial.' Your safety is due to them, and don't forget it."

The total cost of the memorial was around £5,500.

The Inscription

The dedication of the front of the pylon is incised and gilded and reads: IN HONOURED MEMORY OF THE MEN AND WOMEN OF BARNSLEY WHO LAID DOWN THEIR LIVES IN THE GREAT WAR 1914-1918 1939-1945. Above this inscription there is a large wreath carved in relief. On the left face of the pylon the words: THEIR NAME LIVETH FOR EVERMORE is carved: on the right face of the pylon is carved: AND WE IN FAITH KEEP THAT PEACE FOR WHICH THEY PAID.

Barnsley War Memorial (above) from previous page

The lower part of Sheffield War Memorial (below) next page

15. Sheffield War Memorial
Barkers Pool, Sheffield S1 Grade II*

Unveiled by Lt General Sir Charles Harrington MC, General Officer Commanding Northern Command, on 28th October 1925 with the dedication performed by the Bishop of Sheffield. Brief biographical details of Harrington feature on page 80.

Designed by Charles Denny Carus-Wilson (1883-1934) who was born in Sevenoaks, Kent and studied at the Architectural Association Schools. He was admitted by examination as an associate into the Royal Institution of British Architects in 1909. He fought in the First World War and received the Military Cross. Carus-Wilson briefly moved to Sheffield where he was the head of the School of Architecture, before becoming senior lecturer in the College of Art in Edinburgh, where his students found him to be fierce and awe-inspiring. Retiring from lecturing in 1928, he formed a partnership with Frank Mears which lasted until the formers death in 1934.

Sculpted by George Alexander (1881-1942) who was born in Glasgow and worked as an architectural sculptor in the city, prior to moving to London in order to study at the Royal Academy Schools from 1904-07. Alexander undertook a number of important public and private commissions, and was principally noted for his work in metal.

Design Features:

The memorial comprises of an 82ft (25m) tall white flagstaff topped by a gilded orb and crown in bronze. The foot of the flagstaff is held in a large bronze collar into which the dates 1914/1919 and 1939/1945 are cast in relief. The collar itself rises from an orb which is circled with acanthus leaves. Below this on the upper section of the base are four life-sized figures of infantrymen, their rifles reversed; these figures stand between scroll buttresses. The middle section of the base consists of an octagonal pedestal which is draped with floral swags. Four coats of arms, representing the three arms of service and the city facing north, south east and west.

There is skirting at the foot of the base of each panel, which bears one of eight regimental badges: the Yorkshire Dragoons (Queen's Own), Royal Artillery, Royal Engineers, Machine Gun Corps, Tanks Corps, York and Lancaster Regiment, Medical Corps and the Royal Army Service Corps. The whole memorial stands on a splayed octagonal stone plinth which has a circular paved surround.

The Story behind The Memorial:

When the question of a war memorial was first considered following the end of the First World War there was considerable debate regarding the best site for such a memorial with the War Memorial Committee considering no less than fourteen locations before the Barkers Pool site was agreed. It was agreed that the design of the memorial would be decided by competition which would only be open to architects and sculptors working in Sheffield. This decision met with two contradictory disagreements: firstly by people who were not satisfied by the quality of public art in the city and, secondly, by some who thought that there was a suggestion that the city's artists were not good enough to tolerate national competition. The competition was judged by Vincent Harris the architect of the new City Hall. Over 50,000 Sheffield men served during the First World War with over 5,000 making the ultimate sacrifice – the names of these men are recorded on the Roll of Honour. Five hundred and thirty-one men from the 'Sheffield Pals' were killed on the first day of the Battle of the Somme alone. The total cost of the memorial was £5,345.

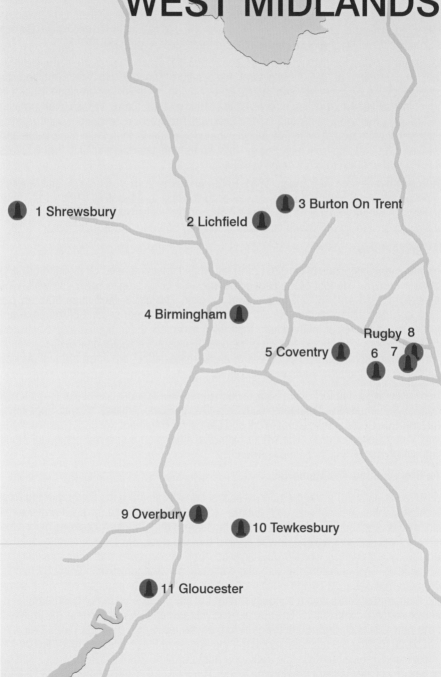

WEST MIDLANDS

1 Shrewsbury

3 Burton On Trent

2 Lichfield

4 Birmingham

Rugby 8

5 Coventry 6 7

9 Overbury

10 Tewkesbury

11 Gloucester

CONTENTS

1. Shropshire War Memorial

The Quarry, St Chad's Terrace, Shrewsbury, SY1
Grade II*

Unveiled on 29th July 1922 by George Herbert, 4th Earl of Powis, who served as Lord Lieutenant of Shropshire from 1896 to 1951. His eldest son had died from wounds received during the Battle of the Somme. The dedication was performed by the Right Reverend John Kempthorne, Bishop of Lichfield.

Designed by George Hubbard (1859-1936), of whom little is known of his early life, although it is recorded that he worked as an architect in London for 50 years, and was twice President of the Royal Institute of British Architects. He designed the Arts School and Stuart House for the Board of Extra Mural Studies at Cambridge University, as well as war memorials in Cambridge, Shrewsbury and Montgomery. Hubbard was a noted connoisseur and collector and a Fellow of the Society of Antiquaries.

Sculpted by Allan Gairdner Wyon (1882-1962) whose father, two of his uncles, his grandfather and great grandfather successively held the position of Chief Engraver of Seals to the monarch. Wyon attended Highgate School and the Royal Academy from 1905 to 1909. From 1924 to 1930 he was the Honorary Secretary of the Art Workers Guild and a fellow of the Royal Society of British Sculptors. Wyon undertook a wide range of sculptures and busts for churches, cathedrals and private clients: in 1933 he took holy orders, and until 1956 he was vicar of St Peter's Church in Newlyn.

Design Features:

The memorial is an open rotunda with a domed stone canopy and entablature resting on six Ionic columns. The internal frieze features the arms of the six boroughs of Shropshire, one above each column. The rotunda itself is on a three-stepped granite plinth and is surrounded by a circle of bronze railings.

Under the centre of the rotunda is a bronze statue of St Michael depicted as the field commander of the Army of God: he is in full gothic plate armour and holds a pennanted lance in his left hand. His right hand is raised in benediction and his halo is in the shape of a solar cross. Large feathered wings act as a frame to the figure.

There are six plaques in front of the statue, one of which carries the inscription, whilst the others show: the arms of the County of Shropshire, a Croix de Guerre, an empty cross in front of a rising sun, the regimental badge of the King's Shropshire Light Infantry and the arms of the town of Shrewsbury.

The richly embellished floor of the memorial shows the County and Regimental arms on a gold mosaic background. The seals or arms of the six boroughs of the County are embossed on the inside frieze.

The Story behind The Memorial:

The memorial cost £4,400 and was paid for by public subscription: more than the cost of the memorial was raised and the surplus was divided between the Royal Salop Infirmary and the Shrewsbury Orthopaedic Hospital.

The memorial was built by Messrs Kirkpatrick and the statue was cast by A B Burton of Thames Ditton.

The Second World War additions were unveiled in 1949 by General Sir Oliver Leese and dedicated by the Suffragan Bishop of Shrewsbury.

The Inscription

The frieze is inscribed: IN MEMORY OF THE MEN AND WOMEN OF SHROPSHIRE WHO FELL IN THE TWO WORLD WARS 1914 – 18 AND 1939 – 45.
In front of the statue, the first plaque is inscribed: REMEMBER + THE GALLANT MEN AND WOMEN OF SHROPSHIRE WHO GAVE THEIR LIVES FOR GOD KING AND COUNTRY 1914 – 18 + 1939 – 45
A brass plaque laid in the ground in front of the gates of the enclosure is inscribed: THIS WAR MEMORIAL WAS BUILT IN 1922-3 IN HONOUR OF THE MEN AND WOMEN OF SHROPSHIRE WHO FELL IN THE GREAT WAR OF 1914-18. THE WAR DEAD OF 1939-45 ARE ALSO COMMEMORATED BY THIS MONUMENT.

2. Lichfield War Memorial
Garden of Remembrance, Bird Street, Lichfield, WS13
Grade II*

Unveiled on 20th October 1920 by the Mayor of Lichfield Cllr H. G. Hall, with the dedication carried out by the Bishop of Lichfield. The band of 2nd Battalion Oxfordshire and Buckinghamshire Light Infantry provided music for the occasion, and the Last Post was sounded by the buglers of the 6th Battalion North Staffordshire Regiment. Major Longstaff, Chairman of the War Memorial Committee, formally handed over the memorial to the Mayor for safe keeping by the city in perpetuity.

Designed by Charles Bateman, a Birmingham architect.

Design Features:

The memorial stands at the east end of the memorial garden, which is part of the Cathedral Close, and takes the form of a large ashlar screen wall in the English Renaissance style. It is built from Guiting stone in the style of a church façade raised on a high plinth.

The centre of the screen is pedimented and raised on reeded and fluted Roman ionic pilasters, which enclose a semi-circular shell-headed niche which contains a Portland stone figure of St George who stands on a dragon. In his right-hand, St George holds a bronze spear and, in his right hand, there is a shield.

The tympanum of the pointed pediment is decorated with a leaf and scallop shell motif carved in relief.

The niche is flanked by panels for the six years from 1914 to 1919 suspended from lion masks, which are interspersed with bunches of fruit and flowers. The side compartments have crowned wreaths in the half gables with swept copings and panelled end piers.

The end piers are topped with tall urn-like pinnacles

finished each with a ball and draped foliage.

The whole of the memorial garden with balustrades, together with the walls, gates and gate piers, are included within the listing.

The Story behind The Memorial:

The war memorial garden is in the north-west corner of Minster Pool and was designed by Bateman as a Garden of Rest. The garden is enclosed to the north and east by walls dating from the eighteenth century, whilst the balustrading and urns are nineteenth century and came originally from Shenstone Court.

The memorial bears the names of 209 men from Lichfield who died in the First World War. It had been decided by the War Memorial Committee that inclusion on the memorial be restricted to those killed who had been born in Lichfield, or who were living in Lichfield at the time they enlisted.

The memorial was constructed by Messrs Robert Bridgeman and Sons.

The Inscription

The principal inscription, which is on the upper middle plaque, is flanked by lists of names and reads: REMEMBER WITH THANKSGIVING THE MEN OF THIS CITY WHO IN THEIR COUNTRY'S HOUR OF NEED WENT FORTH ENDURED HARDNESS FACED DANGER AND FINALLY PASSED OUT OF THE SIGHT OF MEN BY THE PATH OF SACRIFICE AND THE GATE OF DEATH LET ALL WHO COME AFTER SEE TO IT THAT THESE DEAD SHALL NOT HAVE DIED IN VAIN THAT THEIR NAME BE NOT FORGOTTEN AND WHAT THEY STROVE FOR PERISH NOT. A later dedication on the lower middle panel reads: THESE LOWER PANELS ARE DEDICATED TO THOSE WHO DIED IN THE CAUSE OF FREEDOM DURING THE WORLD WAR 1939-1945 AND THE STRUGGLES WHICH FOLLOWED.

3. Burton on Trent War Memorial

Lichfield Street, Burton on Trent, Staffordshire DE13
Grade II*

Unveiled on 2nd August 1922 by William Legge, 7th Earl of Dartmouth, a Conservative politician, who had served with the Staffordshire Yeomanry in the Sinai and Palestine Campaign before commanding the regiment for the last year of the war.

Designed by Henry Charles Fehr.

Design Features:

The joint themes of the memorial are victory and peace, with victory symbolised by a 7ft 6ins (2.3m) tall winged victory standing on a bronze globe. Victory is raising a downward-pointing sword in her right hand, while she holds a laurel wreath in her left hand. The sculpture stands on a square Portland stone pedestal, which stands 14ft 9ins (4.5m) tall and is decorated at each corner with cherubs wearing winged helmets. The pedestal sits on a three stepped base within a spacious enclosure surrounded by a low wall. To the left of the memorial is a bronze figure of St George with his foot on a dragon, symbolic of England crushing evil, whilst to the right is a classical figure of Peace holding a dove.

The Story behind The Memorial:

A War Memorial Committee was set up in Burton on Trent on 9th November 1918 at the suggestion of the then Mayor, Councillor George Hill. A War Memorial fund was established which raised £22,000, including large contributions from Bass and Worthington breweries, both of whom had substantial interests in the town. Of this amount £17,000 went directly to help ex-servicemen, with the balance paying for the memorial.

There was no competition to find the designer of the memorial, although members of the War Memorials Committee visited the Royal Academy War Memorials Exhibition in October 1919.

The Town Clerk of Burton on Trent was impressed with Fehr's work as a result of dealing with him after he had designed a statue of Queen Victoria in Hull, where the Town Clerk had worked before moving to Burton on Trent.

Fehr used a similar winged victory for other memorials that he designed in the United Kingdom and for one in Shanghai. It was a conscious decision not to put the names on the memorial, in order to allow it to speak for itself.

The cost of the memorial, which was cleaned and restored in the year 2000, was £4,630.

The Inscription

The pedestal has bronze plaques to the front and rear with relief inscriptions. The inscription to the front plaque reads: TO THE GLORIOUS AND IMMORTAL MEMORY OF THE OFFICERS NON COMMISSIONED OFFICERS AND MEN OF BURTON ON TRENT WHO SERVED IN THE GREAT WAR 1914 1919 IN DEFENCE OF THEIR KING AND COUNTRY AND GAVE THEIR LIVES FOR THE VICTORY OF HONOUR AND FREEDOM OVER TERROR AND OPPRESSION THEIR IMPERISHABLE NAMES ARE RECORDED ON THE WALLS OF THE TOWN HALL OF THIS COUNTY BOROUGH AN EXAMPLE TO THOSE WHO COME HEREAFTER.

The plaque to the rear of the memorial reads: TO BURTONS HEROES, HONOUR TO THE IMMORTAL DEAD THAT GREAT WHITE COMPANY OF SHINING SOULS WHO GAVE THEIR YOUTH THAT THE WORLD MIGHT GROW OLD IN PEACE 1914-1919.
An additional plaque has been added to the front of the memorial which reads: REMEMBERING ALSO THOSE WHO DIED IN THE WORLD WAR 1939-1945

Trenches: St Eloi
Lt. T.E.Hulme (Died 28th September. Age. 34)

The Germans have rockets. The English have no rockets.
Behind the line, cannon, hidden, lying back miles.
Behind the line, chaos;

My mind is a corridor.
The minds about me are corridors.
Nothing suggests itself,
There is nothing to do but keep on.

4. Hall of Memory

Centenary Square, Broad Street, Birmingham B1
Grade I

The Foundation Stone was laid on 12th June 1923 by the Prince of Wales, and the Hall was opened by HRH Prince Arthur, Duke of Connaught, on 4th July 1925. Prince Arthur, who was the seventh child and third son of Queen Victoria, was a career soldier who served around the world, and was Governor-General of Canada from 1911 to 1916.

A crowd of 30,000 attended the opening. The memorial was "opened" rather than "unveiled" because it takes the form of a building.

Designed by Birmingham architects S.N Cooke and W. N. Twist.

Sculpted by Albert Toft, with the bas-relief work created by William Bloye.

Design Features:

The Memorial is a large and imposing free-standing building of classical design. The land on which the memorial is built was designated for a grand civic area of public buildings, although by the start of the Second World War little had been done and it was not until 1989 that Centenary Square was laid out. The memorial is constructed from Portland stone with bronze statues and doors; it is classical in style and an octagonal shape, with a heavy Doric frieze and attic and a low dome. There are pedimented projections to the four long sides of the octagon, with the one to the south east forming the entrance. The four shorter faces are set back and frame four bronze figures, which represent the Royal Navy, the Army, the Royal Air Force and the Nursing Service.

The statues show a bare-chested sailor in a sitting position, holding a coil of rope in one hand and a ship's wheel in the other. The soldier is also bare-chested and in a sitting position, resting his helmet on his left leg, and his right hand on the barrel of a Lewis gun. In a similar way, the figure representing the Air Force is bare-chested and sitting, and is holding a propeller and cylinders of an aircraft engine in his left hand, while he looks towards the sky. The nurse in the fourth recess is seated, like the other figures, and is holding a wreath in her left hand.

Access to the interior is via huge cast bronze doors. The interior of the Hall has a ribbed and coffered dome and Doric detailing, with a sarcophagus-shaped dais of Sienna marble in the centre of a marble floor. A glass and bronze casket rests on top of the dias, which contains three Rolls of Honour relating to the First and Second World Wars and all campaigns since 1945. Marble paving and seats occupy the angles of the hall with bronze flambeau over them.

Facing the main entrance is a stained glass window by Birmingham artist, Richard Stubington. There are bas-relief Art Deco plaques over each of the other three doors by William Bloye which are entitled "Call", showing men leaving to join the forces; "Front Line", a representation of infantrymen on the firing line; and "Return", which shows a group of men, several of who are badly wounded, returning home.

104

The Story behind The Memorial:

The competition to design the Hall of Memory was only open to Birmingham Architects, and judged by Sir Reginald Blomfield, the architect who designed the "Blomfield Cross", which is also known as the "Cross of Sacrifice".

The original design for the memorial included a colonnade which was situated opposite it but, following the destruction of St Tomas's Church in Bath Street during an air-raid in the Second World War, the colonnade was moved to become a feature in St Thomas' Peace Garden, which is both a monument to peace and a memorial to all those killed in armed conflict.

The total cost of the memorial was £60,000, which was all met by public subscription. The builders were John Barnsley and Sons and John Bowen and Sons.

The Inscription

Bloyes' plaques each have an inscription: Panel 1: OF THE 150,000 WHO ANSWERED THE CALL TO ARMS 12,320 FELL 35,000 CAME HOME DISABLED Panel 2: AT THE GOING DOWN OF THE SUN AND IN THE MORNING WE WILL REMEMBER THEM Panel 3: SEE TO IT THAT THEY SHALL NOT HAVE SUFFERED AND DIED IN VAIN

5. Coventry War Memorial

War Memorial Park, Kenilworth Road, Coventry, CV3

Grade II*

Unveiled on 8th October 1927 by Earl Haig, who had commanded the British Expeditionary Force in France from late 1915 until the end of the war. Haig retired from the Army in 1920 and afterwards devoted his life to the welfare of ex-servicemen, serving as President of the Royal British Legion and establishing the Haig Fund which started the selling of Poppies to raise funds to benefit ex-servicemen.

Designed by Thomas Francis Tickner (1864-1924) a Coventry born architect, although sadly he did not live to see it completed.

Design Features:

Rising to 90ft (27m) this very tall tower is built of reinforced concrete clad in Portland stone and is in the Art Deco style. There are heavy buttresses to the corners and the tower rises to ten tiers. Large bronze doors to both the east and west elevation have a relief image of a cross, with the dates of the First and Second World Wars above. Through these doors, inside the memorial is the Chamber of Silence, which houses the Rolls of Honour for Coventry.

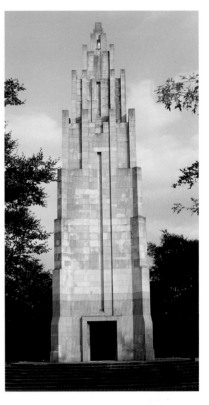

The Chamber of Silence is open to the public on Remembrance Sunday. The north and south elevations each have a plain cross set on a stepped corbel with guttae: on the north side below the cross is a carved wreath with the dates of both world wars and the coat of arms of the City of Coventry below it. There is an Eternal Light on the top of the tower. In 2011 the steps to the monument were replaced and both hand rails and a ramp were added with the steps containing a bronze circle engraved with parts of Laurence Binyon's poem "For the Fallen" together with six bronze discs commemorating Coventry's six Victoria Cross winners.

The Story behind The Memorial:

The park in which the memorial tower was built was an existing park and, as well as the memorial itself, memorial tress were also planted. A Memorial Committee was formed in 1923 and sufficient funds for the memorial had been collected by the following year with building work starting in the autumn of 1925. The decorative bronze doors were added at the end of 1928 as were floodlighting pedestals.

6. 29th Division War Memorial

Junction of the A45 and Fosse Way, Stretton-on-Dunsmore, Rugby, Warwickshire, CV23　　　　　　**Grade II***

Unveiled on 24th May 1921 by William Craven, 4th Earl of Craven, Lord Lieutenant of Warwickshire: Within weeks of unveiling the memorial, Craven had drowned in a sailing accident. Also present was Lord Algernon Percy, a career soldier and politician who had served as High Sheriff of Warwickshire, County Alderman of Warwickshire and Chairman of Warwickshire County Council. Approximately 7,000 people attended the unveiling.

Designed and Built by local Lichfield company, Messrs Robert Bridgeman and Sons.

Design Features:

The memorial comprises a tall, 39ft (12m) tapering square-sectioned monolith of Portland stone surmounted by a square moulded urn finial with a crown, The monolith stands on a pedestal that is moulded and banded with a cornice. Below the panel which bears the inscription is the divisional symbol, a broad based red triangle, whilst around three sides of the base is inscribed the Division's order of battle. From either side of the memorial an avenue of lime trees extends which dates from the early eighteenth century, and has been re-planted at various times including 1920-21 as part of this memorial. Originally the memorial was flanked by two captured field guns, although these were removed during a scrap collection in the Second World War.

The Story behind The Memorial:

The memorial marks the area where, on 12th March 1915, King George V reviewed some 18,000 men and 6,000 horses of the 29th Division before their departure for Gallipoli. Following Gallipoli, the Division served on the Western Front and, after the Armistice in 1918 it moved to the River Rhine. During the whole of the First World War the Division suffered 94,000 casualties and won 27 Victoria Crosses. The Division was disbanded on 15th March 1919.

The Inscription

The moulded panel on the north face of the pedestal carries the following inscription:
HERE IN THE CENTRE OF ENGLAND WHERE TELFORD'S COACHING ROAD FROM LONDON TO HOLYHEAD IS CROSSED BY THE ROMAN FOSSE WAY ON 12TH MARCH 1915 HIS MAJESTY KING GEORGE V REVIEWED HIS TROOPS OF THE IMMORTAL XXIX DIVISION SHORTLY BEFORE THEY EMBARKED FOR ACTIVE SERVICE IN GALLIPOLI. IN MEMORY OF THEIR STAY IN WARWICKSHIRE 1914-15 AND OF THEIR INCOMPARABLE SERVICES SINCE THE AVENUE ON THIS ROAD WAS REPLANTED AND THIS MONUMENT ERECTED BY INHABITANTS OF THE COUNTY.

7. War Memorial Chapel at Rugby School

Rugby School, Dunchurch Road, Rugby, CV22

Grade II*

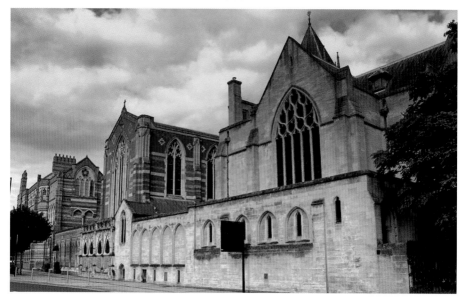

Consecrated on 8th July 1922 by the Bishop of St Edmundsbury and Ipswich, rather than being unveiled, this being a chapel as opposed to being a stand-alone memorial.

Designed by the ecclesiastical architect Sir Charles Nicholson.

Design Features:

The memorial chapel is a freestanding building which is made from the type of limestone known as Beer stone. The plan of the chapel is that of a Greek cross with four equal arms, lit by three large stained glass windows and five lancet lights in the west wall of the cloister. The names of those old boys and masters from the school who died in the war are inscribed on stone tablets under the windows in the north and south transepts. The altar and reredos were given by a single donor, as were the stained glass windows. The north window depicts the Last Supper, the procession to Calvary and the celebration of Holy Communion, whilst one of the outer lights depicts the donor's son who was killed, and his daughter who was a nurse. The east window depicts the crucifixion, whilst the south window depicts the entombment and resurrection. In the lower part of this window are two scenes, one of which represents the burial of a soldier at the front, and the other depicts the vision of St Martin. The west window shows illustrations of the concept of peace and hope. The five lancets each show a figure: the school's founder, Laurence Sheriff; King Oswald; King Alfred; King Edmund; and King Arthur.

The chapel also contains two large decorative wooden cabinets, which hold details of every Rugbeian involved, not only in the First and Second World Wars, but also the Korean War, Egypt and the Suez Crisis of 1951-1956, and the Cyprus Emergency of 1955-1959.

The Story behind The Memorial:

Rugby School has had a long connection of involvement in the military with the Rugby School Rifle Club, which was formed in 1860, being the country's first school cadet force. Over 3,000 Old Rugbeians and masters served during the First World War and suffered total casualties of approximately 1800 – 679 killed and over 1,100 wounded. Major Abel, one of the first British officers killed in the war on 23rd August 1914, was an old boy of the school. Whilst the oldest British casualty of the war, Lt Col J. M. Richardson, killed at the age of 68 had attended Rugby School in the 1860s. The writer and poet, Rupert Brooke, who died of sepsis during the First World War was an Old Rugbeian.

The Inscription

There is an inscription on the outer wall to the east end of the chapel: TO THE GLORY OF GOD IN REMEMBRANCE OF OUR DEAD 1914-1918. A tablet set into the floor of the chapel carries the inscription: THEY WHOM THIS CHAPEL COMMEMORATES WERE NUMBERED AMONG THOSE WHO AT THE CALL OF KING AND COUNTRY LEFT ALL THAT WAS DEAR TO THEM, ENDURED HARDNESS, FACED DANGER, AND FINALLY PASSED OUT OF THE SIGHT OF MEN BY THE PATH OF DUTY AND SELF-SACRIFICE, GIVING UP THEIR OWN LIVES THAT OTHERS MIGHT LIVE IN FREEDOM. LET THOSE WHO COME AFTER SEE TO IT THAT THEIR NAMES BE NOT FORGOTTEN. The lectern has the following inscription: GOD MADE TRIAL OF THEM AND FOUND THEM WORTHY OF HIMSELF. AS GOLD IN THE FURNACE HE PROVED THEM. Above the names of the fallen in the north transept is the inscription: THESE WALLS RECORD THE NAMES OF 679 SONS OF THE SCHOOL WHO GAVE THEIR LIVES IN THE GREAT WAR OF 1914-1918.

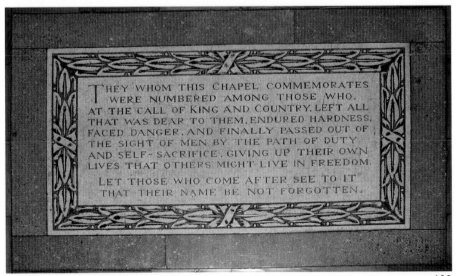

8. British Thomson-Houston Co Ltd War Memorial

Technology Drive, Rugby, CV21 Grade II*

Unveiled by Field Marshal Sir William Robertson, who was a professional soldier who began his career as a trooper in the 16th (The Queens) Lancers in 1877. By 1916 he was Chief of the Imperial General Staff, the professional head of the British Army and the only man ever in the history of the British Army to rise from Private to Field Marshal. Robertson served in India and learned to speak Urdu, Hindi, Persian, Pashto, Punjabi, Gurkhali, French and German.

At the beginning of the First World War, Robertson was appointed Chief of Staff, Quartermaster-General of the British Expeditionary Force. In his retirement Robertson was President of the Royal British Legion. The memorial was dedicated by the Archdeacon of Warwick.

Designed by Sir Edwin Lutyens.

Design Features:

The memorial is constructed of Portland stone, and comprises of a slender 24ft (7m) tall tapering cross. The shaft is lozenge shaped and it has short cross arms linked to the base by stop chamfers and cyma moulding. The base comprises four stepped rectangular blocks, which are of unequal heights and stand on a square plinth, and the whole memorial stands on a square step which is raised on a large circular base 25ft (7.5m) in diameter. Lutyens designed fifteen war crosses of a broadly similar design, although this memorial is the only one that is on a circular base, around which the names of those who gave their lives are inscribed.

The Story behind The Memorial:

British Thomson-Houston was an engineering company principally known for its manufacture of electrical systems and steam turbines. Since the 1890's it had been majority owned by General Electric. The Rugby factory, built in 1902, manufactured electric motors, generators, steam turbines and light bulbs although, during the First World War, this expanded to include lighting, signalling and radio equipment for the Royal Navy.

In 1922 British Thomson-Houston was one of six telecommunications companies that formed the British Broadcasting Corporation. In the 1930s the factory manufactured Frank Whittle's prototype jet engine, the world's first such engine. The company is still in existence on the same site as a division of Alstom Electrical Machines Ltd.

This memorial bears the names of 243 men from the factory who died in the First World War, A further 175 names of those killed in the Second World War were added in 1948, and the company erected other memorials at its other factories.

In 2010, the memorial, including a time capsule that had been included when it was first built, was moved some 438 yards (400 meters) from its original location to facilitate a redevelopment of part of the site, and it now stands on a site that was part of the 1902 factory. The memorial was re-dedicated on 22nd July 2010.

The Inscription

The main inscription is incised into the front of the square plinth: IN MEMORY OF THE MEN OF THE BRITISH THOMSON-HOUSTON COY WHO GAVE THEIR LIVES IN THE GREAT WARS. To one side Roman numbers MCM XIV XIX and the other MCM XXXIX XLV. On the square step is the inscription THEIR NAME LIVETH FOR EVERMORE.

DID YOU KNOW THAT?

Research has shown that the impact of the famous Your Country Needs You poster might have been a myth. In the First World War posters were one of the most important means of spreading propaganda.

On 5th August 1914, the day before Britain declared war on Germany, Field-Marshal Lord Kitchener, who was already a Boer War hero, became Secretary of State for War. He predicted that victory would take several years and require huge new armies. He appealed for volunteers to join the British Expeditionary Force, and by 12th September half-a-million had already joined up. The 'famous poster' did not appear until the end of September, after signing-up had peaked!

Later in the war, there were not enough volunteers joining the forces, and with fears of a mounting crisis, powerful advertising played on the guilt of those who had not volunteered. Even this was not enough and conscription had to be introduced in January 1916.

By 1917 recruitment was not a problem, but the government faced an even more difficult problem. The people of Britain needed to be persuaded to continue supporting a war that was sapping morale. Millions of leaflets were distributed, campaigns were launched which used children to arouse powerful emotions, associated the enemy as evil, and even King George V was used to garner support.

Many believe that World War One propaganda was the birth of 'spin'. Successive governments have used new ways of persuading people to stop smoking, to wear seatbelts and warn about the dangers of AIDS.

9. Overbury and Conderton War Memorial Lych-Gate

St Faith's Churchyard, Church Row, Overbury, Worcestershire, GL20

Grade II*

Unveiled on 12th September 1921 by Michael Furse, Bishop of St Albans. Colonel Allen read the names of those commemorated.

Designed by Sir Herbert Baker

Sculpted by Alec Miller (1879-1961), who was born in Glasgow, the son of a cabinet maker. At the age of 12 he became an apprentice to the woodcarver Miss C P Anstruther, and later to the Kyrle Society.

In 1902 Miller took the position of head of modelling and woodcarving at the Guild of Handicraft. In the late 1920s Miller moved to the United States, where he lectured on art and literature as well as writing several books.

Design Features:

The lych-gate stands to the south of the Church of St Faith, which is Grade I listed and forms the entrance from the lower street level. The lych-gate is built in the English vernacular style, and comprises heavy timber framing on a limestone ashlar base over the churchyard entrance.

The tall chamfered base, with short returns at each end, encloses a stone and timber bench on the outside of the eastern wall, facing the street. There is a similar bench on the western side, inside the churchyard, which is at a higher level than the street.

The stone tiled roof has swept overhanging eaves on shaped brackets. Arch-braced collar trusses form round-headed archways, with additional, smaller, upper collars. The dates 1914– 1918 are carved into the south collar, facing the street, and attached to it is the carved figure of an angel holding a wreath and set in a niche formed by its folded wings. Attached to the north collar is a carved angel with outspread wings. The eastern and western sides of the lych-gate each have a pair of large rectangular open panels.

On the south side, six stone steps lead up from street-level into the gate, whilst inside the churchyard the platform extends beyond the lych-gate, ending in a paved semicircle. Centred inside the gate, raised on the paved platform, a large coffin rest cenotaph in the form of a chest tomb bears some of the inscriptions.

The Story behind The Memorial:

The lych-gate was designed at the instruction of the Holland-Martins of Overbury Court, whose 19 year-old son Geoffrey Holland-Martin had been killed in France in 1918, and has no known grave.

The Holland-Martin family were a wealthy London family who had founded Martins Bank, one of the major component parts of what was to become Barclays Bank. The memorial commemorates all 27 local servicemen who died in the First World War.

The oak for the lych-gate's heavy timberwork came from woodland in Worcestershire: whilst the stone, from Bredon Hill, was given by Robert Holland-Martin. Tiles for the roof were reported to have been collected from old buildings in the village.

Following the Second World War, a plaque commemorating the names of four local servicemen who died in that conflict was added to the lych-gate.

The Inscription

Inscriptions carved into the timbers include GLORY TO GOD IN THE HIGHEST AND ON EARTH, PEACE, GOODWILL TOWARDS MEN and THROUGH THE GATE OF DEATH WE PASS TO OUR JOYFUL RESURRECTION. The principal dedicatory inscription to the south face of the coffin rest reads REMEMBER THE OVERBURY AND CONDERTON MEN WHO GAVE THEIR LIVES IN THE GREAT WAR THAT HONOUR JUSTICE AND LOVE SHOULD RULE MANKIND SEE TO IT YE LIVING THAT YE HERE DEDICATE YOUR LIVES TO THE CAUSE FOR WHICH THEY DIED. The north face of the coffin rest is carved with a quotation from William Blake's poem 'Jerusalem', I WILL NOT CEASE FROM MENTAL FIGHT NOR SHALL MY SWORD SLEEP IN MY HAND TILL WE HAVE BUILT JERUSALEM IN ENGLANDS GREEN AND PLEASANT LAND.

10. Stanway War Memorial

Stanton Road, Stanway, Tewkesbury, Gloucestershire, WR12

Grade II*

Unveiled on 30th October 1920 by Lady Elcho, with the dedication carried out by the Bishop of Gloucester. She was the wife of Lord Elcho who had been killed in Egypt in April 1916. The Countess of Wemyss, who had lost two sons in the war, spoke at the unveiling.

Designed by Alexander Fisher (1894-1926), who was a silversmith, enamellist and metalworker, and worked in the style of the Arts and Crafts Movement. He taught at the London County Council School of Arts and Crafts from 1896-1898, and at other London schools, as well as having his own school in Kensington in London from 1904.

Sir Philip Sidney Stott (1857-1937) acted in an advisory role to the Wemyss family on the positioning and style of the memorial. He was born in Chadderton Lancashire and educated at Oldham High School before joining his father's architectural practice.

In 1883 Stott established his own business specialising in the design of cotton mills and became very wealthy, not so much from his fee income, but from shares he held in mills that he designed. In 1913 Stott moved to Stanton Court in Gloucestershire and was created a Baronet in the 1920 Birthday Honours List.

Eric Gill carved the inscriptions and decorative reliefs.

Design Features:

The memorial is built from North Cotswolds stone which came from the Jackdaw Quarry and was part of the Stanway House estate. The plinth is made from sandstone. The overall height of the memorial is 16ft (5m).

The bronze figure of St George killing a dragon which is coiled around the upper part of the stone column is both dramatic and highly stylised.

The stone column has relief carving of the shield of England and a pilgrim's badge. There is a square-sectioned collar which has the theatres where the local men died engraved into it – FRANCE on one face and EGYPT AND GALLIPOLI on another. The plinth stands on a four stepped base.

The Story behind The Memorial:

Stanway House, which dominates Stanway Village, is the family seat of the Earls of Wemyss and March. Lord Elcho, the eldest son of the Earl and Countess and youngest son, Yvo Alan Charteris, were both killed in the First World War.

Lord Elcho was killed by a shell in Palestine in April 1916 aged 32, whilst his brother was only 19 when he was killed in action in France in October 1915. Yvo had left Eton to join the First Battalion Grenadier Guards, and was shot whilst leading his men out of a trench, having served for only three weeks. His 'battlefield cross' – the wooden gave marker that were used temporarily in France – is in Stanway Church.

The Countess of Wemyss commissioned the war memorial on behalf of a committee, which she chaired, from the nearby villages that was charged with providing a suitable memorial to the fallen of those villages. She knew the sculptor Alexander Fisher, who had carried out work for her mother, and asked him to come up with a proposal. The estimate for the cost of the memorial was around £300, although the final cost was almost £700.

The Inscription

The inscription is incised on the front face of the plinth emanates from Greek poet, Simonides: MEN OF STANWAY 1914-1918 FOR A TOMB THEY HAVE AN ALTAR FOR LAMENTATION MEMORY AND FOR PITY PRAISE.

On the right side of the plinth there are six names, with five on the left side, whilst on the reverse of the plinth the inscription reads: FOR YOUR TOMORROW WE GAVE YOU OUR TODAY taken from J Maxwell Edmund's 'Inscriptions Suggested for War Memorials' HMSO 1919.

11. War Memorial to the Royal Gloucestershire Hussar Yeomanry

College Green, Gloucester, GL1

Grade II*

Unveiled by Deputy Chief of the Imperial General Staff Lt Gen Sir P. W. Chetwode, 1st Baron Chetwode, on 29th April, 1922. He was a career soldier, who saw service during the Second Boer War and in France and Palestine during the First World War.

During his time in Palestine, the Gloucestershire Hussar Yeomanry, as part of the Imperial Mounted Division, would have come under Chetwode's command. However, it is a considerable honour that a serving officer of his rank should unveil a war memorial of what was a Territorial Army unit.

Designed by Adrian Jones (1845-1938) who was born in Ludlow, Shropshire and studied at the Royal Veterinary College before qualifying as a veterinary surgeon in 1866. He served in a number of regiments of the Army from 1867 until 1890 when he retired. Even before his retirement, Jones had been an artist; his best known work is "Peace descending on the Quadriga of War", which was created as a memorial for Edward VII.

This depicted a winged depiction of the angel of peace on a chariot drawn by four very animated horses, which replaced the statue of the Duke of Wellington on the top of the Wellington Arch at Hyde Park Corner in London. Jones was a fellow of the Royal Society of British Sculptors.

Design Features:

The memorial takes the form of a tall stone cross which has a sword carved, in relief, on its front face, together with the regimental badge below the shaft of the cross. The cross stands on a high octagonal plinth which is in the centre of a wider octagonal plinth and the whole memorial sits on a three-stepped base. On each face of the plinth there is a bronze panel, which alternate between four panels giving the names of the 225 men of the regiment who died in the First World War, and four bas-reliefs depicting scenes of regimental life in four different theatres during the war – these panels are inscribed: Gallipoli 1915, Siniae [sic] 1916, Palestine 1917, and Syria 1918.

These latter panels all illustrate specific incidents: the panels depict specific incidents. 'Gallipoli' shows 21 August 1915, with troops climbing a high cliff behind Lala Baba Hill on the shore, before advancing across the dry bed of the Salt Lake, where they sustained heavy casualties. 'Sinai' is sculpted from a photograph taken during the many months the regiment was stationed in the desert, and shows the soldiers, mounted, descending the steep slope of a sand hill with palm trees behind.

'Palestine' shows the scene in February 1918 when the regiment, after three months of fighting, crossed the River Jordan, sending over rafts and setting up pontoon bridges. The final panel, 'Syria', encapsulates much of the regiment's experience, showing as it does, tired and thirsty horses being rested and watered after a long trek through the country.

The Story behind The Memorial:

In 1919 it was resolved to create a memorial to those of the Royal Gloucestershire Hussar Yeomanry who had died during the First World War, and a site outside Gloucester Cathedral was designated for such a memorial. A wooden model of the proposed memorial was set up on the site in October 1920 for approval by the Cathedral authorities, which was granted.

The Second World War addition was designed by Edward Payne, the stained glass artist, painter and sculptor and was installed in 1950.

The Inscription

The faces at the base of the cross have the inscriptions: EGYPT GALLIPOLI SINAI PALESTINE SYRIA. The plinth carries the inscription: IN MEMORY OF THE MEMBERS OF THE ROYAL GLOUCESTERSHIRE HUSSARS WHO GAVE THEIR LIVES IN THE WAR 1939-1945 AND WHOSE NAMES ARE RECORDED IN GLOUCESTER CATHEDRAL.

Women in the First World War

This volume only contains only two memorial dedicated to a woman – Sir George Frampton's impressive memorial to British nurse Edith Cavell in St Martin's Place, London, and Henry Pegram's more modest memorial in Cavell's home town of Norwich. One has to ask oneself if these memorials are, perhaps, more of a propaganda tool more than a genuine desire to memorialise a woman.

In fairness, not many individual men have memorials in the book, and yet it is men that predominate in the statues that adorn many of them. Soldiers in heroic or defiant poses, even a handful of dead and wounded soldiers, yet women are remarkably absent from the vast majority of memorials to the First World War. It is interesting that many of the memorials that do feature women are in the North of England and fall into one of three categories - the family left behind; women serving on the "home front"; and women serving with the armed forces.

A common feature of First World War recruiting and propaganda posters depicted cosy homes and families or German atrocities inflicted on civilians in an attempt to make the fight relevant to the average recruit. If they would not fight for "King and Country", who could argue against defending their family from an enemy that is often depicted in memorials as a "beast"?

If the country went to war for "King and Empire", the concept of going to war for "home and family" was an equally important motivation for many. An heroic soldier defending the women and children 'back at home' may seem an outdated concept now but, at the time, it was an ideal that many men aspired to.

By the time the great memorial building surge was under way, the full horrors of the losses in the war were all too apparent in every community. At the 1920 dedication of the Tomb of the Unknown Warrior in Westminster Abbey, the congregation included around one hundred women who had lost their husband and all their sons in the war. The sacrifice of those "left behind" must have been a life-long burden. Simply managing a home and family with a husband in the forces would have been stressful on its own, without the constant worry that a husband, father or brother might become one of the growing lists of casualties. Many families suffered extreme hardship during the war and welfare committees were established by women in most towns and cities to administer such assistance as they could.

The carnage caused by machine guns and artillery in all theatres of war demanded more and more men, and their place in the factories and elsewhere was increasingly taken by women. Women working was not unknown before the First World War, with domestic service and textile manufacture being major sources of employment. However the war brought new jobs in the vastly expanded areas of munitions and vehicle and aircraft production, whilst other jobs that had always been carried out by men, such as Police officers and bank staff - where women are now everyday sights - were totally unknown before the war. By 1918 almost one million women were employed in the munitions industry alone, but women could also be found working on the buses and railways, construction sites, in agriculture, as teachers and in offices.

Before the war many employers were either reluctant to, or simply refused to employ married women, with jobs only being available to single women or widows. However, with men away in the armed forces, and more women working, there was a constant issue with childcare, which was mainly provided by family members or friends. The government did not intervene in childcare provision until later in the war, when funds were made available to provide day nurseries for munition workers only, and even then it was very limited, with only around 100 day nurseries in the whole country by 1917.

The type of work that women were asked to do was often physically demanding and dangerous, especially for those in the munitions industry, where the modern concept of "health and safety" was unknown, as women handled dangerous chemicals with the minimum of protective clothing. The explosive TNT was poisonous and could cause a potentially fatal condition known as toxic jaundice which turned the skin yellow. In the black humour of the time, the people who suffered from this condition were often known as "canaries".

It is difficult to understand how the United Kingdom could have continued to fight the war without the contribution of women on the "home front".

The millions of men in the forces would be impotent without the continuous supply of ammunition, clothing, and supplies predominately produced by women who, as yet, still have no national memorial. At the end of the war, as the men returned home, they simply went back to the jobs they had

Blyth Spartans Munitions Girls - 1918

left and, to a great extent, women were simply asked to return to their pre-war roles as housewives, with little or no official recognition for their efforts.

If one positive thing did come out of women working in industry during the war it was the start of women's soccer teams. Many factories had been the starting place of men's football teams, and when women began to suggest that they too should form teams, this was officially encouraged, because it was thought that it would be beneficial to health and create a feeling of comradeship in factories. Matches between the numerous women's teams were popular and attended by large crowds until, in 1921, with the "crisis" over and the country returning to 'normal', they were banned from playing in Football League grounds.

For many years before the First World War women had volunteered for organisations as diverse as Queen Alexandra's Imperial Military Nursing Service and the Almeric Paget Military Massage Corps. As may be expected given the period and the military mind, the War Office was initially sceptical of the abilities of women, and thought that the 'horrors of war' would be too distressing for them. However, as the war continued and even the start of conscription in 1916 failed to produce enough men, the military started to consider using women in some roles to release men to the front line.

The initial reluctance and concerns of the military were perhaps understandable to an extent, in as much as the volunteer units that existed before the war were often made up of middle and upper-class women who had to buy their own uniforms and saw volunteering as a social duty. One such unit was the Voluntary Aid Detachment (VAD) which had been formed in 1909 and had 74,000 members by 1915 of whom two thirds were women. The unit aimed to offer volunteer nursing care, although there were issues caused by class and perceptions in several hospitals where they worked; the trained professional nurses resented volunteers who only had rudimentary training and tended to pick and choose which duties they performed, whereas the members of the VAD thought the professional nurses 'common' or rude.

In 1915 The Agricultural Organisations Society (AOS) agreed to setting up Women's Institutes, following the Canadian pattern, as they could see the value of harnessing rural women to help to grow and preserve food to help the war-torn nation. They invited Lady Denman to become the Chairman of the WI sub-committee. Gertrude Mary Pearson was born in 1884, the daughter of Weetman Pearson (later Baron Cowdray) the wealthy

industrialist. In 1903 she married Thomas, the third Baron Denman. In 1911 Lord Denman was appointed Governor General of Australia and so, at a very young age, she became First Lady. They and their two children returned in 1914 to find Britain on the brink of war.

She was an ideal person to lead the Women's Institutes. Owning her own estate at Balcombe in Sussex, she saw how hard life could be for countrywomen. She had already become President of the Women's Section of the Poultry Association and had plans for promoting small holdings, she believed strongly in the right and ability of women to conduct their own affairs.

By 1917 there were 137 WIs in different parts of the country and the responsibility for forming them was handed from AOS to the newly formed Women's Branch of the Board of Agriculture which was tasked with setting up the Women's Land Army. The National Federation of Women's Institutes (NFWI) was set up

Lady Denman in 1928

and Lady Denman became the first National Chairman (a post she would hold until 1946). At the same time she was made Honorary Assistant Director of the Women's Branch. In this role she was part of the recruiting team for Land Girls, but was also able to encourage WI members to encourage and support them.

The major role of WI members during the war was to bottle, jam and preserve all the surplus fruit and vegetables they could to be supplied to these who did not have enough, to keep poultry and collect eggs to be given to hospitals and convalescent homes where wounded troops were being cared for, and to fulfil many roles in the community left when the men had entered the armed services.

When the war was over Lady Denman gave the Victory Hall at Balcombe as their war memorial. Ever a practical women she saw this as of more value to the community than a monument.

A blue plaque for Lady Denman was unveiled at the hall in September 2017, with 132 WI members in attendance (along with one man - this book's Editor!). She went on to lead the WI to play an important role in the reconstruction of the countryside and to encourage women to play their part in improving the conditions of rural life for themselves and their families.

At the outbreak of the Second World War Lady Denman was invited by the Minister of Agriculture to become the Director of the Women's Land Army, as she had been involved with it during the First World War. She made her house, Balcombe Place, the Headquarters and for this work she was awarded the Grand Cross of the British Empire in 1951.

She finally retired as Chairman of NFWI in 1946:

"I think that countrywomen are the salt of the earth. I do not feel they get a fair deal, and I have always thought that if we got together we could do something about it; and it has been extraordinarily satisfactory to me because we have been able to do something about it. It has given me the very greatest happiness."

The WI College was about to be opened, and was named Denman College in her honour, eight years before she died.

Several women's units such as the First Aid Nursing Yeomanry, the Women's Hospital Corps and Scottish Women's Hospitals took official rejection very personally and, instead, offered their services to the armed forces of other countries, who were pleased to accept their offer and, indeed, many were decorated for bravery in the service of other armies.

The first women's unit raised as part of the British Army was the Women's Army Auxiliary Corps (WAAC) announced in February 1917. It was made up entirely of volunteers and by the end of the war some 57,000 women had served in its ranks. As early as the end of March 1917, the first WAACs moved to France where they were engaged in some very unglamorous roles which were, maybe, not unlike what they did at home.

Cooking, storekeeping, acting as waitresses and clerical work, although some were also involved in vehicle maintenance and driving, and a large detachment provided administrative support to the American Expeditionary Force. By early 1918 some 6,000 WAACs were serving in France, while the rest served in various locations throughout Britain. The Women's Army Auxiliary Corps was followed, very quickly, by the Women's Royal Naval Service and in 1918 the Women's Royal Air Force.

The work of women, as either volunteers or members of the services, was not without danger, and many made the supreme sacrifice with their names being recorded on war memorials and Rolls of Honour across the country. Whilst it can be argued that the country had to wait sixty years for the somewhat impersonal memorial to 'The Women of World War II' in Whitehall, surely a national memorial to the service and sacrifice of women in many different ways during the First World War is even longer overdue?

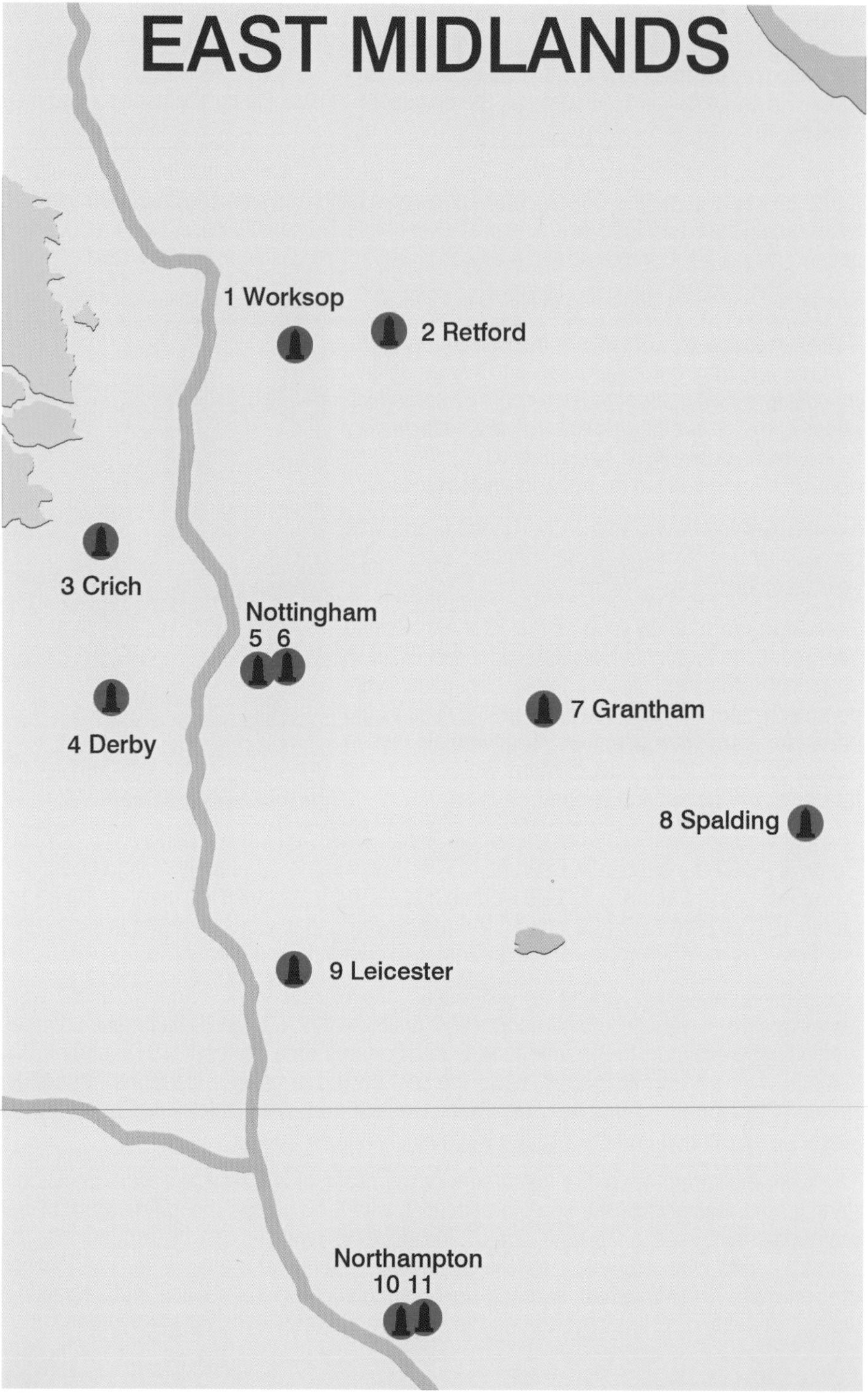

EAST MIDLANDS

1 Worksop

2 Retford

3 Crich

Nottingham
5 6

4 Derby

7 Grantham

8 Spalding

9 Leicester

Northampton
10 11

CONTENTS

Map reference and Memorial Name   Page

1. Worksop War Memorial
Memorial Avenue, Worksop, Nottinghamshire, S8
Grade II*

Unveiled by General Sir Horace Smith-Dorrien on 30th May 1925, who was a career soldier, and the twelfth of sixteen children. He was one of the few British survivors of the disastrous Battle of Isandlwana in 1879 during the Zulu War, and a veteran of the Second Boer War.

During the First World War, Smith-Dorrien had been a Corps commander in the early battles of the war, despite the fact that he had had a personality clash with Sir John French, commander of the British Expeditionary Force, going back a number of years. In spring 1915, he commanded the Second Army at the Second Battle of Ypres: however he was relieved of his command by French when he asked permission to withdraw to a more easily defended position.

In November 1915, Smith-Dorrien was sent to East Africa as General Officer Commanding; however he contracted pneumonia on the voyage to South Africa and was not well enough to take up his command. He did not regain his health enough to take on a field command, and in January 1917 he was appointed Lieutenant of the Tower of London. Consecration of the memorial was by the Right Reverend Edwyn Hoskins, Bishop of Southwell.

Designed by A. H. Richardson, a local architect.

Design Features:

Constructed from Portland stone and set on a base of Aberdeen granite, the memorial is a cenotaph which comprises a rectangular block in two stages, topped by a rectangular domed cap, with moulded cornice. The memorial is supported by diagonal flying buttresses, each with two set-offs with scrolled feet, domed caps and cross motifs.

On each face of the memorial there are inscribed stone plaques with elliptical pediments. On all four faces there are bronze plaques with the names of those who died in the various wars.

The memorial stands on a traffic island surrounded by an oval kerb, which has dwarf railing and spiked chains, whilst to both north and south there are carved and panelled piers, each carrying a three-branched lamp standard: all of these works are included within the listing.

The Inscription

: On the south face the inscription is: THEIR NAME LIVETH FOR EVERMORE TO THE GLORY OF GOD/AND TO THE EVERLASTING MEMORY OF THE MEN OF WORKSOP WHO FELL IN THE GREAT WAR 1914-1918 1939-1945. On the north face the inscription reads: THEIR GLORY SHALL NOT BE BLOTTED OUT. FOR GOD AND COUNTRY 1939-1945/Korea 1950-1953. On the west face there is the single word; COURAGE and on the east face is the single word FAITHFULNESS.

The Soldier
Rupert Brooke (1887-1915) wrote this poem not long before he was killed.

If I should die, think only this of me
That there's a corner of a foreign field
That is for ever England.
In that rich earth a richer dust concealed
A dust whom England bore, shaped, made aware,
Gave, once, her flowers to love, her ways to roam,
A body of England's breathing English air,
Washed by the rivers, blessed by sons of home

And think, this heart, all evil shed away,
A pulse in the eternal mind, no less
Gives somewhere back the thoughts by England given;
Her sights and sounds, dream happy as her day;
And laughter, learnt of friends, and gentleness,
In hearts at peace, under an English heaven

2. Retford War Memorial
The Square, Market Place, Retford, Nottinghamshire, DN22
Grade II*

Unveiled on 14th September 1921 by Sir Frederick Milner Bt, a former Conservative Member of Parliament who, after losing his seat in 1906, retired from politics due to deafness. During the First World War he committed himself to helping disabled ex-servicemen. He founded the first hostel for shell-shocked soldiers in Hampstead during the war, followed by Enham Village Centre, and a similar establishment at Papworth, which still exists. The dedication was performed by The Venerable the Archdeacon of Newark, Egbert Hacking.

Designed by Leonard W Barnard of Cheltenham, who also designed the memorial at Prestatyn, Denbighshire in a similar style.

Design Features:

The basic design of the memorial is that of an Eleanor Cross, although it also includes elements of a medieval 'Lantern of the Dead' and a Roman milestone. A three stepped base is topped with a four stage plinth, on top of which is an elaborately carved upper section with trefoils, gargoyles, finials and a domed cap. On the second stage of the plinth, the names of 304 men who died in the First World War are inscribed on each face, whilst on the third stage an addition has been made in respect of those killed in the Second World War. The names of the 112 killed in this conflict are included on bronze plaques on the other seven elevations, and these plaques were unveiled on 6th May 1951.

On the fourth stage, east elevation is a further addition is a plaque inscribed: KOREA 1950-1953. This plaque was unveiled and dedicated on 1th August 2008.

On the lowest stage of the base are two recently added stone boxes, one on the east side and one on the west side on which is carved: WE WILL REMEMBER THEM. These boxes are specifically excluded from the listing.

The Story behind The Memorial:

The concept of the Roman milestone is illustrated by the list of place names on the memorial, which are those of actions where men from Retford lost their lives, many volunteers or conscripts met their deaths a long way from home.

The lantern at the top of the memorial echoes the medieval tradition of having a 'Lantern of the Dead', in which a light would be put at sundown, in order that the dead will be remembered at night as well as during the day.

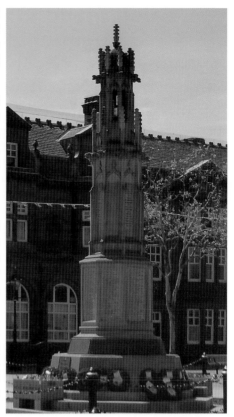

The Inscription

On the lower section of top stage of the plinth there are the following inscriptions: North elevation – ERECTED BY PUBLIC SUBSCRIPTION IN MEMORY OF THE MEN OF RETFORD AND DISTRICT WHO GAVE THEIR LIVES DURING THE GREAT WAR 1914-1918. South elevation: THEY WILLINGLY LEFT THE UNACHIEVED PURPOSE OF THEIR LIVES IN ORDER THAT ALL SHOULD NOT BE WRENCHED FROM ITS PURPOSE. West elevation: BELLENGLISE STATUE MILES 297, GOMMECOURT 270, HOOGE 240, LENS 258, LE VERGUIER 295, RANICOURT 198, YPRES 237. To the east elevation there is the following inscription: GALLIPOLI (SOUTH END OF PENNINSILA STATUE MILES 1552, STRUMA VALLEY (NORTH END OF LAKE TACHINOS) 1414, BEERSHEBA 2346, BIER EL TAHTR (BERT UR ET TAHTA) 2312, JERUSALEM 2329, ES SALT 2342, HAIFA 2276, ALEPO 2173. The numbers after the various battles refer to the number of miles they are from the memorial.
There are further inscriptions, on the south-west elevation: TO THE GLORY OF GOD AND IN PROUD REMEMBRANCE OF THE MEN AND WOMEN FROM THIS BOROUGH WHO GAVE THEIR LIVES FOR FREEDOM IN THE WORLD WAR, 1939-1945.

3. Crich Stand (Sherwood Foresters Regimental Memorial)

Plaistow Green Road, Crich, Derbyshire, DE4   Grade II*

Unveiled on 6th August 1923 by the Honorary Colonel of the Regiment, General Sir Horace Smith-Dorrien. (Further information about him is shown on page 144. Also present at the unveiling were the Dukes of Portland and of Devonshire, together with Admiral Salmon. The dedication was performed by Edwyn Hoskins, Bishop of Southwell.

Designed by Lt Col A. W. Brewill DSO (1861-1923) and Capt. L. C. Brewill (1889-1943). Arthur and Lionel Brewill were father and son and practiced architecture together in Nottingham. Arthur studied architecture at the Nottingham School of Art becoming a Fellow of the Royal Institute of British Architects in 1892. He served with the 7th (Robin Hood) Battalion of the Sherwood Foresters and commanded the Battalion from 31st July 1915. Arthur was mentioned in despatches and won the Distinguished Service Order.

He carried out considerable work on churches in the area around Nottingham as well as public buildings and private commissions. Lionel Brewill was educated at Uppingham School, Nottingham School of Art and University College, Nottingham. He was appointed an Associate of the Royal Institute of British Architects in 1919 having served through the First World War in the same battalion as his father, rising to the rank of Captain.7th (Robin Hood) Battalion. Sherwood Foresters became a Territorial unit and Lionel was appointed a Major in it in 1927 and Lieutenant Colonel in 1929.

Design Features:
The memorial stands in a prominent position on Crich Hill. It comprises a 62 feet (19m) tall circular tower of Derbyshire Gritstone with ashlar dressing, standing on a battered square platform of rock-faced sandstone. The platform has large flat copings which support wrought-iron railings and gates – these railings and gates were added in 1929. There are stone steps to the platform from the south. The tower has a doorway surrounded with heavy stone jambs and a deep lintel and pediment, which bears a bronze wreath. Above the doorway is the regimental badge of the Sherwood Foresters and the dates 1914-18 and 1939-1945 in bronze letters. Higher on the south face is a Latin cross with an inverted broadsword set into it reminiscent of the sword on the Bromfield Cross. At the top of the tower is an open arcaded lantern with fluted Doric columns, a circular stone frieze and cornice beneath an ashlar dome and flaming finial. The lantern provides a viewing gallery and is approached by an internal spiral staircase. There is a powerful electric light in the lantern, which is lit at night, and is visible for as much as 35miles around.

The Story behind The Memorial:

There has been a tower on the site of this memorial since at least 1760, when a wooden tower was built to celebrate the accession of George III to the throne. In 1788 a limestone tower with a wooden top was built, although this had fallen into disrepair by 1843, and a further replacement was built in 1851. A landslide at a nearby quarry in 1882 caused the collapse of the tower. A further rebuild was delayed by the First World War and it was not until 1922 that the stones started to be removed.

In 1921 a committee of the Sherwood Foresters Old Comrades Association was created with the brief to consider a permanent memorial to the 11,409 men of the regiment who had died during the First World War. The initial thoughts were that two separate memorials should be created, one in Nottinghamshire and one in Derbyshire, until General Smith-Dorrien, the Colonel of the Regiment, suggested one memorial close to the boundary between the two counties. Crich Stand was suggested as a site and that a tall tower would be appropriate. The company that owned the site donated the stonework from the old tower, paid to move the materials and donated £200 to the appeal fund. The builder was Joseph Payne of Crich and the total cost of the memorial was £2,382, which was raised by public subscription.

The Inscription

The lintel over the tower doorway contains an inscription in incised lettering: TO THE MEMORY OF 11409 MEN OF ALL RANKS OF THE SHERWOOD FORESTERS (NOTTINGHAMSHIRE AND DERBYSHIRE REGIMENT) WHO GAVE THEIR LIVES FOR THEIR KING AND FOR THEIR COUNTRY IN THE GREAT WAR 1914 - 1919 AND IN HONOUR OF 140000 OF THEIR COMRADES WHO SERVED DURING THE WAR IN THIRTY TWO BATTALIONS OF THE REGIMENT THIS MONUMENT IS GRATEFULLY ERECTED BY THE PEOPLE OF THE COUNTIES OF NOTTINGHAM AND DERBY. TO REMIND US OF THEIR SACRIFICE AND OUR DUTY.

A plaque to the left of the main gateway, added in 1952, contains a cast bronze commemorative plaque bearing the words, in raised lettering: TO THE GLORY OF GOD AND IN HONOURED MEMORY OF THE 1520 SHERWOOD FORESTERS WHO GAVE THEIR LIVES IN THE WAR OF 1939-1945 & IN HONOUR OF THEIR COMRADES WHO SERVED IN THE 13 UNITS OF THE REGIMENT.

A plaque to the right contains the regimental badges. There are three further bronze panels either side of the tower door; two to the left and one to the right. The upper panel on the left is inscribed, in raised lettering: THIS MEMORIAL TOWER IS ALSO DEDICATED TO THE MEMORY OF THOSE OF THE SHERWOOD FORESTERS WHO GAVE THEIR LIVES IN THE SERVICE OF THEIR COUNTRY FROM 1945 TO 1970. The lower panel is inscribed: THIS MEMORIAL TOWER IS FURTHER DEDICATED TO THE MEMORY OF THOSE MEMBERS OF THE MERCIAN REGIMENT WHO GAVE THEIR LIVES IN THE SERVICE OF THEIR COUNTRY SINCE THE FORMATION OF THE REGIMENT IN 2007.

The panel to the right is inscribed: THIS MEMORIAL TOWER IS ALSO DEDICATED TO THE MEMORY OF THOSE OF THE WORCESTERSHIRE AND SHERWOOD FORESTERS REGIMENT WHO HAVE GIVEN THEIR LIVES IN THE SERVICE OF THEIR COUNTRY SINCE THE FORMATION OF THE REGIMENT ON 28 FEBRUARY 1970.

4. Midland Railway War Memorial
Midland Road, Derby, DE24
Grade II*

Unveiled by Charles Booth, Chairman of the Midland Railway on 15th December 1921, with the Right Reverend Edwyn Hoskins, Bishop of Southwell, leading the service of dedication.

Designed by Sir Edwin Lutyens.

Design Features:

The memorial is a 33ft (10m) high cenotaph made from Portland stone, flanked by a 6ft 6ins (2m) screen wall. The wall forms rectangular alcoves on each side of the cenotaph. The cenotaph is topped with an effigy of an unknown soldier lying and partially covered with his greatcoat, and his helmet and bayonet lie at his feet.

The body lies on a raised bier mounted on the heads of four lions. On two faces of the shaft is a carving of the Midland Railway's coat of arms enclosed in a wreath, and on the sides are the Roman numerals MCM XIV-XIX (1914-19). Bronze plaques are attached to the alcoves created by the screen wall, and contain the names of the staff of the Midland Railway Company killed in the First World War: the names are listed alphabetically, with no indication of rank or arm of service.

The memorial was built by J Parnell and Son Ltd at a cost of £10,309 which was fully met by the company.

The Story behind The Memorial:

At the time of the First World War, the Midland Railway was the largest employer in Derby, and employed around 60,000 staff across England and Wales. With the coming of the war, the company released some 23,000 staff of whom 2,833 were killed and 7,068 were wounded.

As well as the memorial, the company published a Book of Remembrance and sent a copy to the family of each of the men named on the memorial. Unlike the anonymity of the memorial, the book gave details of the occupation of each man, where he worked, the name of his regiment or unit and his rank.

In the foreword to the book, the memorial is described as "… the triumphant end of the war, as well as the sadness and sorrow it entailed, and is intended to embody the whole meaning of those troubled years which have bequeathed to us the memory of so many

130

good lives lost and stout hearts which no longer beat. It marks the victory which crowned their whole efforts, and the pride with which the Midland Railway can truly affirm – 'our men did not a little to that end'."

In 2010 two men were jailed for stealing four bronze plaques from the memorial: thankfully the plaques were recovered. Restoration was carried out by Network Rail and the Railway Heritage Trust at a cost of £18,000. When the plaques had been restored to their rightful place, a service of re-dedication was held on 17th December 2010, using the original Prayer of Dedication from the 1921 unveiling ceremony.

After nationalisation of the railways in 1947, and the gradual retreat from Derby by railways works and offices, a large number of plaques that related to staff from specific workshops became 'homeless' – in an imaginative move, after cleaning and restoration, these have been fixed adjacent to each other on platform 1 of Derby Station.

The Inscription

On the face of the cenotaph that faces the road is the inscription: TO THE BRAVE MEN OF THE MIDLAND RAILWAY WHO GAVE THEIR LIVES IN THE GREAT WAR.

DID YOU KNOW THAT?

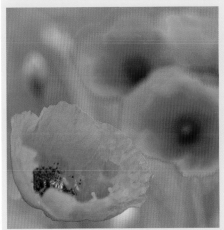

The poppy became a symbol of remembrance of those killed in the war as a result of American professor and humanitarian, Moina Michael, (image below) who wrote in 1918 - 'And now the Torch and Poppy Red, we wear in honor of our dead...' - and she campaigned to make the poppy a symbol of remembrance of those who had died in the war.

She was responding to the famous poem In Flanders Field, which was written by John McCrae as a tribute to his fellow Canadian Forces comrade Alexis Helmer, who had been killed near Ypres on 2nd May 1915. His poem had been inspired by the appearance of poppies near to the graves. Poppies have been sold in Britain since 1921 to support ex-servicemen and women and their families.

5. Lenton War Memorial

Adjacent to the Albert Ball Memorial Homes, Junction of Church Street and Sherwin Road, Old Lenton, Nottingham, NG7   Grade II*

Unveiled on 29th May 1920 by Major General the Honourable Edward Montague-Stuart-Wortley, a career soldier who had seen service around the world. At the time of the outbreak of the First World War, Stuart-Wortley was General Officer Commanding the 46th (North Midland) Division. He was dismissed after the opening days of the Battle of the Somme, when he was made the scapegoat when a diversionary attack had failed: he retired from the army in 1919.

Designer: The name of the designer of the memorial is not recorded, although the adjacent memorial homes were designed by local architects, Brewill and Bailey. The memorial homes were built three years later, and no direct connection can be made with the memorial.

Design Features:

The memorial is situated in a small memorial garden in front of the Albert Ball Memorial Homes, which were built three years after the memorial.

A bronze cross with a sunburst stands on top of a tall, Aberdeen granite, fluted ionic column, on top of a square pedestal with a moulded top and cornice. There are large bronze plaques on each face of the memorial. The plaque to the front of the memorial bears the main inscription, whilst those to each side give the names of the 287 people from the village who gave their lives in the First World War. The plaque on the rear of the memorial is a key to the abbreviations used in the memorial.

The Story behind The Memorial:

The memorial was built in 1919 by public subscription, although the money for the bronze cross was donated by Alderman A Ball, a local estate agent and chairman of the memorial committee. Alderman Ball was the father of Albert Ball, arguably Britain's most famous First World War fighter pilot, who was killed in action in France on 7th May 1917 aged 20, having previously shot down 44 enemy aircraft. Ball was awarded a posthumous Victoria Cross having already received a Distinguished Service Order and two bars.

Also included on the memorial is Dorothea Crewdson, who was a nursing sister as a member of the Voluntary Aid Detachment. Sister Crewdson was awarded the Military Medal, a very rare honour for a woman, for continuing to treat the wounded, despite being wounded herself, during a German air raid on the hospital at Etaples in France. She was already a recipient of the Royal Red Cross Medal, and died from peritonitis resulting from her wounds: she is buried at Etaples Military Cemetery.

The Inscription

The main inscription of the memorial is on the front plaque: TO THE GLORIOUS AND UNDYING MEMORY OF THE MEN OF LENTON WHOSE NAMES ARE HERETO AFFIXED WHO LAID DOWN THEIR LIVES FOR THEIR COUNTRY'S HONOUR AND FREEDOM IN THE GREAT WAR 1914-1918 THIS MEMORIAL IS ERECTED BY THE INHABITANTS OF LENTON 1919.

My Boy Jack

Rudyard Kipling (1865-1936).
Many believe this poem reveals his feelings of guilt in getting his son John a commission in the army.

Have you news of my boy Jack?
Not this tide.
When do you think that he'll come back?
Not with this wind blowing, and this tide

Has any one else had word of him?
Not this tide
For what is sunk will hardly swim,
Not with this wind blowing, and this tide.

Oh, dear, what comfort can I find?
None this tide
Nor any tide.
Except he did not shame his kind –
Not even with that wind blowing, and that tide.

Then hold your head up all the more,
This tide,
And every tide;
Because he was the son you bore,
And gave to that wind blowing and that tide.

6. Statue of Albert Ball

Nottingham Castle Gardens, Nottingham, NG1
Grade II*

Unveiled by Sir Hugh Trenchard on 8th September 1921, who had been a career army officer, although he only just managed to meet the minimum standard for a commission. After service during the Second Boer War, when he was critically wounded, and further service in Nigeria, in 1912 Trenchard learned to fly and transferred to the Royal Flying Corps, rising to command it in France from 1915 to 1917.

Although he opposed the formation of the Royal Air Force, by combining the Royal Flying Corps and Royal Naval Air Service, Trenchard realised that it was necessary and supervised the transition, although he resigned almost immediately afterwards, following a disagreement with Lord Rothermere, the Air Minister. After resolution of this disagreement, which saw Rothermere resign, Trenchard finished the war as Commander of the Independent Air Force in France.

Designed by Edwin Alfred Rickards (1872-1920) who was born in London and became apprenticed to an architect at the age of 15. Following studies at the Royal Academy Schools, Rickards worked for several architects until, in partnership with H V Lanchester and James Stewart, he won the competition to design Cardiff City Hall and Law Courts, which was one of a number of Neo-Baroque buildings designed by the partnership, with others including the Methodist Central Hall in London and Deptford Town Hall.

Rickards volunteered for the army during the First World War, but was invalided back to England in 1916 after only a few months on the Western Front. Rickards final architectural work was the design of the Army Transport Depot in Slough.

Sculpted by Henry Poole.

Design Features:

The memorial consists of a cast bronze statue of Captain Albert Ball in his flying uniform of helmet and coat, with his hands on his belt, whilst behind him is an allegorical figure of a woman in flowing clothes representing Air. The woman has one hand pointing to the sky and the other on Ball's shoulder. This group stands on a moulded stone plinth, with inscriptions on two of the four sides both in auricular cartouches. On the other two sides of the plinth are reliefs of an SE5a bi-plane. On the north side the aircraft is depicted flying over trenches, whilst on the south side it is shown flying above the clouds.

134

The plinth stands on a wider tiered base which, in turn, stands on three lobed steps with smaller interlocking circles at each lobe. At the base of the plinth there is further bronze ornamentation which includes eternal flames, a feather, a laurel wreath, scrolls draped in foliage, and scrolled and fanned bronze feet which appear to support the base.

The Story behind The Memorial:

This is a highly unusual memorial, one of only three in this book, in as much as it commemorates an individual – the others are to Edith Cavell and Earl Haig. Albert Ball was one of Britain's most famous fighter pilots of the First World War: he had achieved 44 confirmed "kills" and a further 25 unconfirmed within one year. Ball was killed in action on 7th May 1917 at the age of 20. It is not just Ball's extraordinary ability as a pilot that single him out, but his lengthy letters to his parents do not reveal the slightest hint of malice towards the enemy. David Lloyd George wrote a tribute to Albert Ball:

"This war has revealed many stirring examples of heroic simplicity, but seldom have I come across so fine a spirit of devotion to freedom, home and country as is reflected in Captain Ball's letters to his family. In all his fighting record there is no trace of resentment, revenge or cruelty…What he says in one of his letters, 'I hate this game, but it is the only thing one must do just now', represents, I believe, the conviction of those vast armies who, realising what is at stake, have risked all and endured all that liberty may be saved. I am sure nobody can read these letters without feeling that it is men like Captain Ball who are the true soldiers of British democracy. It is their spirit of fearless activity for the right, in their daily work, which will lead us through victory into a new world in which tyranny and oppression will have no part."

During his short career Ball won the Military Cross, three DSO's (Distinguished Service Orders) and he was awarded a posthumous Victoria Cross, which was presented to his parents by King George V in the market place in Nottingham.

The memorial was commissioned by Nottingham City Council and was paid for by public subscription.

The Inscription

The inscription to the front reads: CAPT. ALBERT BALL V.C. 7TH ROBIN HOOD BATTALION SHERWOOD FORESTERS ATTACHED ROYAL FLYING CORPS, DSO (2 BARS) MC CROIX DE CHEVALIER, LEGION D'HONNEUR, ORDER OF ST GEORGE (RUSSIAN) HON. FREEMAN OF THE CITY OF NOTTINGHAM PER ARDUA AD ASTRA. To the back of the plinth the inscription reads: IN THE AIR HE GAVE MOST CONSPICUOUS AND GALLANT SERVICE TO HIS COUNTRY AND WAS KILLED IN ACTION FIGHTING GLORIOUSLY MAY 7TH 1917 AGED 20 YEARS PER ARDUA AD ASTRA. [Per ardua ad astra is the Latin motto of the Royal Air Force and can be translated as 'Through adversity to the stars' or 'Through struggle to the stars'.]

7. War Memorial in the Churchyard of St Wulfram's Church

St Wulfram's Church, Church Street, Grantham, Lincolnshire, NG31

Grade II*

Unveiled on 27th November 1920 by local clergy and dignitaries.

Designed by Sir Charles Nicholson Bt

Sculpted by Mr Phillips, who worked for the builders Messrs Bowman & Sons.

Design Features:

This highly detailed Gothic style 30ft (9m) memorial is octagonal in plan and consists of four stages and made from Clipsham stone. The octagonal plinth, which is decorated with a blind Gothic arcade, rests on a two-tier octagonal base. Each side of the plinth is decorated with three trefoil-headed arches except one which holds a stone tablet bearing the inscription.

Above the plinth the broached column is an eight pointed star on plan, forming 16 Gothic-panelled faces, surmounted by a square, moulded capital embellished with a four leaf clover motif. The top stage has four richly canopied niches facing the four cardinal points with moulded and crocketed pinnacles at each corner and an octagonal, ribbed and crocketed pinnacle rising from the centre. The niches for the four figure sculptures contain, on the west side Christ on the cross with Mary and St John flanking him, on the north side is St Wulfrum, to the east, St Michael, and to the south, St George.

The Story behind The Memorial:

Architecturally, St Wulfrum's is widely considered to be one of the most important parish churches in the country and it was important, therefore, that the war memorial should complement the existing design. Nicholson was the leading ecclesiastical architect of the early 20th Century and took his inspiration from the 14th Century spire of the church.

The total cost of the memorial was £1,517.00. The memorial was cleaned and re-dedicated in 2012.

The Inscription

A stone panel on one side of the plinth carries the following inscription: IN GRATEFUL MEMORY OF THE GRANTHAM MEN WHO SACRIFICED THEIR LIVES IN THE GREAT WAR 1914-1919 WHOSE NAMES ARE INSCRIBED ON THE WAY WITHIN THE CHURCH. IN MEMORY ALSO OF THOSE WHO GAVE THEIR LIVES IN THE SECOND WORLD WAR 1939-1945.

DID YOU KNOW THAT?

"Fighting Germans, Austrians and Drink"

Alcohol consumption was a major worry for the British Government in the First world war, not only with those fighting in the field of battle, but also at home.

In January 1915, Lloyd George said that Britain was "Fighting German's, Austrians and Drink, and as far as I can see the greatest of these foes is Drink," as well as "Drink is doing us more damage in the war than all the German submarines put together."

He campaigned to persuade key public figures to take a pledge that they would not drink alcohol during the war, and this was taken up by King George V, on behalf of the Royal household. But the Prime Minister Lord Asquith, reputedly a heavy drinker, did not sign the pledge. The quarterly magazine National Review commented, "The  failure of the Prime Minister to take the King's Pledge has naturally aroused comment." To which Asquith retorted angrily, that Lloyd George had "completely lost his head on drink."

In the 19th Century English breweries typical produced various strengths of the most popular "Mild Ale" with the gravity ranging from 5.5% and 7% ABV (Alcohol By Volume).

The Government introduced a number of measures during the War including higher taxes on beer, "licensing hours" in cities and industrial areas, and a "No Treating Order".

The higher taxes resulted in breweries reducing the gravities of their beer to an ABV of between 3.5% and 4%, which meant it became exempt from taxation. These at some stage became known, as they area today, as "sessions beers"

Before the law change in August 1914, public houses in Britain could open from 5 am in the morning to half past midnight, but now opening times in cities and industrial areas (adjacent to munition factories) were reduced to 12.00 noon to 2.30 pm and 6.30 to 9.30 pm. However, in most rural areas, people could continue to buy alcoholic drinks throughout the day.

Munition workers, most of whom were women and were called "Munitionettes", were key patrons to the new strength beers and licensing hours and The Times reported that "we do not all realise the increase in drinking there has been among the mothers of the coming race, though we may yet find it a circumstance darkly menacing to our civilisation".

The "No Treating Order" meant that a person could only buy alcohol for their own consumption, rather than in "rounds". Whilst a drink could cost only sixpence (2.5p), fines of £1 were imposed on the purchaser and £5 on the barperson.

Convictions for drunkenness fell, spirit consumption radically declined, and beer consumption reduced in the war period – from 89m gallons in 1914 to 37m in 1918.

8. Spalding War Memorial

Ayscoughfee Hall Gardens, Ayscoughfee Hall, Church Gate, Spalding, Lincolnshire PE11

Grade I

Unveiled on 8th June 1922 by General Sir Ian Hamilton, whose biographical details are included on page 44. The memorial was consecrated by the Rev Alfred Jarvis, Assistant Chaplain-General to Northern Command. At the deremony three ex-servicemen unveiled the three inscribed panels inside the pavilion. At the end of the service a lone bugler played the Last Post and the congregation sang the National Anthem.

Designed by Sir Edwin Lutyens

Design Features:

The memorial garden lies within the southern garden area of Ayscoughfee Hall, which is listed Grade I and the gardens are listed Grade II. The Temple of Remembrance is at the head of the Garden of Remembrance and comprises a brick pavilion with three Tuscan stone arches to its front face and single arches to each side face. The roof, which is hipped, is covered in red pantiles. The floor has panels of red herringbone bricks set within stone surrounds. On the rear wall there are two painted stone flags of the sort much favoured by Lutyens in other memorials. The flag to the left is the Union Flag whilst that to the right is the White Ensign. There are three panels set into the inner rear wall, the central panel has the main dedication together with 24 names that had been omitted from the memorial and were added in 2015. The names were added following research by a volunteer from the local branch of the Royal British Legion. The panels to the left and right have names of 224 men from Spalding who were killed in the First World War. Leading from the Stone of Remembrance is a canal, which was re-worked by Lutyens to form a reflecting pool. The canal has ashlar walls and a stone flagged surround.

The Story behind The Memorial:

The proposal for a war memorial for those from Spalding killed during the First World War came in January 1918 from Barbara McLaren. Her husband, Francis, who was Spalding's Member of Parliament, had been killed in an accident in 1917 whilst serving with the Royal Flying Corps.

Mrs McLaren was a niece of Gertrude Jekyll, the celebrated Scottish garden designer, who had collaborated with Lutyens' many times on the design of country houses and Lutyens had designed the McLaren's London home. Mrs McLaren wrote to Spalding Council in January 1922 to say that she had already engaged Lutyens to design a suitable memorial for the fallen of the town. Lutyens designed an elaborate U-shaped cloisters, however when this was presented to the town council there was considerable debate, and at a public meeting in August 1919 a number of other proposals were put forward. The result of the ballot was the scaled-down design described above, together with a carillon which was to be built on the roof of the town's Corn Exchange.

To raise the £3,500 cost of the memorial the Spalding War and Victory Memorials Committee was formed in September 1919.

Mrs McLaren donated £1,000 which was matched by £1,000 from her father-in-law, whilst the late Francis McLaren's brother donated the two painted flags. Fund-raising proved slow and the memorial was not completed until 1922. It can only be speculation now, however, but were Mrs McLaren's actions in engaging Lutyens before informing the Town Council, together with pursuing the memorial as a personal one for her late husband, partly to blame?

Sufficient money was raised to buy 23 bells for the carillon however installation had to wait until a bell tower was built on the Corn Exchange in the 1930's. The mechanism for the carillon fell into disrepair and was not restored to full playing condition until 1998 when it was installed in the newly refurbished South Holland Centre.

The Inscription

The main dedication reads: IN LOVE AND HONOUR OF THOSE WHO GAVE THEIR LIVES FOR THEIR COUNTRY IN THE YEARS OF WAR MCMXIV – MCMXIX / THIS MEMORIAL IS RAISED IN THEIR HOME BY THE MEN AND WOMEN OF SPALDING. Inside the pavilion there is a frieze that includes the inscription: ETERNAL REST GRANT TO THEM O LORD AND LET LIGHT PERPETUAL SHINE UPON THEM. There is a further stone within the pavilion which bears the inscription: THIS STONE COMMEMORATES FRANCIS WALTER STAFFORD McLAREN MEMBER OF PARLIAMENT FOR THE SPALDING DIVISION 1910–1917 WHEN HE FELL IN THE SERVICE OF HIS COUNTRY AT THE AGE OF 31.
In front of the pavilion, raised on a three stepped base, there is a Stone of Remembrance which is inscribed: THEIR NAME LIVETH FOREVER MORE together with 1914 1918 to the left and 1939 1945 to the right.

9. The Arch of Remembrance

War Memorial Approach, Victoria Park, Leicester LE1

Grade I

Unveiled on 4th July 1925, in the presence of Sir Edwin Lutyens, by two local widows, Mrs Elizabeth Butler, who had lost four of her eight sons in the war, and Mrs Annie Glover, who had lost three sons. The dedication of the memorial was performed by Cyril Bardsley, the Bishop of Peterborough who, in 1927, became the first Bishop of Leicester in modern times

Designed by Sir Edwin Lutyens.

Design Features:

The memorial is a 69ft (21m) high, Portland stone, triumphal arch, which is square in plan with tall, wide, open arches to the north-east and south-west, whilst the arches to the north-east and south-west are smaller. Lutyens was, of course, working in imperial measurements and the arches are formed in simple multiples: the larger arches are 18ft wide, 36ft tall and 9ft deep with the smaller arches 12ft wide, 24 ft tall and 6ft deep.

There are stone wreaths which flank the arches both to the front and the rear. The wreaths to the left of the arches have the inscriptions MCMXIV in them, whilst those to the right have MCMXIX. Above the arches is a heavy attic, which bears the arms of the city of Leicester suspended from large swags. The arch is topped with a low dome.

The main arch has a barrel vault ceiling with similar, but lower, vaults to each side arch. Painted stone flags are feature of a number of Lutyens' memorials, and there are four set on corbels in the main arch: the flags are the Union Flag, the Royal Navy, the Army and the Royal Air Force.

The Story behind The Memorial:

A War Memorial Committee was set up in Leicester following a public meeting on 14th May 1919, Lutyens was suggested as a possible architect, and Victoria Park as a site. The initial design involved avenues of lime trees, a cenotaph and a circular walled enclosure. By late 1920 only £4,000 of the anticipated costs of £20,000 had been raised, and in March 1923 the original scheme was abandoned, although as much for lack of public enthusiasm as for shortage of funds. At the request of the committee Lutyens produced an alternative design for a memorial arch, which he estimated may cost £25,000.

When work started on the memorial in 1923 the committee had still not raised sufficient cash, so it was necessary to raise a bank loan to cover any potential shortfall. The loan was secured by five guarantors from the committee. Upon completion of the memorial, the final cost was over £27,000, which meant that there was a shortfall of £5,532 which the five guarantors were called upon to meet. Lutyens' fee for designing the memorial was £1,635.

The positioning of the Arch of Remembrance is such that as the sun rises on 11th November it shines directly through the arch. Whilst many similar claims are nothing more than urban myths, this has been tested and proved, both visually and astronomically, by an academic from De Montfort University.

The Inscription

Over the main arch facing War Memorial Approach the words: GLORY TO GOD IN THE HIGHEST AND ON EARTH PEACE are inscribed whilst, on the opposite side that faces into the park is a very poignant inscription: ALL THEY HOPED FOR, ALL THEY HAD, THEY GAVE/ TO SAVE MANKIND - THEMSELVES THEY SCORNED TO SAVE. The dates of the Second World War are carved in Roman numerals towards the base of the piers, facing into the park.

Above the arch to the north-east face is inscribed: REMEMBER IN GRATITUDE TWELVE THOUSAND MEN/ OF THIS CITY AND COUNTY/ WHO FOUGHT AND DIED FOR FREEDOM./ REMEMBER ALL WHO SERVED AND STROVE/ AND THOSE WHO PATIENTLY ENDURED. Over the arch on the south-west face are the words: I WILL NOT CEASE FROM MENTAL FIGHT/ NOR SHALL MY SWORD SLEEP IN MY HAND/ TILL WE HAVE BUILT JERUSALEM/ IN ENGLAND'S GREEN AND PLEASANT LAND.

The memorial is set in a park and surrounded by a circle of iron railings. There are four pairs of rusticated stone gate piers decorated with a Greek key pattern and swags. On top of each of the piers is a short pillar topped with an urn.

10. The Town and County War Memorial

Wood Hill, Northampton, NN1
Grade I

Unveiled on 11th November 1926 by Lord Horne. General Henry Sinclair Horne, 1st Baron Horne, was a career soldier who had received his commission in May 1880 and had served throughout the Second Boer War in the cavalry under the command of Sir John French. In 1912, Horne was promoted Brigadier and appointed Inspector of Artillery. He commanded a force of artillery under General Haig at Mons at the beginning of the war, but also served at Gallipoli, Egypt and back on the Western Front. It was Horne who invented the "creeping barrage", whereby the artillery fire fell just in front of advancing infantry. Thousands of local residents attended the ceremony, including some 5,000 school children. There was a procession led by survivors of the battle of Mons, as well as nurses from Northampton General Hospital, and civil and military representatives. The memorial was dedicated by the Suffragan Bishop of Leicester before Lord Horne committed the memorial into the care of the Mayor and the County Council.

Designed by Sir Edwin Lutyens.

Design Features:

The memorial is made from Portland stone and stands in a garden that is surrounded by a stone wall and a yew hedge, with gates to the north and the south. The gates are ornamental and made from wrought iron, and hang from stone gate piers that have urn finials. The wall around the memorial is made from stone and is just over 3ft (1 meter) tall topped by a chamfered coping. The memorial itself stands on a paved platform in the centre of which is a Stone of Remembrance, which is raised on three steps. To north and south of the Stone of Remembrance is a tall obelisk: each one raised on a tall, square four staged corniced column. Each of the columns stands on a square, undercut plinth.

Round arched, curved niches are carved into the major stage of each column. Tall stone flags topped with gilded laurel wreaths flank each obelisk. The flags are painted and similar flags can be seen on other Lutyens memorials. The northern obelisk is flanked by the Red Ensign to the north and the Union Flag to the south, whilst the southern obelisk carries the White Ensign to the north and the RAF Ensign to the south.

The Story behind The Memorial:

It was felt very soon after the end of the First World War that some form of memorial to those from Northampton and Northamptonshire who had died in the war was needed. Consequently a wooden cenotaph was erected in Abington Street in July 1919, until a decision about a formal memorial could be made. Early discussions involved something practical such as a concert hall, although these were abandoned in favour of a formal memorial. Sir Edwin Lutyens was commissioned to design the memorial and a site was chosen. The preferred site for the memorial was in the centre of the town and comprised what was then part of the churchyard of the Church of All Saints. Although Lutyens had completed the design work in 1920, the memorial was not able to be built and unveiled until 1926, because permission had to be sought to remove some graves from the churchyard.

The Inscription

Dedications are inscribed into each element of the memorial. On the east side of the northern obelisks is carved MCMXIX and below this is the coat of arms of the town with MCMXXXIX MCMXLV below that. To the west side is MCMXIV. These inscriptions are repeated on the southern obelisk. The Stone of Remembrance is inscribed: THE SOULS OF THE RIGHTEOUS ARE IN THE HANDS OF GOD on the west side while on the east side is inscribed THEIR NAME LIVETH FOR EVERMORE. There is a dwarf stone wall on the western side of the garden which is inscribed TO THE MEMORY OF ALL THOSE OF THIS TOWN AND COUNTY WHO SERVED AND DIED IN THE GREAT WAR.

11. Edgar Mobbs War Memorial
Garden of Remembrance, Kettering Road, Northampton, NN1
Grade II*

Unveiled on 17th July 1921 by John Powys 5th Baron Lilford. Lilford was a keen amateur cricketer who played for Northamptonshire in 1911, making a first-team appearance against the touring Indian cricket team. The unveiling was also attended by G.S. Whiting, Mayor of Northampton, together with representatives of the English Rugby Union.

Sculpted by Alfred Turner (1874-1940), who studied at the South London Technical Art School in Lambeth and from 1895 at the Royal Academy Schools. He taught sculpture at the Central School of Arts and Crafts in London from 1907. Turner produced statues for private and corporate clients as well as undertaking relief work, and was involved with the design of a number of war memorials. He was an Associate of the Royal Academy from 1922 and a full member from 1931, as well as being one of the early members of the Royal Society of British Sculptors, being a Fellow from 1923 until his death.

Design Features:

The memorial comprises a draped female figure in bronze, who represents either the Goddess of Fame, or the Glory of the Dead – contemporary records are not clear on the matter. The figure is holding a laurel wreath in her left hand and a staff in her right. The statue stands on a 20ft (6m) tall Portland stone pillar, which stands on a three stepped base. The front (east) face of the pillar holds a bronze bust of Lt Col Mobbs in uniform, with a wreath behind his head; the south face depicts a rugby match, whilst the north face depicts men in battle. Contemporary reports state that the central figure in each represents Mobbs, but the depictions are not rendered in enough detail to identify individuals.

The Story behind The Memorial:

This memorial is one of only four in this book dedicated solely to an individual – the other three are Edith Cavell; Earl Haig and Captain Albert Ball. Edgar Roberts Mobbs (1882–1917) was a native of Northampton and captained the Northampton rugby union side from 1907 to 1913. During his career, Mobbs scored 177 tries and also captained the Barbarians, the East Midlands (1906–13), and led the joint West Midlands/East Midlands side which, on 2 December 1908, beat the Australians 16–5 at Leicester, their only defeat in England. Not only was Mobbs a great individual player, he also captained London and the Midlands against the West; the South against the North at Twickenham; and England against France in Paris. He won seven England caps and he also played for Toulouse, where he became a great favourite. As well as his rugby successes, Mobbs also played county cricket for Buckinghamshire.

When the First World War started Mobbs, then 32, was refused a commission on the grounds that he was too old. Mobbs joined the Northamptonshire Regiment as a Private and set about raising his own company of over 250 men, which formed D company of the 7th Battalion, of the regiment. Mobbs leadership abilities were recognised and he was commissioned in October 1914. By April 1916 he had risen to the rank of Lieutenant-Colonel and had become Battalion Commander. Wounded three times, he was gazetted Distinguished Service Order on 1 January 1917. Returning to his battalion for the third battle of Ypres, Passchendaele, Mobbs was killed in action at Zillebeke, Belgium, on 31 July 1917. His body was never found and his name is on the Menin Gate

The memorial, which cost £1000, was funded by subscriptions from around the world, and cost £1500. The remaining £500 raised was donated to the East Midlands Rugby Union and funded a trophy at Bedford Modern School. The memorial was originally located in the Market Square, Northampton, but was moved to Northampton's new Garden of Remembrance in time for the dedication of the garden on 1st January 1937.

The Inscription

The east face of the pillar carries the inscription: LIEUT – COL EDGAR R MOBBS D.S.O. COMMANDING OFFICER 7TH BATTALION NORTHAMPTONSHIRE REGIMENT KILLED IN ACTION JULY 31ST 1917 AGED 35 O VALIANT HEARTS WHO TO YOUR GLORY CAME, THROUGH DUST OF CONFLICT AND THROUGH BATTLE FLAME TRANQUIL YOU LIE YOUR KNIGHTLY VIRTUE PROVED YOUR MEMORY HALLOWED IN THE LAND YOU LOVED.
The inscription on the bust reads: HE DID HIS DUTY EVEN UNTO DEATH.
The reverse of the monument is inscribed: ERECTED BY SUBSCRIPTIONS OF ADMIRERS THE WORLD OVER TO THE MEMORY OF A GREAT AND GALLANT SOLDIER SPORTSMAN WHEN THE GREAT WAR BROKE OUT HE FOUNDED "MOBBS COMPANY" JOINED AS A PRIVATE AND ROSE TO COMMAND THE BATTALION TO WHICH IT BELONGED.

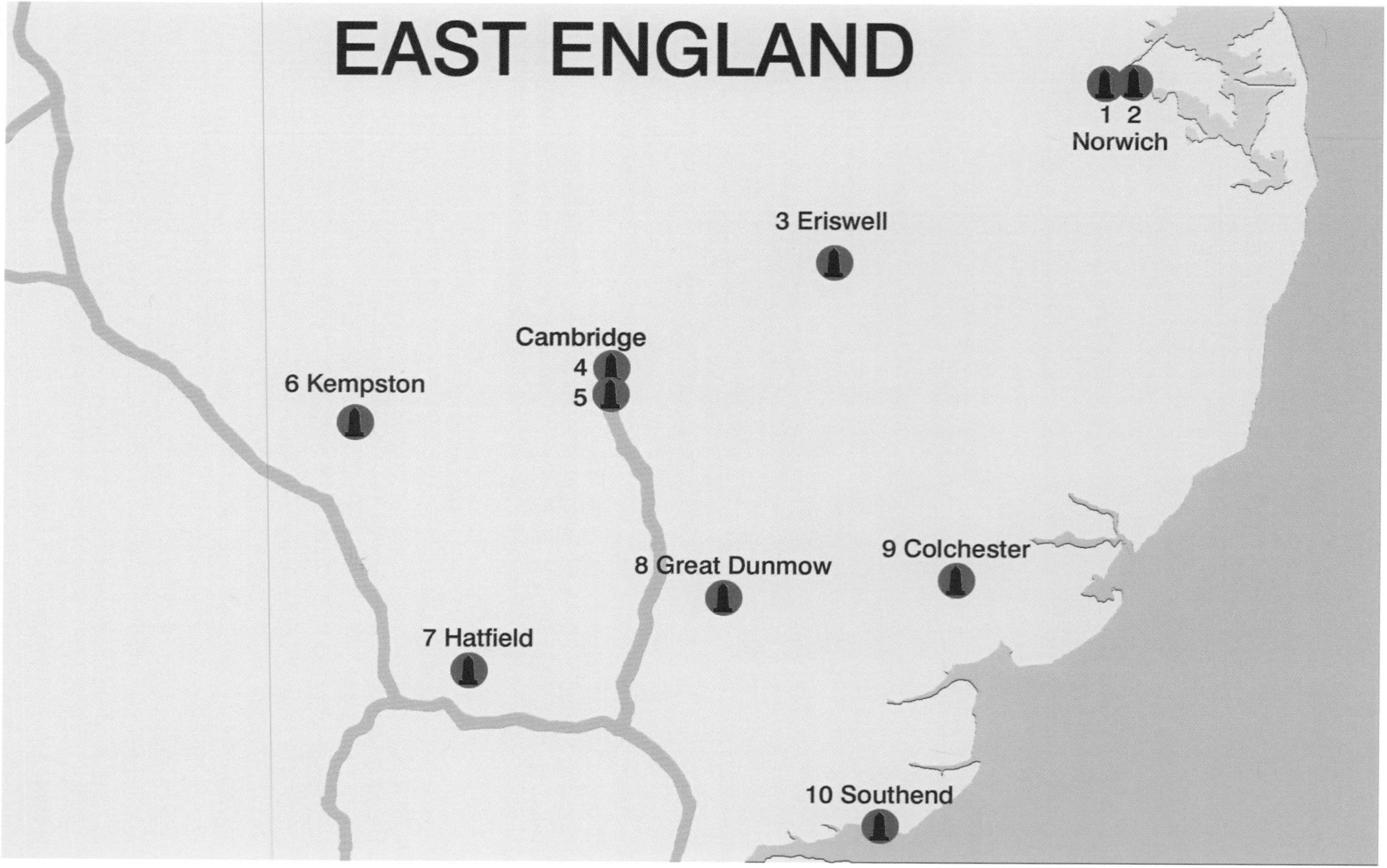

EAST ENGLAND

1 2 Norwich

3 Eriswell

Cambridge
4
5

6 Kempston

7 Hatfield

8 Great Dunmow

9 Colchester

10 Southend

CONTENTS

Map reference and Memorial Name   Page

1. Norwich Memorial and War Memorial Garden Terrace

St Peters Street, Norwich, NR2

Grade II*

Unveiled by Bertie Withers, a disabled veteran, who carried out the unveiling on 9th October 1927 during a ceremony led by General Sir Ian Hamilton. Hamilton was a career soldier, and further information about him is shown on Page 44.

Designed by Sir Edwin Lutyens, with this being the last of his eight cenotaph designs. The memorial gardens were designed later by C.H. James and S. R. Pierce.

Design Features:

The memorial is made from Portland Stone and topped by bronze flambeaux. Like many of Lutyens' designs it is the uncluttered simplicity of the memorial that makes it so striking. A low screen wall is topped in the centre by a wreath topped sarcophagus, which has the carved and painted city arms, supported by two angels, on the front. Pedestals on either end of the screen wall support gilt bronze flambeaux, which have gas feeds, that would have enabled a flame to be lit at night. Lutyens suggested this feature on other memorials that he designed, but Norwich was the only city to accept the concept.

Coming out from the centre of the screen wall is a Stone of Remembrance. Lutyens designed the Stone of Remembrance to be free standing, and this example is the only one that is attached to another structure.

The Story behind The Memorial:

Norwich's attempts to decide on a war memorial that pleased everyone were not simple. The first idea put forward was a plan to build an agricultural college which would serve as a war memorial. Donations were requested, but these had to be returned, because it was realised that the scheme would cost too much and there were suggestions that it would not appeal to everyone.

In 1926 when Charles Bignold, who was from the family that founded Norwich Union Insurance, was elected Lord Mayor of Norwich, he resolved that the city would have a war memorial before he left office. Bignold instructed Lutyens who had a considerable reputation, and the two men decided on a site near the Guildhall. Bignold wanted the scheme to benefit the living as well as commemorating the dead, so established a Joint Hospitals and War Memorial Appeal with the aim of raising £35,000. £4,000 was to be allocated to a memorial, and the balance to be split between the Norfolk and Norwich Hospital and the Jenny Lind Children's Hospital.

The memorial proposed by Lutyens would not have space for the names of the 3,544 people of Norwich who had died in the war. so an additional £800 to £1,000 was allocated to pay for Lutyens to design and build a set of oak panels, that would fold out to reveal the names. The memorial was built at a total cost of £2,700 including Lutyens' fee of £270.

It was decided that a disabled veteran should unveil the memorial and Bertie Withers was chosen at random from a list of men who met four criteria. They had to be natives of Norwich, had to have been a volunteer and not conscripted, to have served overseas

and be permanently disabled. Withers had lost the lower part of a leg at the First Battle of Gaza and had spent a year in the Norwich and Norfolk Hospital.

The issues around the memorial did not end with it being unveiled. The market area of Norwich was redeveloped in 1938 and the memorial was moved to sit in a newly designed Memorial Garden. The memorial and garden were officially opened by King George VI on 29th October 1938. Even this proved not to be the last chapter in story of the memorial, as in 2004 the garden was closed and fenced off after structural problems were found with the undercroft. The fences remained in place for a number of years during which the condition deteriorated further, until work started on the garden in 2008 and the memorial in 2009. During the repairs, the memorial was rotated to face the city hall. The memorial garden and memorial were re-dedicated on 11th November 2011 after a spend of £2.6 million.

The Inscription

The inscription over the Stone of Remembrance reads: OUR GLORIOUS DEAD whilst on the stone itself it says: THEIR NAME LIVETH FOR EVERMORE. There is a further inscription on the base of the stone and in a smaller font: REMEMBERING ALSO ALL OTHERS OF THIS CITY WHO HAVE GIVEN THEIR LIVES IN THE SERVICE OF THEIR COUNTRY. This latter inscription was added after the Second World War, when the dates of the two world wars were added to the screen wall on either side of the Stone of Remembrance.

2. Edith Cavell Memorial

Adjacent to the Erpingham Gate, Norwich, NR3
Grade II*

Unveiled on 12th October 1918, the third anniversary of Edith Cavell's death, by Queen Alexandra, widow of King Edward VII and mother of King George V. Queen Alexandra would also unveil the memorial to Edith Cavell in London, which was unveiled on the fifth anniversary of her execution in 1920.

Sculpted by Henry Pegram (1862-1937), who was born in London and attended the West London School of Art. In 1881 he entered the Royal Academy schools, became a member of the Art Workers Guild in 1890, an Associate of the Royal Academy in 1904, and a Royal Academician in 1922. Pegram's war memorial work includes the Preston War Memorial, also featured in this book, together with 'Victory' on the memorial at the Cunard Building in Liverpool.

Design Features:

. The memorial comprises of a bronze bust of Edith Cavell wearing a nurses' uniform, which stands on a stone pyramidal plinth set on a square base. On the plinth there is a life-sized carving of a soldier in high relief. The soldier is reaching upwards towards Cavell, presenting a wreath to add to the one already portrayed under the bust. In his left arm the soldier is holding his rifle, the butt of which rests on the base of the memorial.

The Story behind The Memorial:

Edith Cavell was born in the village of Swardeston near Norwich, where her father was the Vicar. Following an education at Norwich High School for Girls and boarding schools at Clevedon, Somerset and Peterborough, she became a governess for a number of families, including one in Brussels. After successfully caring for her father and nursing him back to health from a serious illness, Edith decided to become a nurse and started training at the Royal London Hospital in Whitechapel, London, before working in other hospitals and caring for a number of patients in their own homes. In 1907 Edith was recruited to establish a nursing school in Brussels and, by 1910, she was the training nurse for three hospitals, 24 schools and 13 kindergartens in Belgium.

Following the occupation of Brussels during the early months of the First World War, Edith became involved in assisting British and French soldiers, as well as French and Belgian civilians of military age, to escape to neutral Netherlands. She had been working for the Red Cross since the start of the war and it would appear that her motivation was purely humanitarian because she dealt with all her patients equally, whether German or Allied. In August 1915 Edith was arrested by the Germans on charges of harbouring Allied soldiers and was tricked into writing a confession. Tried by a German military court, she was sentenced to death and shot by firing-squad on 12th October 1915.

One account of the story of Edith's execution tells of a German soldier by the name of Rammler, who was part of the firing party, although he found that he could not execute a woman. Rammler was court martialled and executed for refusing to obey orders.

The memorial was commissioned during the year that J G Gordon-Munn was Lord Mayor of Norwich, which suggests that it was on the wave of patriotic uproar following Cavell's execution because her family, as in the case of the London memorial, had not wanted Edith's death to be marked by a memorial. The propaganda value of the Germans executing a British woman who was a nurse was seized upon by the government, and it was calculated at the time, that this single act brought about the enlistment of an additional 40,000 recruits to the armed forces.

Despite her family's reluctance to have Edith's death memorialised, her life and death are remembered in several plaques in Britain and memorials in Belgium, France and Australia.

In 1993 the memorial was moved from its original site at Tombland in Norwich to its present site, which is closer to the cathedral where Cavell is buried following her exhumation from Belgium in 1919. The memorial was restored in 2014.

The Inscription

The front of the base is inscribed 'EDITH CAVELL NURSE PATRIOT AND MARTYR' the inscription on the rear face reads 'ERECTED BY PUBLIC SUBSCRIPTION J.G. GORDON MUNN ESQ MD FRSE LORD MAYOR 1914 - 1915'. The right-hand side of the plinth and the base of the bust are inscribed 'HENRY PEGRAM SC 1918'.

3. Elveden War Memorial

Adjacent to the A11, Eriswell, Suffolk, IP27
Grade II*

Unveiled by Field Marshal Sir Henry Wilson on 21st November, 1921 with the dedication being carried out by the Bishop of Edmundsbury and Ipswich. Field Marshal Wilson was a professional soldier, although he failed the examinations at both the Royal Military Academy and the Royal Military College more than once. He subsequently entered the Army by way of obtaining a commission in the Militia. Wilson was wounded over the left eye while serving in India leading him to be rather unkindly called "Ugly Wilson" and "the ugliest man in the British Army". After further service in India, and during the Second Boer War, he held a number of senior staff appointments during the First World War. Always a strong Irish Unionist, Wilson was assassinated outside his London home by two members of the IRA in June 1922, as he returned home from unveiling the war memorial at Liverpool Street Station.

Designed by Clyde Francis Young (1871-1948), who was born in 1871, the son of architect William Young. Young was educated privately and, between 1890 and 1894, he was articled to his father during which time he attended a course at University College, London. He became a partner in his father's practice in 1898 and in 1900 Young was admitted into the RIBA. Young continued his father's practice and also his editorship of Spons's 'Practical Builders Pocket Book' - the 'Architects and Builders Price Book' - which his father had started. This publication is still produced today and is seen as the 'architect's bible'. Young became a Fellow of the RIBA in 1910.

Design Features:

The memorial stands on the A11 where the parishes of Elveden, Icklingham and Eriswell meet. It is a very tall 128ft (39m) Corinthian column with a base, pedestal, shaft and capital, all in Weldon Stone with a stone funerary urn at the top made from Portland Stone. The urn, with fluting up to its widest point, is a copy of a smaller urn from Mount Edgcumbe, Plymouth which dates from 1791.

The rectangular pedestal has an inset door with simple projecting, low-pediment architrave which is approached by steps on the north side. The door leads to a staircase of 148 steps which rise the full height of the monument. On the other three sides of the pedestal, there are name panels for the dead of the parishes, each facing their respective parishes. There are 48 names from the First World War and six names from the Second World War noted.

The Story behind The Memorial:

The Elveden estate, on whose land the memorial stands, was owned by Edward Cecil Guinness of the famous brewing family, who had bought it from the executors of the late Maharajah Duleep Singh, the last Maharajah of the Sikh Empire. Guinness had employed William Young to extend the hall by adding another wing in the classical style, but he died before the work was completed, and his son and business partner, Clyde, finished supervising the building. It was Clyde Young to whom Guinness turned to design the memorial. There is a monument to Coke of Norfolk on the estate of nearby Holkham Hall, and Guinness asked that the Elveden memorial be taller than that, but not as tall as Nelson's Column.

It took two years to build the monument. The memorial was mainly paid for by Guinness, although there were donations from the parishioners of the three parishes.

The unveiling was attended by Prince Frederick Duleep Singh, the younger son of Duleep Singh.

The Inscription

The main inscription is on the south-east side and reads: HERE WHERE THE PARISHES OF ELVEDEN ERISWELL AND ICKLINGHAM MEET, THE INHABITANTS HAVE ERECTED THIS MONUMENT TO THE GLORIOUS MEMORY OF THE MEN OF THESE VILLAGES WHO GAVE THEIR LIVES FOR FREEDOM AND HONOUR IN THE GREAT WAR 1914-1919.

4. Clare College Memorial Court

Clare College, Queens Road, Cambridge CB3
Grade II*

Opened on 11th November 1924: there was no formal dedication ceremony.

Designed by Sir Giles Gilbert Scott.

Design Features:

This is a court of nine sides, open on the west side, built of grey brick with a pantile roof. The principle building is the east wing, through the centre of which is a round-headed rusticated archway, enclosing fluted columns with an opening in the head of the arch. There is a block of 3 storeys and 9 windows on each side of the arch, ending in L-shaped end portions of the lower elevation,

which are 2 storeys and 3 windows, with the end window bays being flanked by fluted columns. Behind the main building there are right-angled sections, which lead to longer parallel wings running east-west.

The Story behind The Memorial:

Clare, one of the colleges of the University of Cambridge, expanded quickly after the First World War requiring an increase in accommodation. The whole of the accommodation block is designated as a war memorial, as it is dedicated to the men of Clare College who gave their lives in the First World War and, later, those from the Second World War. Given that the majority of Clare College students would have become junior officers in the First World War their losses, which are not recorded on the memorial, would have been considerable, because the losses among junior officers were proportionately the highest during the war. It is interesting to note that whilst the inscription relating to the First World War is in Latin, that for the Second World War is in English.

The Inscription

Dedicatory plaques are fitted to inward-facing sides of the arch. There are two plaques, one bearing the words: SUI MEMORES ALIOS FECERE MERENDO (Make others remember you, by deserving it) and the other: TO THE MEMORY OF THOSE CLARE MEN WHO GAVE THEIR LIVES FOR FREEDOM 1939-1945.

5. Trumpington War Memorial

Junction of Church Lane and High Street, Trumpington, Cambridge, CB2

Grade II*

Unveiled by Charles Adeane C.B. J.P., Lord Lieutenant of Cambridgeshire on 11th December 1921, following a service led by the vicar of Trumpington, Reverend Moule. Moule had been one of the principle forces behind the creation of the memorial, and was formerly Professor of Chinese at Cambridge University.

Designed by Eric Gill.

Design Features:

The memorial consists of a 19ft (6m) tall, four-sided, tapering cross with relief carvings on the lower half of the shaft. The shaft rises from a square plinth that sits on a three-stepped base, and the Latin cross head is inscribed KR – an abbreviation of the Greek, Christos.

The shaft is wider at the bottom and reduces slightly around halfway up. On the wider section are moulded oval cartouches and arched panels to all four sides: these arched panels each have a small cross at the top and bottom, and contain nine names of those from the village who died in the First World War – 36 men in total. Below these oval panels are arched panels, each with a religious image carved in relief.

One shows a seated Mary in front of a cradle and a lily, with the infant Jesus in her arms; a second shows a winged and haloed Saint Michael thrusting a sword into the mouth of a dragon which represents the Devil; the third panel depicts Saint George also slaying a dragon, and behind Saint George is a haloed female figure who is tied to a tree; the final panel shows a war weary soldier, weighed down by his greatcoat, rifle and helmet, walking into the sunset through a battle-torn landscape. The plinth has a moulded colonnade of three arches on each side which contains the inscriptions.

The Story behind The Memorial:

In September 1915, a Roll of Honour was unveiled in the parish church of St Mary and St Michael, which had the names of the 69 men from the village who had already enlisted, and of whom two had already been killed. One of those killed was Captain Francis Percy Campbell-Pemberton, 2nd Life Guards, the only son of Canon and Mrs Pemberton of Trumpington Hall, who was killed in Belgium on 19th October 1914. Eric Gill was commissioned to make a memorial tablet and this was installed in the church in 1915. In May 1919 Trumpington Parish Council formed a War Memorial Sub-Committee to decide on what form a fitting memorial should take, and suggestions included a garden with tennis courts, a clock tower and an obelisk, before the cross was agreed upon.

Half of the total cost of £400 came from the Pemberton family, with the balance being raised by public subscription. The memorial was cleaned and restored in 2014 in anticipation of the First World War centenary commemoration.

The Inscription

Under the relief of Saint Michael the three panels contain – left panel – 1914; central panel MEN OF TRUMPINGTON WHO GAVE THEIR LIVES IN THE GREAT WAR and in the right panel – 1918. On the plinth below the relief of Saint Mary in the central arch is inscribed FOR LIBERTY AND JUSTICE.

Trumpington War Memorial (left)
previous page

Bedfordshire and Hertfordshire
Regimental War Memorial (below)
next 3 pages

6. Bedfordshire and Hertfordshire Regimental War Memorial

Bedford Road, Kempstone, Bedfordshire, MK42

Grade II*

Unveiled on 11th November 1921 by Mrs Whitbread, wife of the Lord Lieutenant of Bedfordshire, Samuel Whitbread, head of the brewing company that bears his name. The dedication was by the Bishop of St Albans.

Designed by George Allen, a local architect.

Design Features:

The memorial stands to the north side of Bedford Road opposite the site once occupied by Kempston Barracks. The memorial is in the neo-classical style, and takes the form of a circular memorial temple flanked to the front by two obelisks, and the rear by a low screen wall, with square piers at each end and a seat, with dividers, projecting from the screen wall.

The two piers have carved rectangular panels and two reliefs in a form to imitate classical military trophies. The left-hand panel comprises: a rose and garland, Lewis gun, entrenching tool, a base plate for a trench mortar, a laurel wreath and four hand grenades.

The panel to the right has: a rose and garland, Vickers machine gun, entrenching pick axe, water bottle, haversack, laurel wreath, helmet and four hand grenades. There is a semi-circular portico to the temple which is supported by two ionic pilasters which hold up a frieze, dentilled cornice and a dome, which is slated and ends in a gilded cross. When the memorial was first built there was only one obelisk which was placed centrally, and the second obelisk was added in 1950 to commemorate the dead of the Second World War. When the second obelisk was added the original one was moved and positioned to maintain the symmetry of the memorial. The obelisks are inscribed 1914 and 1919 and 1939 and 1945 respectively.

Beneath the portico is a wall with two ionic pilasters and two niches either side of a central doorway, with a moulded architrave and eight panelled bronze door. Internally, the temple is lit by three stained glass windows of Jesus Christ, St Alban and St George. The floor is paved in three types of marble: Dove colour, pale Sienna and white Sicilian: there is a moulded and ribbed plaster ceiling.

On the left of the temple is the First World War obelisk which has a two-tiered stepped base, pedestal and a shaft decorated with a Sword of Sacrifice, and the regimental badge carved in relief and surrounded by a laurel wreath. On the right of the temple is the Second World War obelisk, which matches the design of the adjacent obelisk with a stepped base, pedestal and a shaft decorated with a Sword of Sacrifice and regimental badge.

Behind the memorial is a garden of remembrance.

The Story behind The Memorial:

A successful appeal for donations towards the cost of a regimental memorial was made in 1921, and the land on which it is built was given by Mr and Mrs Harold Howard of Kempston Grange, in memory of their son Lieutenant Addison J. Howard, who died whilst serving with the regiment on the Somme in 1916.

The roll of honour book, which is bound in red Morocco leather, lists all those who lost their lives in the First World War. It originally rested on an oak altar inside the temple, although it was later removed to Warley Barracks for safe-keeping.

The memorial was built by local builder, Samuel Foster.

The Inscription

The frieze around the portico carries the inscription: THEIR NAME LIVETH FOR EVERMORE. This inscription is, of course, very well-known and was chosen by Rudyard Kipling when he was a member of the Imperial (now the Commonwealth) War Graves Commission. The source is Biblical – Ecclesiasticus 44:1-15.

There are extensive and detailed inscriptions on the memorial. On the front of the First World War pedestal is the inscription: TO THE SACRED AND GLORIOUS MEMORY OF THE OFFICERS WARRANT OFFICERS NON-COMMISSIONED OFFICERS AND MEN OF THE BEDFORDSHIRE REGIMENT WHO FELL IN THE GREAT WAR THIS MONUMENT HAS BEEN ERECTED BY THEIR COMRADES AND FRIENDS OF THE REGIMENT.

On the east side of the pedestal is the inscription: THE NUMBER OF THOSE WHO FELL IN THE WAR OVERSEAS WHILE THEIR NAMES WERE ON THE ROLLS OF THE BEDFORDSHIRE REGIMENT WAS 366 OFFICERS AND 5745 OTHER RANKS, BUT THE ROLL OF HONOUR INCLUDES HUNDREDS MORE NAMES OF THOSE WHO HAVING SERVED IN THE REGIMENT DURING THE WAR WERE TRANSFERRED TO OTHER REGIMENTS IN WHICH THEY GAVE UP THEIR LIVES FOR KING AND COUNTRY.

The west side is inscribed: THE BEDFORDSHIRE REGIMENT DURING THE GREAT WAR CONSISTED OF TWENTY-TWO UNITS, NAMELY 1ST BATTALION 2ND BATTALION 3RD RESERVE BATTALION 4TH EXTRA SPECIAL RESERVE BATTALION 5TH TERRITORIAL FORCE BATTALION 6TH SERVICE BATTALION 7TH SERVICE BATTALION 8TH SERVICE BATTALION 9TH SERVICE BATTALION 10TH SERVICE BATTALION THE BEDFORDSHIRE TRAINING DEPOT 2/5TH TERRITORIAL FORCE BATTALION 3/5TH TERRITORIAL FORCE BATTALION 1ST GARRISON (F.S.) BATTALION 2ND GARRISON (F.S.) BATTALION 3RD GARRISON (F.S.) BATTALION 11TH TERRITORIAL FORCE BATTALION 12TH TRANSPORT WORKS BATTALION 13TH TRANSPORT WORKS BATTALION 51ST GRADUATED BATTALION 52ND GRADUATED BATTALION 53RD YOUNG SOLDIERS' BATTALION.

The names and dates of the battles and operations in which the regiment were engaged are carved into three sides of the obelisk.

On the east side: 1914 MONS LE CATEAU THE MARNE THE AISNE LA BASSEE MESSINES ARMENTIERES YPRES 1915 NEUVE CHAPELLE HILL 60 AUBERS RIDGE FESTUBERT GIVENCHY YPRES LOOS SULVA BAY ANZAC. On the west side: 1916 THE SOMME MONTAUBAN LONGUEVAL TRONES WOOD THIEPVAL RIDGE THE ANCRE SCHWABEN REDOUBT SINAI PENINSULA 1917 ARRAS MESSINES YPRES CAMBRAI UMBRELLA HILL GAZA JAFFA. On the north side: 1918 THE SOMME THE LYS AMIENS ARRAS HINDENBURG LINE THE SELLE MEGIDDO.

On the Second World War obelisk are the following inscriptions: TO THE SACRED AND GLORIOUS MEMORY OF THE OFFICERS WARRANT OFFICERS NON-COMMISSIONED OFFICERS AND MEN OF THE BEDFORDSHIRE AND HERTFORDSHIRE REGIMENT AND THE HERTFORDSHIRE REGIMENT WHO DIED IN THE SECOND WORLD WAR THIS MONUMENT HAS BEEN ERECTED BY THEIR COMRADES AND BY THE MEN AND WOMEN LIVING IN THE COUNTIES OF BEDFORDSHIRE AND HERTFORDSHIRE.

The west side is inscribed: THE NUMBER OF THOSE WHO WERE KILLED IN ACTION OR WHO DIED OF TERRIBLE PRIVATIONS IN ENEMY HANDS WAS 1074 ALL RANKS.

The names and dates of the battles and operations in which the regiment were engaged are carved into two sides of the obelisk.

On the west side: DUNKIRK 1940 N. W. EUROPE 1940 TOBRUK 1941 TOBRUK SORTIE BELHAMED TUNIS NORTH AFRICA 1941-43 CASSINO II TRASIMENE LINE ITALY 1944-45 ATHENS GREECE 1944-45 SINGAPORE ISLAND MALAYA 1942 CHINDITS 1944 BURMA 1944. On the east side: NORMANDY LANDING N.W. EUROPE 1944 MONTOR SOLI GOTHIC LINE MONTE GAMBERALDI MONTE CECO MONTE GRANDE ITALY 1944-45.

On the plinth below is a list of battalions of the regiment during the Second World War: THE BEDFORD AND HERTFORDSHIRE REGIMENT 1ST BATTALION 2ND BATTALION 5TH BATTALION (TERRITORIAL ARMY) 6TH BATTALION (TERRITORIAL ARMY) 7TH BATTALION 8TH BATTALION (BECAME 14TH BEDS. AND HERTS. MEDIUM REGT. R. A.) 9TH BATTALION 30TH BATTALION 70TH BATTALION 71ST BATTALION HERTFORDSHIRE REGIMENT. 1ST BATTALION (TERRITORIAL ARMY) 2ND BATTALION (TERRITORIAL ARMY).

On the north side of the obelisk is the inscription: UNVEILED BY HER MAJESTY QUEEN ELIZABETH COLONEL IN CHIEF OF THE REGIMENT ON 11TH NOVEMBER 1950.

7. Hatfield War Memorial

Great North Road, Hatfield, Hertfordshire, AL9
Grade II*

Unveiled on 12th June 1921 by the Lord Lieutenant of Herefordshire, Thomas Brand, 3rd Viscount Hampden. Hampden had been the Commanding Officer of the 1st Battalion Hertfordshire Regiment from 1913 to 1915, when he was promoted to Brigadier General and commanded the 126th (East Lancashire) Brigade at Gallipoli and, later, the 185th (2/1st West Riding) Brigade on the Western Front. The dedication was performed by

the Bishop of Exeter, Lord William Cecil, brother of the 4th Marquis of Salisbury, who had donated the land on which the memorial was built. Lord Salisbury read out the names of those killed in the First World War.

Designed by Sir Herbert Baker

Design Features:

The memorial is in a memorial garden which lies adjacent to the north-east gates of Hatfield Park. As well as the memorial cross in the garden, there is a pavilion which houses the commemorative tablets. The memorial itself is a 'Baker Cross', a wheel-headed cross which rises from a moulded collar on an octagonal shaft. The circlet of the head of the cross is formed of roses and lilies (representing England and France) and these trail down the shaft. The cross shaft ends in a moulded foot which rests on an octagonal plinth which, in turn, stands on a low octagonal pavement. The cross is constructed of Portland stone.

The pavilion, which is at the north end of the garden, is rectangular comprising three bays, and projects northwards outside the garden area. The general form of the pavilion is that of a shelter, and it is built of red brick with red tile details. The two side walls and the rear wall are solid, whereas the front wall has three round-headed arches. The central arch extends to the ground and the two side ones are closed by dwarf walls. The pavilion has a hipped roof of plain clay tiles and is open inside to reveal the timber frame. The floor of the pavilion is brick in a herringbone pattern. The memorial garden is enclosed by brick walls with gates and brick gate piers which are included in the listing.

The Story behind The Memorial:

The memorial commemorates 139 local servicemen killed in the First World War with a further two names being added in 2014 following research carried out by the Hatfield Local History Society. Repairs were carried out to the memorial in 1998 and 2015. The original cost of the memorial was £1,500.

The Inscription

Portland stone tablets in the pavilion, supported by shallowly projecting brick piers, are fixed to the west, north, and east interior walls. These bear the inscriptions:

(West) WE WILL REMEMBER THEM 1939 – 1945
(North) THANKS BE TO GOD WHICH GIVETH US THE VICTORY MCMXIV – MCMXIX
(East) WE WILL REMEMBER THEM 1939 – 1945 VICTIMS OF ENEMY ACTION ON 3RD OCTOBER 1940 VICTIMS OF ENEMY ACTION ON 22ND SEPTEMBER 1944 VICTIMS OF ENEMY ACTION ON 10TH OCTOBER 1944
The names of service personnel are recorded with rank, unit, date and place of death. The dedication on the rear walls spans three separate tablets of names.

In Flanders Fields

Lt.Col John McCrae
(Died 28th January 1918. Age 45)
First published in Punch magazine, and within months came to symbolize the sacrifice of all who were fighting in the First World War.

In Flanders fields the poppies blow
Between the crosses, row on row,
That mark our place, and in the sky
The larks, still bravely singing, fly
Scarce heard amid the guns below.

We are the Dead. Short days ago
We lived, felt dawn, saw sunset glow.
Loved and were loved, and now we lie
In Flanders fields.

Take up our quarrel with the foe:
To you from failing hands we throw
The torch; be yours to hold it high.
If ye break faith with us who die
We shall not sleep, though poppies grow
In Flanders fields.

8. Great Dunmow War Memorial

Junction of High Street and New Street, Great Dunmow, Essex CM16

Grade II*

Unveiled by General Lord Byng, 1st Viscount Byng of Vimy, a former resident of Dunmow, on 17th July 1921, only two weeks before taking up his appointment as the 12th Governor-General of Canada. Known to his friends as "Bungo", Lord Byng was a career soldier who served in Egypt and the Sudan as well as with the British Expeditionary Force in France at the start of the First World War.

Byng fought in Gallipoli and was Commander of the Canadian Corps at Vimy Ridge, and when he returned from Canada in 1926, he became Commissioner of the Metropolitan Police. The memorial was dedicated by the Bishop of Chelmsford.

Designed by Basil Oliver (1882-1948), who attended Liverpool University School of Architecture from 1900 to 1902, before moving to London where he continued his studies at the Architectural Association and Royal Academy Schools. In 1905 Oliver assisted in the drawing office of Holloway Brothers, builders in London who were, after the First World War, major creators of war memorials. He also worked in the offices of Arthur Blomfield & Sons in 1906: Blomfield would achieve fame following the First World War for his design of what became known as the Blomfield Cross or the Cross of Sacrifice which is present in any cemetery containing 40 or more war graves. Oliver later became a Fellow of the Society of Antiquaries, Master of the Art Workers' Guild, and a member of various building preservation bodies.

Sir George Clausen – a painter and official war artist who volunteered for the Civic Arts Association's war memorials committee and assisted in the design of the memorial, as well as making a model of it before its construction.

Sculpted by Eric Gill and his apprentice Joseph Cribb.

Design Features:

Made from Portland stone standing on a Cornish granite base, the memorial consists of a three sided pillar almost 20ft (6m) tall. There are Latin crosses carved in relief around the head of the pillar, underneath three projecting arches and above a narrow collar. The plinth has two steps and is on a three-stepped base; the lowest step is round and the top two are hexagonal.

The Story behind The Memorial:

Great Dunmow Parish Council decided in April 1918 that the village should have a war memorial, and a sub-committee of 25 members was formed which first met in October of that year. As in other places, it was not a foregone conclusion that the dead would be remembered by way of a monument: among other suggestions were a memorial institute, a library, a reading room, a cottage hospital, a social club and a public hall. Also, as in other places, a monument was finally agreed and fund-raising began with a view to raise £1,000.

The Civic Arts Association offered free advice to war memorial committees which requested help, and Great Dunmow took advantage of this offer, which resulted in the involvement of George Clausen and the recommendation that Basil Oliver be instructed as architect.

Holloway Brothers (London) Ltd for whom Oliver once worked, and who were well experienced in memorial construction, carried out the building work. The final cost of the memorial was £760 and the additional monies raised - £315 – was diverted to the memorial social club.

On the same day that the memorial was unveiled, a memorial plaque was also unveiled inside the church, with the same names as were recorded on the pillar.

The Inscription

The inscription on one face of the plinth reads: REMEMBER THE MEN OF THIS PLACE WHO DIED FOR FREEDOM AND HONOUR A 1914 – 1918 D and A 1939 – 1945 D.
The names of those from the area killed in the two world wars are inscribed on the faces of the pillar and the plinth – 84 from the First World War on the pillar and 25 from the Second World War on the plinth.

9. Colchester War Memorial

Colchester Castle, Cowdray Crescent, High Street, Colchester, CO1

Grade II*

Unveiled on 24th May 1923 by Field Marshal Sir William Robertson Bt. He achieved the unique distinction of rising from private soldier to Field Marshal – the highest rank in the British Army. Further biographical details can be found on page 110.

Designed by Duncan W. Clarke, a local Colchester based architect

Sculpted by Henry Fehr.

Stone carved by Carlo Magnoni, the Italian anarchist, noted for his sculpting of the Waggoners' Memorial at Sledmere, which is shown on page 78.

Design Features:

The memorial stands at the centre of Cowdray Crescent at the entrance to Castle Park, and consists of a tall Portland stone pedestal set on a three-stepped granite base, topped by a statue of winged Victory cast in bronze. Victory is holding an inverted sword in her right hand and a laurel wreath in her left hand. There are curved projections on the sides of the pedestal support: on the east side there is a bronze statue of St George with a sword and shield, whilst on the west side Peace is depicted holding a dove. The upper angles of the pedestal are carved with festoons and cherub heads with elongated wings.

The wrought-iron gates, flanked by walls in multi-coloured brick, together with railings and piers around the memorial, are all included in the listing.

164

The Story behind The Memorial:

The site chosen for the memorial was part of a town planning scheme that saw the demolition of some buildings in the High Street in order to extend Castle Park and open up the approach to Colchester Castle. The castle itself was purchased with money donated by Lord Cowdray, who also paid for the ornate gates. The cost of the war memorial was met by public subscription. The associated works around the memorial include a pier, which is surmounted by a stone urn, made by Doulton & Co This was paid for by Mr W H Shephard of Colchester, a local undertaker with offices in High Street, and the name is still in existence although now part of a larger company.

The Inscription

The main inscription is on the front, south face of the memorial, which has a raised bronze plaque with a wreathed head bearing the city arms. The inscription reads: TO THE GLORIOUS MEMORY OF THE MEN OF COLCHESTER WHO FELL IN THE GREAT WAR 1914-18 THEY STROVE FOR PEACE THEY SERVED FOR FREEDOM THEY DIED TO LIVE. Beneath this plaque a further plaque is inscribed: THE NAMES OF 1263 MEN OF COLCHESTER HERE COMMEMORATED ARE INSCRIBED ON VELLUM AND DISPLAYED INSIDE THE PRINCIPAL ENTRANCE AT THE TOWN HALL.

On the north face, a further bronze plaque is inscribed: TO THE HONOUR OF THE MEN & WOMEN OF COLCHESTER WHO STOOD FOR KING & COUNTRY & BEARING ARMS OR BY THEIR WORK HELPED TO WIN THE WAR 1914-18. THANKS BE TO GOD WHO GAVE US THE VICTORY. A plaque beneath which was added later reads: AND TO HONOUR ALSO THOSE WHO WORKED, SERVED AND DIED IN THE FURTHER WAR OF 1939-1945. A third plaque, also added later, reads: TO MEMBERS OF THE ARMED FORCES FROM COLCHESTER KILLED ON DUTY OR AS A RESULT OF TERRORIST ACTION SINCE THE END OF THE SECOND WORLD WAR.

DID YOU KNOW THAT?

For the first two years of the First World War the British Government did not encourage an official war artist programme. This painting by Eric Kennington exhibited in 1916 prompted the government to encourage images of the war to be painted by returning soldiers.

THE KENSINGTONS AT LAVENTIE. 1915 'A platoon of British soldiers standing in a French village street'.

10. Southend-on-Sea War Memorial

Clifftown Parade, Southend-on-Sea, Essex, SS1
Grade II*

Unveiled on 27th November 1921 by Lord Lambourne, Lord Lieutenant of Essex, with the dedication performed by the Bishop of Chelmsford. D Company, 6th Essex Regiment formed the Guard of Honour.

Designed by Sir Edwin Lutyens.

Design Features:

The memorial is made from Portland stone with bronze plaques and fittings, and stands in an elevated position overlooking the Thames estuary. Lutyens planned the gardens in front of the memorial, which takes the form of a tapered obelisk 36ft (11m) tall, with a square base that incorporates a moulded cornice set on a square pedestal rising in six unequal sections. The lowest of the six sections is incorporated into low surrounding walls, which form an enclosure incorporating a flight of six broad steps. A platform and two further steps approach the memorial from the north. Bronze mounts for flags are fixed at either end of the surrounding wall.

On the north face of the base of the obelisk there is a carved stone laurel wreath, and on either side painted stone flags rise from the lower stage of the pedestal, with the Union Flag on the west side and the White Ensign on the east side. The painted stone flags are a feature of a number of Lutyens' memorials.

There is a garden between the memorial and Clifftown Parade comprising of a lawned area, flower beds and paths, all enclosed by low chains suspended from bollards, whilst a hedge separates the memorial from the footpath to the south. The words LEST WE FORGET are picked out in Portland stone in the lawn in front of the memorial.

The Story behind The Memorial:

Lutyens' original plan was for a cenotaph topped by an urn and surrounded by lamps, although it was decided that the prominent position chosen for the memorial would better suit an obelisk. Southend's memorial was the first of six broadly similar obelisks designed by Lutyens with the last being in Northampton in 1926. The total cost of the memorial was £5,521 15s.

The Inscription

The inscriptions are carved into the north face of the memorial. At the base of the obelisk are the dates MCMXIV MCMXIX (1914 1919) whilst on the upper tier of the pedestal – added later – MCMXXXIX MCMXLV (1939 1945). On the centre tier of the pedestal: OUR GLORIOUS DEAD. On the lower tier of the pedestal the principal inscription is carved: THE NAMES OF THE 1338 MEN of SOUTHEND-ON-SEA IN HONOURED MEMORY OF WHOM THIS MEMORIAL WAS ERECTED BY GRATEFUL RESIDENTS ARE RECORDED UPON A TABLET PLACED IN THE REFECTORY AT PRITTLEWELL PRIORY. On the lowest tier of the pedestal is inscribed: AT THE GOING DOWN OF THE SUN AND IN THE MORNING WE WILL REMEMBER THEM.

In 1998 a further plaque was added to the pedestal which reads: THIS PLAQUE IS DEDICATED TO THE MEN AND WOMEN OF SOUTHEND WHO HAVE SERVED THEIR COUNTRY IN ALL WARS AND CONFLICTS TO PRESERVE PEACE AND FREEDOM FOR ALL. WE WILL REMEMBER THEM. FUNDED BY SOUTHEND-ON-SEA BOROUGH COUNCIL ON BEHALF OF THE ROYAL BRITISH LEGION (SOUTHEND BRANCH) 1998.

A small metal plaque has been added to the north facing pier at the east end of the wall by the Association of Jewish Ex-Servicemen and Women and reads: AJEX SOUTHEND AND DISTRICT BRANCH IN MEMORY OF OUR FALLEN COMRADES WHO GAVE THEIR LIVES IN THE SERVICE OF THEIR COUNTRY.

To Germany

Capt. Charles Sorley (Died 13th October 1915. Age 20)
The first soldier poet to reject romantism for reality

You are blind like us. Your hurt no man designed.
And no man claimed the conquest of your land.
But gropers both through fields of thought continued
We stumble and we do not understand.
You only saw your future bigly planned,
And we, the tapering paths of our own mind.
And in each others dearest wars we stand,
And hiss and hate. And the blind fight the blind.

When it is peace, then we may view again
With new won eyes each other's truer form
And wonder. Grown more loving kind and warm
We'll grasp firm hands and laugh at the old pain.
When it is peace. But until piece it is the storm.
The darkness and the thunder and the rain.

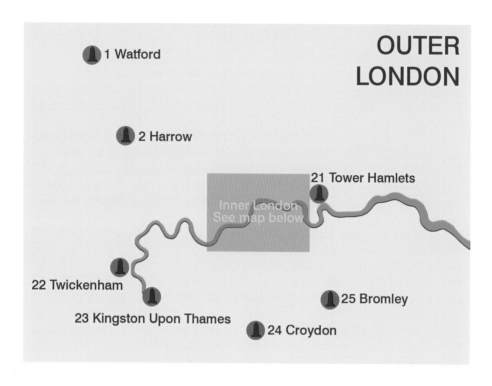

OUTER LONDON

1 Watford

2 Harrow

21 Tower Hamlets

Inner London
See map below

22 Twickenham

25 Bromley

23 Kingston Upon Thames

24 Croydon

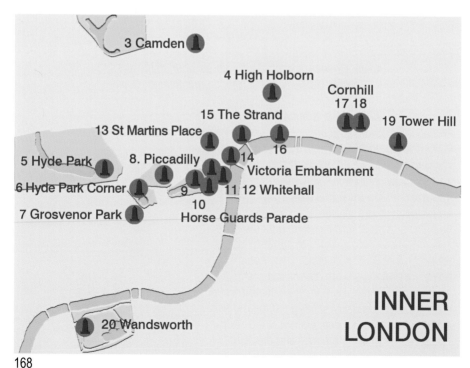

3 Camden

4 High Holborn

Cornhill
17 18

15 The Strand

19 Tower Hill

13 St Martins Place

16

5 Hyde Park

8. Piccadilly

14

Victoria Embankment

6 Hyde Park Corner

9

11 12 Whitehall

7 Grosvenor Park

10

Horse Guards Parade

20 Wandsworth

INNER LONDON

CONTENTS

1. Watford Peace Memorial

The Parade, Watford, Hertfordshire WD17

Grade II*

Unveiled on 18th July 1928 by the Earl of Clarendon. Robert Herbert Hyde Villiers, 6th Earl Clarendon, who was a Conservative politician, and at the time of the unveiling was Chairman of the BBC Board of Governors, and would later serve as Governor-General of South Africa.

Sculpted by Mary Pownall (1862-1937), who was born in Leigh, Lancashire although by the 1890s she was living in Birkenhead, Cheshire. After studying in Frankfurt in 1896, she moved to Paris from 1897 to 1898 where she was tutored by the celebrated French sculptor, Auguste Rodin. In 1902 she married a barrister, Alfred Bromet, although she continued to use the name Mary Pownall professionally. From 1903 to 1931 Pownall lived in Watford and died in Oxhey, Hertfordshire.

Design Features:

The monument comprises of a semi-circular stepped plinth with three pedestals that support three bronze male nude sculptures. Viewed from the front, the left-hand figure is of a seated male who is leaning on this left knee, head bent and representing a mourner. The central figure is a standing male, his right arm raised and head tilted slightly back representing victory, whilst the figure on the right is another seated male figure with open hands coming forwards over his right knee, representing a blinded or wounded man. All the figures are signed by the sculptor, and there are relief carved wreaths to the flanking low walls.

The Story behind The Memorial:

This monument is unique, within those covered by this book, in as much as it is called a 'peace' memorial rather than a 'war' memorial. The memorial is also one of only two in this book that was designed by a woman. The local newspaper, The Watford Observer, had started to ask the question as early as 1915 as to how the fallen of the town were to be commemorated. By 1917 the proposal to replace Watford District Cottage Hospital had been accepted, and the Peace Memorial Hospital was opened in 1925. The cost of £90,000 for the new hospital was met by public subscription. In 1922 a Roll of Honour in the form of a book was compiled by the local authority and was inscribed by students from the College of Art.

The local sculptor, Mary Pownall Bromet, offered the hospital three plaster figures that she had made during the war which she called, collectively, the Spirit of War and a public appeal was launched to have them cast in bronze. The casting was carried out by Morris Singer & Co Ltd at a cost of £800.

In 1971 the memorial was moved a short distance to allow for road widening and it now stands on the Parade outside Watford Town Hall.

In 2012 War Memorials Trust made a grant of around £5,000 to cover the cost of lightly cleaning the statues, removing bronze staining from the plinth and protecting the statues with microcrystalline wax.

The Inscription

Under the three figures are simple inscriptions: under the statue to the left is inscribed: TO THE FALLEN; under the statue to the right: TO THE WOUNDED and under the central statue: VICTORY 1914-1918   1939-1945. There is a stone tablet at the base of the memorial in front of the central figure with the following inscription: AND IN REMEMBRANCE OF ALL OTHER CITIZENS OF THIS BOROUGH BOTH MILITARY AND CIVILIAN WHO HAVE GIVEN THEIR LIVES IN THE SERVICE OF HUMANITY.

For the Fallen

Laurence Binyon (1869-1943) wrote this poem, which is widely used in Remembrance Day services, in 1914

They shall not grow old, as we that are left grow old:
Age shall not weary them, nor the years condemn.
At the going down of the sun and in the morning
We will remember them.

2. Harrow School War Memorial Building

Harrow School, Grove Hill, Harrow-on-the-Hill, HA1
Grade II*

Unveiled on 3rd June 1926 by the Rt. Hon. Stanley Baldwin MP, Conservative Prime Minister and Old Harrovian. He served as Prime Minister three times and has the unique distinction of being the only Prime Minister to serve three monarchs - George V, Edward VIII and George VI.

Designed by Sir Herbert Baker.

Design Features:

The memorial as listed comprises a shrine, building, ceremonial staircase, forecourt and retaining wall. Some of the interior fittings come from Brooke House, Hackney and the floorboards are oak timbers from HMS St Vincent, which had been built in 1815.

The building is in the neo-Jacobean style built on a sloping site, and consists of two storeys with a basement to the centre and north. The entrance to the building is through the south elevation which takes the form of a loggia-style shrine. Decorative wrought-iron gates lead to a buttressed round-arched entrance arcade with decoratively carved heraldic panels.

The upper floor is taller and has a central multi-light oriel window, flanked by 6-light windows. The wall height is accentuated by a parapet. There is 5-bay elevation to the High Street / Grove Hill façade with gabled outer bays, each with multi-light window to upper floor. Basement windows 3-light strips by pavement. There are round-arched windows above the ground and multi-light oriel to the upper floor flanked by 9-light windows. The terrace to the north elevation is accessed through an arched doorway: central round-arched doorway with 6-light windows flanking, multi-light window at centre to upper floor above, flanked by 6-light windows. The rear west elevation with multi-light canted window to centre and blind bays flanking: brick terrace with balustrade retaining wall to northern end, which has steps leading down to Church Hill.

The tripartite, dome-vaulted stone shrine contains, in the apsidal west end, an ashlar cenotaph (sarcophagus), with an ornate sword carved on top, and dedicatory inscription in memory of the sons of Harrow who died in the Great War 1914-1919, with carved wreaths on flanking ends.

The interior of the building has a polished ashlar dome-vaulted gallery at ground floor level. There is a bow-ended display loggia to east, which has a bronze dedicatory wreath at centre on stone flags, bronze inscribed panels to bowed walls, and inscribed memorial dedications in ashlar walls and timber-panelled double staircase, bow-ended, to west. There is a ladies rest room, which is accessed from the gallery, in a vaulted room with a scalloped octagonal ceiling light at centre.

The gallery features busts of: Viscount Palmerston by R Jackson, 1870; Sidney Herbert by Foley, 1865; Bishop Perry by G Summers, 1876; Winston Churchill by Clare Sheridan, 1942; and 4th Earl of Aberdeen by W Theed. The staircase has a bust of Sir Robert Peel by M Noble, 1850. The rooms to north have keystoned doorways, panelled doors and herringbone parquet floors, together with fireplaces with decorative tiles.

The upper floor has a reception room above the gallery with a multi-light window to the roadside, boarded floor, panelled dado and niched sections to end walls, corniced ceiling with plasterwork wreath to central oval domed recess. There are bronze busts of Stanley Baldwin and Archbishop Davidson by Newberry A Trent, given in 1927.

Decorative timber saloon-style doors with newelled upper panels lead to steep, narrow alternative stairs to the floor below. The masters' room, which is at the north end, has a boarded floor, tailored postal gantries, with a panelled front to service lift and trabeated timber ceiling. The Fitch Room is lined with decorative oak panel work from Brooke House, Hackney, circa 1580, a scalloped motif, fluted pilasters and decorative carving. The stone mantelpiece is of the period of Henry V and VII.

There is a four-centre-arched ceiling with architraved mantel, strapwork carvings and small masque carvings. There is decorative stained glass to all windows: one dedicated to Alex Fitch, with heraldic and figurative designs: modern stained glass to the canted window to the southern forecourt end. The basement contains a kitchen with modern fittings, boiler room and storage rooms, which were refurbished in 2014.

A double perron of steps leads from the High Street, with a landing which gives access to the higher level of Church Hill. There is Portland stone balustrading to both streets over retaining walls faced in flint with stone insets. At the apex of the site where the streets converge is a lamp on octagonal base dated 'MCMXIX' [1919]. A rectangular slab milestone is incorporated in the High Street face stating '10 miles to London'. There is a balustraded retaining wall to the higher ground of Church Hill at the west of the forecourt, to the right of the steps with buttress-flanked ashlar niche. A flagged court has a circular granite metal-cross-embossed marker at centre (site intended for memorial cross). There are decorative metal lamps to High Street entrance.

The Story behind The Memorial:

In May 1917 Harrow school formed a committee to decide on a form of memorial and to undertake the necessary fund-raising. The considerable funds required to buy the land and build the memorial came from a combination of subscriptions and donations, together with a bequest from Mr J A Apcar, a member of an Anglo-Indian merchant family, who showed great generosity to the school over more than one generation. The site of the building was purchased for £6,975 and construction costs totalled £38,680. Although the whole building is included in the listing, the committee was very precise in specifying that only the shrine should be considered the war memorial and the wider building an accessory.

A foundation stone was laid on 6th October 1921 by Randall Thomas Davidson, Archbishop of Canterbury and an Old Harrovian. The shrine itself was completed by July 1923 and was open for visits, whilst the rest of the building work proceeded. The original plans specified a cross in front of the shrine and, although this was amended, the intended site is marked with a cross-embossed roundel in the stone-flagged forecourt.

Lady Fitch funded the decoration in the room above the shrine in memory of her 20-year-old son, Alex, who was killed while serving with the Royal Artillery. A lamp was placed over the fireplace which dates from the reign of Henry V, which was to be kept lit constantly in honour of her son and all fallen soldiers.

During the Second World War, Harrow was declared a neutral zone with no requirement to evacuate children. The basement of the War Memorial Building was used as the Air Raids Precautions Wardens Post for the school, heavily reinforced with steel joists and columns which were mostly removed in a refurbishment in 2014.

The Inscription

The walls of the loggia contain panels inscribed with the names of the fallen, each surmounted by a gilded inscription, reading: 'BE THOU STRONG AND OF GOOD COURAGE BE NOT AFRAID NEITHER BE THOU DISMAYED' 'BE THOU FAITHFUL UNTO DEATH AND I WILL GIVE THEE A CROWN OF LIFE' 'REMEMBER THOSE WHO DIED FOR FREEDOM AND HONOUR AND SEE YOU TO IT THAT THEY SHALL NOT BE FORGOTTEN'.

3. London and North Western Railway War Memorial

Euston Station, London, NW1 (On a roundabout in front of the station)

Grade II*

Unveiled on 21st October 1924 by Field Marshal Douglas Haig, 1st Earl Haig, the commander of British forces on the western front during the war. The dedication was performed by Randall Davidson, the Archbishop of Canterbury

Designed by Reginald Wynn Owen (1876-1950), architect to the London & North Western Railway (LNWR). He trained as a diocesan architect, worked at the Liverpool University School of Architecture, and was elected as a Fellow at the Royal Institute of British Architects in 1930.

Sculpted by Ambrose Neale (1868-1930), chief artist at L.Boulton & Sons, who also sculpted a statue of King Edward VII and a Boar War Memorial in Cheltenham

Design Features:

The most striking element of the memorial is the over-life-sized bronze statues representing the Royal Navy, the Artillery, the Infantry and the Royal Air Force. Each statue stands with its head bowed, resting on an upturned rifle. It is unusual to see the air force featured so prominently on a First World War memorial. The memorial consists of a tall 43ft (13m) obelisk of Portland stone, which stands on a grey granite circular stepped base, just below which the obelisk is moulded to the pedestal. Buttresses extended from the pedestal act as steps, and four crosses in relief with bronze wreaths encircling their feet are carved at the top of the obelisk.

The Story behind The Memorial:

The memorial's site was originally in the centre of Euston Square on the approach to the station, and on an axis with the Euston Arch. The arch had been built in 1838 and was one of the few remnants of the original grand station complex, which was demolished to much consternation in 1961. There are moves afoot to rebuild it as part of a major upgrade of the area.

The memorial was paid for mainly by donations from LNWR staff to commemorate the 3,719 employees who died in the war. It is one of a number of memorials for LNWR employees erected across the country.

The Inscription

The south-facing front of the obelisk is inscribed IN/ MEMORY/ OF OUR/ GLORIOUS / DEAD. A granite tablet in front of the memorial contains the inscription IN GRATEFUL MEMORY OF THE 3719 MEN OF THE/ LONDON AND NORTH WESTERN RAILWAY COMPANY/ WHO FOR THEIR COUNTRY, JUSTICE AND FREEDOM/ SERVED AND DIED IN THE GREAT WAR/ 1914-1919/ THIS MONUMENT WAS RAISED BY THEIR/ COMRADES AND THE COMPANY AS A / LASTING MEMORIAL TO THEIR DEVOTION.

Stone inscription panels on the east and west sides commemorate employees of the London Midland and Scottish Railway Company (into which the LNWR was absorbed in 1921) who died in the Second World

London and North Western Railway War Memorial (left) from previous page

Royal Fusiliers War Memorial (below) details on next page

4. Royal Fusiliers War Memorial

High Holborn, London, EC1N   Grade II*

Unveiled on 4th November 1922 by Sir Edward Moore 1st Baronet, Lord Mayor of London. The dedication was performed by Arthur Winnington-Ingram, Bishop of London

Designed by Cheadle & Harding & Co   **Sculpted by** Albert Toft

Design Features:

The memorial stands on a traffic island on High Holborn at one of the 'entrances' to the City of London. The principal feature of the memorial is an 8'6" (2.6m) tall statue of an infantryman of the Royal Fusiliers in full First World War battle dress. He carries a rifle and bayonet in his right hand whilst his left fist is clenched. The infantryman's head is turned and his right leg raised on a rock in a pose suggesting that he is guarding the City of London.

The figure stands on a Portland stone 16ft (5m) tall pedestal. On the front (west) face of the pedestal is the regimental badge, a Tudor rose enclosed by a garter and bearing the inscription: HONI SOIT QUI MAL Y PENSE – [shamed be he who thinks evil of it] - surmounted by the Royal Crown. On the rear (east) side of the pedestal there is a bronze plaque bearing a list of the 53 regular, service, and territorial battalions of the regiment that served in the First World War. The base of the statue is inscribed Albert Toft Sc.

The Story behind The Memorial:

21,941 men of the Royal Fusiliers died during the First World War – to put that into perspective some 17,000 men from the City of Liverpool died in the conflict. A permanent memorial to the dead was first proposed in 1919 with a site in one of the royal parks as the preferred site, although this was later changed to Hounslow Barracks, the depot of the regiment. As well as the memorial, a Roll of Honour in London's Guildhall was proposed, together with a brass memorial in the garrison church of St Paul, Hounslow. The £3,000 cost of the memorial was raised by public subscription in 1920, although it was felt that a more prominent site would be better for the memorial, and Major-General Sir Geoffrey Barton, Colonel of the Regiment, wrote to the Lord Mayor of London requesting a 'conspicuous site….to commemorate the sacrifice of those who gave their lives for King and Country, to bring home to the public the great services rendered by the City during the War, and as an incentive for citizens of all times to patriotism and national duty'. The request was accepted and Holborn Bars, one of the entry points to the city, was chosen.

The memorial includes men of the 45th and 46th Battalions who lost their lives in the 1919 intervention in the Russian Civil War. The bronze figure was cast by A B Burton at the Thames Ditton Foundry, London. The memorial underwent cleaning and restoration work in 2003.

The Inscription

Beneath the badge on the west face of the pedestal, is the inscription: THE ROYAL FUSILIERS (CITY OF LONDON REGIMENT) TO THE GLORIOUS MEMORY OF THE 22,000 ROYAL FUSILIERS WHO FELL IN THE GREAT WAR 1914-1919 AND TO THE ROYAL FUSILIERS WHO FELL IN THE WORLD WAR 1939-1945. On the chamfered top of the base is a stone block, inserted later, inscribed in small lettering: AND THOSE FUSILIERS KILLED IN SUBSEQUENT CAMPAIGNS.

5. Royal Artillery Memorial
Hyde Park Corner, London, SW1   Grade I

Unveiled on 18th October 1925 by Prince Arthur, Duke of Connaught, and Anglican priest Rev.Alfred Jarvis. Arthur was the seventh child of Queen Victoria and entered the Royal Military Academy at Woolwich at the age of 16. After forty years service in the Army, during which time he served in the Corps of Royal Engineers, the Royal Regiment of Artillery and the Rifle Brigade, he was appointed Governor-General of Canada in 1911, which post he held until November 1916. Following the death of his wife in 1917, Arthur largely withdrew from public life, although his service with the Royal Regiment of Artillery made him the perfect choice to unveil this memorial.

Designed by Lionel Pearson (1879-1953) who trained in Liverpool and then practiced in London.

Sculpted by Charles Sergeant Jagger

Design Features:
The Memorial is a large and striking one, set on a cruciform base with a number of stepped-back upper sections, on top of which is a stone depiction of a full-sized 9.2 inch howitzer. On each face of the memorial, supported by projecting blocks, are bronze larger-than-life-sized figures. On the north side is a recumbent corpse, draped in an overcoat with a helmet on his chest – although fundamentally all memorials are about death, it is very rare for a corpse to feature. The south face has an Artillery lieutenant, holding an overcoat. The east side has a carrier with panniers filled with shells, whilst on the west side there is a driver wearing a cape and leather puttees, whilst holding a harness in his outstretched arms.

Around the principal level of the base there is a frieze comprising four depictions of the artillery in action. On the north-east face a battery of 60 pounder heavy guns in action is depicted, whilst the south-east face there are anti-aircraft gunners. The south-west face has artillerymen shell-spotting and signallers, whilst on the north-west face there is a depiction of bringing up a horse-drawn 13 pounder battery into action.

The Story behind The Memorial:
At the time of the First World War, The Royal Artillery was the largest regiment of the British Army. Its regimental motto - "UBIQUE" ("everywhere" in Latin) - was given to them by King William IV in 1832, indicating that it fought in all the various theatres of the war. The Royal Artillery War Commemoration Fund sub-committee for the erection of a memorial was established in May 1919 and quickly secured a site from the Office of Works on a traffic island. They wanted a design with a 'realistic gun', and the original sculptors struggled. Jagger was approached for a design early in 1921 and a definitive design was presented in September 1921. A howitzer was selected as he believed it was the only gun suitable to treat as a sculpture. Jagger had been an infantryman and he wanted to distance the sculpture from the symbolic and idealised approach of most contemporary war memorials. In view of the fact that the central sculpture was a large howitzer, the orientation was changed on the advice of architects Sir Edwin Lutyens and Sir Reginald Blomfield to point the gun to the south, so that it was not aiming directly at the Wellington Arch.

When it was unveiled the memorial was not universally appreciated. Lord Curzon, Leader of the House of Lords and a former Viceroy of India, dismissed it as "a toad squatting, about to spit fire out of its mouth ... nothing more hideous could ever have

been conceived". The arts establishment, however, was impressed and Jagger was awarded the Gold Medal of the Royal Society of British Sculptors and, a short time later, was elected an Associate of the Royal Academy. Perhaps most importantly, the memorial was well-received by the regiment and veterans of the war, who had wanted a monument that should be clearly defined as an artillery monument.

The Inscription

Given the size of the memorial, and the fact that the Royal Artillery was involved in all the major actions of the First World War, the inscriptions are extensive. On the east and west sides of the projecting arm of the base is inscribed – IN PROUD REMEMBRANCE OF THE FORTY NINE THOUSAND & SEVENTY SIX OF ALL RANKS OF THE ROYAL REGIMENT OF ARTILLERY WHO GAVE THEIR LIVES FOR KING AND COUNTRY IN THE GREAT WAR 1914-1919. Around the upper level of the base are listed some of the countries/theatres in which the Royal Artillery served, the names run clockwise from the north-east face and some are repeated – FRANCE, AFRICA, PERSIA, EGYPT, CENTRAL ASIA, PALESTINE, RUSSIA, ITALY, INDIA, ARABIA, MESOPOTAMIA, FLANDERS. From the south end are listed - FRANCE, AFRICA, PERSIA, EGYPT, CENTRAL ASIA, PALESTINE, RUSSIA, ITALY, ARABIA, EGYPT, MACEDONIA, DARDENELLES, FLANDERS. At the suggestion of the sculptor the inscription under the corpse reads – HERE WAS A ROYAL FELLOWSHIP OF DEATH, which was taken from Shakespeare's Henry V. At the north end of the memorial an inscription refers to the roll of honour which is buried below, and on the south side there are panels commemorating the 29,924 members of the regiment who were killed in the Second World War, which were added in 1949.

9. The Guards Memorial

Horse Guards Parade, Horse Guards Road, London SW1

Grade 1

Unveiled on 16th October 1926 by the Duke of Connaught, who was the senior Colonel in the Guards and General George Higginson, who was 100 years old and a veteran of the Crimean War. The dedication was by the Rev. H.J. Fleming, who was senior chaplain to the Guards Division upon its foundation in 1915, and the benediction was given by Rev. Alfred Jarvis, the then Chaplain-General to the Forces. There was a march-past by 15,000 serving or former guardsmen.

Designed and Sculpted by Gilbert Ledward and Harold Chalton Bradshaw, who had met at the British School in Rome before the war, and also collaborated on other memorials.

Bradshaw (1893-1943) was born in Liverpool and served in the Army in the First World War, where he was gassed and wounded. His principal works for the Imperial War Graves Commission were the Cambrai Monument in France, on which he worked with Charles Sargeant Jagger, and the Ploegsteert Memorial to the Missing in Belgium, in collaboration with Gilbert Ledward.

Bradshaw was the first Secretary of the Royal Fine Arts Commission, which was established in 1924, and was a Fellow of the Royal Institution of British Architects. He was awarded an honorary Masters in Architecture by the University of Liverpool in 1930.

Design Features:

The memorial is constructed of Portland stone with bronze figure: it is classical in design and 3ft (12m) tall. The central pylon, which stands on three white stone steps, is a broad squat obelisk, and an incised string course of five lines, one for each of the Foot Guards regiments, caps the memorial. On a raised step on the east side of the memorial are five larger than life-sized – 7'3" (2.2m) – figures of guardsmen standing easy.

The figures of the representatives of five regiments of the Foot Guards – the Grenadiers, the Coldstream, the Scots, the Irish and the Welsh – are modelled on actual soldiers from their respective regiments.

184

The Story behind The Memorial:

The main inscription was written by Rudyard Kipling whose son, John, had been killed whilst serving with the Irish Guards at the Battle of Loos in 1915.

The cost of the memorial was £22,000, and fundraising for a memorial to the approximately 14,000 guardsmen killed, began in 1920. The memorial is the result of a 1921 competition that was won by Bradshaw and Ledward. The original idea for the plaque to the west face of the memorial to represent dead and dying soldiers was later dropped, not because the subject was thought unsuitable, but because of the sculptor's fundamental conservatism.

The guardsmen used as models for the sculptors were: Sergeant R. Bradshaw MM of the Grenadier Guards; Lance-Corporal J. S. Richardson of the Coldstream Guards; Guardsman J McDonald of the Scots Guards; Guardsman Simon McCarthy of the Irish Guards although for some unexplained reason the legs are those of Lance-Sergeant W. J. Kidd and Guardsman A. Comley of the Welsh Guards. Ledward, the sculptor, insisted on the soldiers being naked when he made the sculptures. and the lettering was cut by Ernest Gillick. During the Second World War the memorial was damaged by shrapnel from bombing, whilst some of it was repaired, some of the damage was left as "honourable scars".

The Inscription

The Guards lost approximately 14,000 killed in the war, and although there are no names inscribed on the memorial, there is an inscription under a cross that fills the east face of the obelisk: TO THE GLORY OF GOD/ AND IN MEMORY OF THE/ OFFICERS WARRANT OFFICERS/ NON COMMISSIONED OFFICERS &/ GUARDSMEN OF HIS MAJESTY'S/ REGIMENTS OF FOOT GUARDS/ WHO GAVE THEIR LIVES FOR THEIR/ KING AND COUNTRY DURING THE/ GREAT WAR OF 1914 - 1918 AND OF THE/ OFFICERS WARRANT OFFICERS/ NON COMMISSIONED OFFICERS AND/ MEN OF THE HOUSEHOLD CAVALRY/ ROYAL REGIMENT OF ARTILLERY/ CORPS OF ROYAL ENGINEERS/ ROYAL ARMY SERVICE CORPS ROYAL/ ARMY MEDICAL CORPS AND OTHER/ UNITS WHO WHILE SERVING WITH/ THE GUARDS DIVISION IN FRANCE &/ BELGIUM 1915 - 1918 FELL WITH THEM IN/ THE FIGHT FOR THE WORLD'S FREEDOM. The west face of the memorial also bears a cross and a list of the battle honours of the five regiments.

Beneath each of the figures is a carving of the regimental badge of the respective regiments and beneath that is the following inscription which was added after the Second World War: THIS MEMORIAL ALSO COMMEMORATES ALL THOSE MEMBERS/ OF THE HOUSEHOLD DIVISION WHO DIED IN THE SECOND WORLD WAR/ AND IN THE SERVICE OF THEIR COUNTRY SINCE 1918. On the bottom step is the inscription: THIS MONUMENT WAS ERECTED BY THEIR FRIENDS AND COMRADES. Each of the other faces has a bronze plaque: those on the north and south depict equipment carried by guardsmen, whilst the plaque on the west side has an 18 pounder field gun being loaded.

11. Statue of Field Marshall Earl Haig
Whitehall, London, SW1
Grade II*

Unveiled on 10th November 1937 by Prince Henry, the Duke of Gloucester. He was the third son of King George V and Queen Mary, and the first son of a British Monarch to be sent to school rather than being educated at home. After Eton College and the Royal Military Academy, Sandhurst, Prince Henry was commissioned into the Kings Royal Rifle Corps and, subsequently, the 10th Royal Hussars. He had to attend to so many royal duties that he gained the nickname "the unknown soldier".

Designed by Stephen Rowland Pierce (1896-1966), who won the British Prix de Rome in architecture in 1921, which enabled him to study architecture at the British School at Rome. He was elected an Associate of the Royal Institute of British Architects in 1929 and a Fellow in 1938. From 1936 to 1942 Pierce was director of architectural studies at the Hastings School of Art and he lectured at the School of Architecture at Manchester University from 1941 to 1942. He was a member of the Council and Vice-President of the R.I.B.A. from 1951–55.

Sculpted by Alfred Hardiman (1891-1949) who was born in London. In 1912 he won a London County Council scholarship to the Royal College of Art, and in 1915 moved to the Royal Academy School. Service in the Royal Flying Corps interrupted Hardiman's training, which resumed in 1920 when he was awarded the British Prix de Rome, and he spent two years studying at the British School at Rome.

Hardiman was elected an Associate of the Royal Academy in 1936 and a full member in 1944. In 1938 he became a fellow of the Royal Society of British Sculptors and received their silver medal for his statue of Earl Haig.

Design Features:

The memorial comprises an equestrian statue standing on a Portland stone pedestal. Earl Haig wears an open greatcoat over his uniform and is bare-headed. In his right hand he carries a scroll, and the reins of the horse are in his left hand. The horse is a powerful animal and has its left foreleg raised, whilst its neck is arched, with its head drawn on a short rein. The statue is on a bronze rising base signed Alfred Hardiman 1936 to the front.

The pedestal is oblong in plan and the inscription is on the front, or south end beneath a cartouche bearing the Haig arms, surrounded by the Order of the Thistle and topped by a coronet.

The Story behind The Memorial:

This is one of only four memorials to individuals in this book: the other three being Edith Cavell, Edgar Mobbs and Albert Ball and, technically, it is not a war memorial because it does not commemorate a person killed in the war. The memorial has, however, been included because of Haig's crucial importance in the story of the First World War. A career soldier with considerable military experience, Haig entered the First World War as commander of the First Army before replacing Sir John French and rising to Commander-in-Chief British Expeditionary Force in France from mid-1915 until the end of the war.

Haig's reputation has been the subject of debate over many years, although he never lost the confidence of the army and became very involved in the welfare of ex-servicemen following the war. Haig replied by hand to any letter that he received from an ex-serviceman.

Soon after Haig's death in early 1928 the Prime Minister, Stanley Baldwin, suggested that a monument be raised to him and a competition was won by Alfred Hardiman.

Haig's widow did not like the horse which she felt was too stylised: however no changes were made to the design.

The Inscription

The inscription of the front of the pedestal reads, simply: FIELD MARSHALL EARL HAIG, COMMANDER-IN-CHIEF OF THE BRITISH ARMIES IN FRANCE 1915-1918. On the rear of the pedestal the inscription reads: ERECTED BY PARLIAMENT.

12. The Cenotaph

Whitehall, London SW1A 2ET
Grade I

Unveiled on 11th November 1920 by King George V, and was part of a larger ceremony that was also to see the internment of the Unknown Soldier in Westminster Abbey. The coffin of the Unknown Soldier was carried on a gun carriage as part of a solemn procession which halted at The Cenotaph. The King placed a wreath on the gun carriage and then unveiled the memorial, which was draped in large Union Flags. He subsequently joined the procession to take the Unknown Soldier for burial in Westminster Abbey.

Designed by Sir Edwin Lutyens.

Design Features:

The Cenotaph stands on hollow steps in the centre of Whitehall and is, by comparison with many others, simple. It embraces a plain tomb chest with a large laurel wreath on a rectangular top and with a three staged base which, in turn, stands on a tall shaft on which are inscribed the dates of the two World Wars – those for the First World War on either end and those for the Second World War on the sides. On either end, at the upper corners of the shaft are carved stone bosses with laurels suspended by stone fillets, which were carved by Francis Derwent Wood RA. The flags of each of the three branches of the armed forces are installed on each side of the base.

The Story behind The Memorial:

The Cenotaph is probably the most famous memorial from the First World War, but is not the first memorial on that site that was designed by Lutyens. Following the formal end of the First World War by the signing of the Treaty of Versailles on 28th June 1919, a London Victory Parade was to be held in on 19th July 1919. There were to be series of temporary wooden monuments along the route of this parade, one of which was to be in Whitehall. Only two weeks before the parade, Lutyens was invited to Downing Street to meet Prime Minister, Lloyd George. Lloyd George wanted a catafalque similar to the one that was being constructed adjacent to the Arc de Triomphe in Paris. Lutyens, instead, proposed a structure identical to the present memorial, only with the wreaths made from laurel rather than stone.

The 'temporary Cenotaph' – at this stage that there was no plan for a permanent memorial on the site - was unveiled quietly on the day before the victory parade. For some time after the parade, the base of the memorial was covered with wreaths and flowers and had caught the imagination of the public. By 30th July 1919 the War Cabinet had decided that the temporary structure should be replaced with a permanent one, and designated as the United Kingdom's "official" national war memorial.

It had been Lutyens' plan that the flags on the sides of the memorial should be carved in stone and then painted as they are on his memorial in Rochdale [see page 14]. However, Lutyens was overruled and cloth flags were used instead. Initially the flags on the Cenotaph were, on one side, the Union Flag, a White Ensign and a Red Ensign with

a Union Flag, a White Ensign and a Blue Ensign. Currently the flags on the Cenotaph in addition to the two Union Flags are those of the Royal Navy, The Army, the Royal Air Force and the Merchant Navy.

The memorial was not dedicated at the unveiling ceremony, as it commemorated all British, Empire and Dominion soldiers who died in the First World War, but not all were Christian. The people honoured by the memorial have gradually been increased, to include those of the Second World War and all subsequent conflicts.

The build cost for the Cenotaph was £7325.

The Inscription

The only words on the memorial are - THE GLORIOUS DEAD.

13. Edith Cavell Memorial

St Martin's Place London WC2

Grade I

Unveiled on 12th October 1920 (the fifth anniversary of her execution) by Queen Alexandra, widow of Edward VII and mother of George V. Queen Alexandra also unveiled the memorial to Edith Cavell in Norwich.

Designed and Sculpted by Sir George Frampton RA (1860-1968) who was born in London By the age of 18 he was working as a stone carver on the Hotel de Ville in Paris, before studying first at the South London Technical School of Art, then later at the Royal Academy Schools. Frampton's work fused sculpture with the decorative arts and often his pieces combined a number of different materials. Sir George Frampton was commissioned in 1915 to design the memorial, even though it was not completed for almost five years.

Design Features:

This memorial comprises a marble statue of Cavell dressed in a nurses' uniform as she was dressed when she met her end in front of a German firing squad. The statue stands on a two-stage plinth in front of a tall grey granite pylon. On the rear of the pylon, a British lion stands triumphant over a serpent to represent British triumph over the envy, malice, spite and treachery of the German Empire. The top of the pylon is cruciform in shape, with a Geneva Cross in relief, and crowned with a depiction of a woman and child depicting 'humanity'.

The Story behind The Memorial:

Immediately following her execution, Edith Cavell's family asked for there not to be a memorial. However, the outpouring of public indignation meant that the case was taken up by Viscount Burnham, owner of the Daily Telegraph, together with the then Lord Mayor of London, the Bishop of London and the Chairman of the London County Council, and a fund was established because so many members of the public wished to subscribe. Although not universally liked at the time of its unveiling, Frampton's design was striking in its austerity and monumentality, and he refused to take a fee for his work on the memorial. For Cavell's face, Frampton used family photographs initially but later asked her sister to sit for him.

The Cavell's Nurses' Trust was established in Edith's memory and still supports nurses, midwives and healthcare assistants who are suffering hardship. She is buried in the grounds of Norwich Cathedral, close to the Grade II* Memorial that was erected in her honour, and on page 136 there are more details of her life.

The Inscription

At frieze height around the memorial are inscribed the words HUNANITY, SACRIFICE, DEVOTION, FORTITUDE. Between the top of the statue and the cruciform shape the inscription FOR KING AND COUNTRY is between two wreaths. The inscription under Cavell's statue states simply EDITH CAVELL BRUSSELS DAWN OCTOBER 12th 1915. The inclusion of the word "dawn" a perpetual reminder that Nurse Cavell was executed rather than killed in action.

The memorial is unusual in as much as there was an addition to the inscription after its completion and unveiling. Reverend Stirling Gahan, who was an Anglican priest, was permitted by the Germans to give her Holy Communion the night before her execution, and she memorably forgave her executioners saying – "Patriotism is not enough I must have no hatred or bitterness for anyone" – and these words were added to the front of the memorial in 1924 at the request of the International Council of Women, a group founded in 1888 by women from many countries which advocates human rights for women.

14. Belgian Monument to the British Nation
Victoria Embankment, London WC2
Grade II*

Unveiled by Princess Clementine of Belgium on 12th October 1920, the fifth anniversary of the execution in Brussels of Nurse Edith Cavell. In his speech, Belgian Prime Minister, Leon Delacroix, referred to the self-sacrifice of British troops serving in Belgium. A parallel memorial, sculpted by Charles Sargeant Jagger was unveiled in 1923, and another to the gratitude of Belgian refugees was erected at Milford Haven, in Wales.

Sculpted by Belgian sculptor, Victor Rousseau (1865-1954), who was descended from a line of stonemasons, and began carving at the age of eleven.

Architectural setting by Sir Reginald Blomfield RA

Design Features:

The memorial consists of a bronze

figural group set on a rectangular stone base. The group represents a mother, drapery-clad and with an elongated neck, encouraging two garland-bearing children forward. The group stands on a broad paved area reached via steps. Behind it is a stone screen, classical in design, with a taller central section flanked with curved wings. On the left is a relief carving depicting Justice, which is shown holding the 1837 Treaty of London, which guaranteed Belgium neutrality. On the right is a matching relief depicting Honour, which is represented as St. George. At the top of the inset panels to the wings are relief carvings of the provinces of Belgium. The rear of the memorial incorporates a seat.

The Story behind The Memorial:

This memorial was a tribute to Great Britain from the people of Belgium, in recognition of the welcome given to Belgians seeking refuge from the German invasion of Belgium in August 1914. This invasion led to Britain's entry into the First World War, and the acknowledgement reflects the impact on civilian populations, movingly expressed through the fatherless group. The memorial is a rare example in England of continental public statuary, and is located opposite Cleopatra's Needle. Subscriptions were raised from Belgium troops, along with donations from the Belgian royal family.

Rousseau observed:-"I designed the group representing Belgium as a woman draped in mourning, in the act of telling her children that Belgians will never forget their debt of gratitude to Great Britain. The garlands and other floral offerings borne by the children are symbolical of the wealth of the nine Belgian provinces. As for the children themselves, the lad and the little girl are designed to typify the spirit of youth and the confidence of the future, which is the most marked characteristic of the Belgian nation"

194

15. The Civil Service Rifles War Memorial
Somerset House, (The Riverside Terrace), Victoria Embankment,
London WC2E   Grade II*

Unveiled by the Prince of Wales, the regiment's Honorary Colonel, on 27th January 1924. A guard of honour was formed by the two Civil Service Companies of the regiment to commemorate the 1,240 men who fell during the war. A roll of honour was placed inside the memorial when it was dedicated by Rev. E H Beattie, the chaplain to the 1st Civil Service Rifles in France and Flanders.

Design Features:
The memorial consists of a Portland stone square column 16ft (5m) high, with a shallow cornice upon which stands a plinth and an urn. The plinth is decorated with laurel leaf swags and panels carrying the inscription MCM/XIV and MCM/ XIX (1914 and 1919). The column stands on a square, undercut, plinth which rests on a platform of two steps. The flags on either side of the central column were originally completed in copper, but were replaced with carved stone in 2002. To the west is the Union Flag, and to the east, the regimental colours.

The Story behind The Memorial:
The Civil Service Rifles was more accurately known as the 15th (County of London) Battalion, the London Regiment (Prince of Wales Own Civil Service Rifles). It was created from the members of the Civil Service for which Somerset House had originally been built. The memorial was suggested by Colonel Parish, DS, MC, who had served as the Commanding Officer of the 1st Battalion.
The Committee on Sites for Monuments suggested that the memorial should be located in the entry to Somerset House's central quadrangle, behind Neptune's statue. At that time, Somerset House was still used as civil service offices, and when Lutyens viewed the site, he suggested that it would be more appropriate to place it in the centre of the quadrangle, as this had acted as the parade and drill ground for the regiment. The memorial was moved to its present location in 2002.

The Inscription

On the south face there is an inscription - IN MEMORY/ OF THE/ 1240 MEMBERS/ WHO FELL/ WHILE SERVING/ WITH/ THE REGIMANT/ IN/ THE GREAT WAR/ THEIR NAMES/ ARE RECORDED/ ON A SCROLL/ PLACED WITHIN/ THIS COLUMN/ ALSO IN MEMORY / OF MEMBERS OF/ THE CIVIL SERVICE/ CADET BATTALION
On the north face the inscription reads THIS COLUMN/ WAS ERECTED/ BY THE 15TH/ COUNTY/ OF LONDON/ BATTALION/ THE LONDON/ REGIMENT/ PRINCE OF WALES/ OWN/ CIVIL SERVICE/ RIFLES
Battle honours are inscribed into the face of the upper edge of the undercut plinth: - on the south face – FESTUBERT 1915 LOOS SOMME 1916-1918 FLERS COURCELETTE; on the west face – DORIAN 1917 LYS KEMMEL GAZA NEBI SAMWIL JERUSALEM; on the north face – ST QUENTIN ALBERT 1918 ANCRE 1918 BAUPAUME 1918 SELLE; on the east face TRANSLOY MESSINES 1917 1918 YPRES 1917 1918 CAMBRAI 1917

The Civil Service Rifles War Memorial (left) previous page

The National Submariners' War Memorial and its inscription (below) next page

The Inscription

In relief letter on the frieze is the following inscription: ERECTED TO THE MEMORY OF THE OFFICERS AND MEN OF THE BRITISH NAVY WHO LOST THEIR LIVES SERVING IN SUBMARINES 1914-1918 AND 1939-1945.
Below the main plaque is a smaller one topped by a rendition of the badge of the Submarine Service. The plaque reads: NATIONAL SUBMARINE WAR MEMORIAL (1922) THIS PLAQUE COMMEMORATES THE MEMORIAL'S SEVENTIETH ANNIVERSARY AND THE CONTRIBUTION BY THE MEMBERS OF THE SUBMARINERS OLD COMRADES, LONDON, IN THEIR DEVOTION TO THE UPKEEP OF THIS MEMORIAL, UNVEILED BY PETER P RIGBY CBE JP.

16. The National Submariners' War Memorial
Victoria Embankment, (Temple Pier), London, EC4Y
Grade II*

Unveiled by Admiral Sir Hugh Sinclair, known as Quex Sinclair, who enlisted with the Royal Navy at the age of 13 in 1886. At the outbreak of the First World War he joined the Naval Intelligence Division, becoming its Director in 1919. From 1921 to 1923 Sinclair was Chief of the Submarine Service, and in 1923 he became head of the Secret Intelligence Service. In 1938, using £6,000 of his own money, he bought Bletchley Park to be an intelligence station. The dedication of the memorial was performed by Archdeacon Charles Inglis, Chaplain of the Fleet.

Designed by A.H. Ryan Tenison (1861-1930) for whom few records survive, although it is known that he was born in Towcester and, in 1881, he was an architecture student living in Wolverton, Buckinghamshire. By the age of 30 he was already a widower and living in London. Tenison designed the cricket pavilion at Radley College, Oxfordshire and was a Fellow of the Royal Institute of British Architects.

Sculpted by Frederick Brook Hitch (1897-1957). His father was the architectural sculptor Nathaniel Hitch, who, although he had no formal training, worked on many churches in Britain and around the world. Frederick Hitch worked with his father and attended the Royal Academy School, becoming a Fellow of the Royal Society of British Sculptors, and sculpted both statues and bas-relief work.

Design Features:

This substantial stepped, granite pier is an integral part of the Victoria Embankment. At the centre of the pier there is a large bronze plaque with a frame which has, at its centre, a bas-relief image showing a Captain and three crew members in the control room of a submarine. Around the central image sea spirits are tugging at nets which ensnare the submarine. The cornice is crowned by an escutcheon which resembles the Dolphin badge of the Submarine Service, and the base has a bas-relief of a submarine cruising on the surface, together with the dates 1914 and 1918.

To the left, the pilasters have the names of 50 submarines lost in the First World War and, to the right, the 82 submarines lost in the Second World War. The capitals are decorated with the insignia of the Royal Navy and the bases with laurel wreaths. Supporting the sides of the plaque are the allegorical figures, Truth and Justice, who are supported on miniature pedestals with dolphin consoles.

Attached to both the face of the memorial and walls to each side of it are 40 bronze wreath hooks in the form of anchors.

The Story behind The Memorial:

The First World War was the first conflict in which submarines played a significant role. At the beginning of the war Britain had 57 operational submarines with a further 15 being built but, by the end of the war there was a fleet of 137 with another 78 under construction. During the First World War 54 boats were lost with a loss of 138 officers and 1,225 other ranks, and these losses represented around one-third of the total personnel of the submarine service. The nature of the submarine service, in common with all maritime losses, is that there was seldom the opportunity for a burial, so a memorial would be the only physical commemoration.

17. The City and County of London Troops War Memorial

Cornhill, London EC3V
Grade II*

Unveiled by the Duke of York, on behalf of the Duke of Connaught, on November 12th 1920, the day after the ceremony for the burial of the Unknown Warrior at Westminster Abbey. Soldiers from the Royal Fusiliers (City of London Regiment), the 56th (1st London) and 47th (2nd London) Divisions on parade, with a guard of honour from 3rd Battalion (Grenadier Guards) at the Mansion House. The service was led by the Bishop of London and attended by the Lord Mayor of London, civic dignitaries and ex-servicemen.

The scheme to erect the memorial in front of the Royal Exchange involved improvements to the space, including the railings at the underground railway station entrances to the west, with Portland stone parapets with bronze railings and lamps.

Designed by Sir Aston Webb (1849-1930), the London-born, prolific architect, who designed the principal façade of Buckingham Palace, the Admiralty Arch in the Mall, and the main building of the Victoria & Albert Museum.

Sculpted by by Alfred Drury (1856-1944) a Londoner, who was one of the central figures in the New Sculpture movement at the end of the 19th century. He worked with Webb at the Victoria & Albert Museum, and constructed the figure of Prince Albert above the entrance.

Design Features:

Standing 21ft (7.5m) high, it comprises a finely detailed Portland stone pier with two rounded buttress plinths to the base, each of which supports a life-sized bronze statue of a soldier. The front face of the central pier presents a carving in relief of the coat of arms of the City of London.

Around the base, two rows of bronze pegs ornamented with crossed rifles carry chains for the suspension of wreaths. On the rear of the central pier, the heavily mantled coat of arms of the County of London is displayed. The inscriptions to front and rear are in attached metal lettering, some of which is flush with the stonework, and some of which stands proud from the surface.

Each side of the pier has carvings in low relief of three standards, each surmounted by a wreathed crown and topped with a lion. On the left (north) buttress stands the bronze statue of a Royal Artilleryman, standing at ease with his rifle in his right hand. On the right (south) buttress is the corresponding bronze statue of a Royal Fusilier, standing easy with both hands resting on the muzzle of his rifle.

The corniced top of the pier is surmounted by a moulded stone pedestal on which stands a bronze of a lion holding a shield. The shield is ornamented with a relief of St George, mounted, killing a dragon with the legend ST GEORGE FOR ENGLAND.

Two images of The City and County
of London Troops War Memorial

The Story behind The Memorial:

The memorial stands in the heart of the City of London, within a group of buildings including the Grade-I listed Mansion House, Bank of England, and Royal Exchange and the Grade II-listed equestrian statue of the first Duke of Wellington.

The Rifle Volunteer Corps was created in 1859 by residents of the City of London and the surrounding counties of Middlesex, Surrey and Kent, in order to secure their home defence. As a result of the Territorial and Reserve Forces Bill in 1907, the Volunteers was abolished, but a year later the London Regiment was formed as a Territorial regiment for the new County of London, comprising 26 battalions. The first eight were the City of London battalions and the remaining 18 in County battalions.

By the end of 1914, following the outbreak of the First World War, 58 battalions had been raised. and by May 1915 the regiment had expanded to 82 battalions, of which 56 were involved across every theatre of the war. At the end of the First World War, the battalions were re-formed in the Territorial Army.

The City and County of London Troops memorial reflects the London units as they were organised at the end of the First World War. This includes the eight City of London battalions, an additional City battalion (33rd Rifle Brigade), the 18 County battalions and one additional County battalion (34th Kings Royal Rifle Corps), the Royal Fusiliers and the Honourable Artillery Company; four Yeoman battalions; eight artillery brigades and two heavy artillery batteries; and the London units of the Royal Engineers, the Electrical Engineers, the Royal Army Service Corps, the Royal Army Medical Corps, the Royal Army Veterinary Corps, the Territorial Force Nursing Services, and the Voluntary Aid Detachments. A number of the battalions were originally raised by specific localities or communities: for example, the 11th County of London Battalion was known as the Finsbury Rifles, the 14th was the London Scottish, the 28th was the Artists. Although many of the units represented also had their own memorials, this memorial commemorates all those men and women who served in the City and County of London Troops.

The Inscription

Three inscriptions on the central pier read TO THE/ IMMORTAL HONOUR/ OF THE OFFICERS/ NON-COMMISIONED/ OFFICERS AND MEN/ OF LONDON/ WHO SERVED THEIR/ KING AND EMPIRE/ IN THE GREAT WAR/ 1914-1919/ THIS MEMORIAL IS/ DEDICATED IN PROUD &/NAME LIVETH/ FOR EVERMORE/ UNVEILED ON NOV 12TH 1920/ BY HRH THE DUKE OF YORK/ ON BEHALF OF/ FIELD-MARSHAL HRH/ THE DUKE OF CONNAUGHT/ K.G., K.T., K.P/ AND/ ALBEIT MANY UNITS / NAMEWD HEREON/ HAVE CHANGED IN/ DESIGNATION AND ROLE/ WE HONOUR AND/ REMEMBER THE MEN/ AND WOMEN WHO SERVED/ IN ALL THE UNITS OF/ THE CITY AND COUNTY/ OF LONDON IN THE WAR OF/ 1939-1945.

Below this is an inscription on a small bronze plaque, added after 1945 when the Second World War dedication above replaced the original record reads RAISED BY PUBLIC SUBSCRIPTION/ AT THE MANSION HOUSE IN THE/ PEACE YEAR 1919 DURING THE / MAYORALTY OF COL THE RT HON/ SIR HORACE BROOKS MARSHALL/ K.C.V.O. LL.D

18. St Michael, Cornhill War Memorial

Abutting the western pier of the porch of the Grade I listed
Church of St Michael, Cornhill EC3V
Grade II*

Unveiled by the Lord Mayor of London, James Roll, on 1st November 1920, with a service conducted by the Rector, Rev. J H Ellison and Ernest Holmes, the Archdeacon of London.

Designed by Richard Reginald Goulden, and the bronze work was cast by A B Burton of Thames Ditton.

Design Features:

The memorial consists of a narrow, tapering Portland stone pedestal on a deep plinth, the latter set at the height of the plinth of the adjacent Gothic porch, and with a matching hollow-chamfer moulding. Above is a bronze sculptural group with the youthful figure of St Michael, the Archangel, and symbol of the triumph of good over evil.

The Archangel, with wings outstretched stands poised as in victory, holding a blazing sword aloft. Below to his right is a pair of ferocious lions, one with its teeth sunk into the neck of the second, symbolizing war. To the left, representing peace, is a cluster of four cherubic children gazing upwards to seek St Michael's protection.

The Story behind The Memorial:

The memorial commemorates the City employees who worked within the parish of St Michael, Cornhill which, since 1906 had incorporated the adjacent parishes of the demolished churches of St Peter le Poer and St Benet Fink. 2130 men are commemorated, with the 170 who were killed in the war listed on a Roll of Honour in the church.

The Grade I listed St Michael Church was designed by Christopher Wren, and between 1857 and 1869 was remodelled by Sir George Gilbert Scott.

The Inscription

A bronze tablet reads DURING THE/ GREAT WAR/ 1914-1918/ THE NAMES WERE/ RECORDED ON THIS/ SITE OF 2130 MEN/ WHO FELL FROM OFFICES/ IN THE PARISHES OF/ THIS UNITED BENEFICE/ VOLUNTEERED TO/ SERVE THEIR COUNTRY/ IN THE NAVY AND/ ARMY + OF THESE /IT IS KNOWN THAT/ AT LEAST/ 170 GAVE/ THEIR LIVES FOR THE/ FREEDOM OF/ THE WORLD.

19. The Mercantile Marine First World War Memorial

Trinity Square Gardens, Trinity Square, Tower Hill, London EC3N

Grade I

Unveiled on 12th December 1928 by Queen Mary deputising for King George V who was unwell. The ceremony was submitted live on radio and was the Queen's first broadcast.

Designed by Sir Edwin Lutyens.

Sculpted by Sir William Reid Dick (1879-1961) who was born in Glasgow, and at the age of twelve was an apprentice stonemason. He took drawing and modelling classes at the Glasgow School of Art, and in 1911 his first commission was a marble portrait of the Scottish music hall entertainer, Harry Lauder. In 1914 Dick joined the Territorial Army and served in the Royal Engineers in France and Palestine.

His work as a prolific sculptor included the lion for the Menin Gate at Ypres and the Franklin D Roosevelt statue in Grosvenor Square, London . Dick was elected as a Fellow of the Society of British Sculptors in 1923, became its President from 1933 to 1938, and was a member of the Royal Academy. The memorial was built by Holloway Brothers (London).

Design Features:

This large memorial is raised on a platform above street level and takes the form of a temple with three bays. Each bay is formed by piers and columns in the long side walls which flank the central open space. The piers have external round arch curved niches made from Portland Stone. These niches are clad with rectangular bronze panels, which are laid in a pattern like stretcher bond, and bear the names of the missing arranged by vessel. A low-pitched roof with side parapets is capped with a low, flat, circular dome, and there are pedimented gable ends over the entrance arches to the east and west ends of the memorial.

Attached to the wall is a User's Guide to the memorial, with a ground plan and the names of the dead under the names of the ships in which they were serving.

The floor of the temple is laid with black and white paving in a chequerboard pattern. A flight of five stone steps which have iron gates leads from the street at either end of the temple. From the platform there are steps that lead into a garden and the Second World War Memorial which is on the north side.

The Story behind The Memorial:

The role of the Merchant Navy during the First World War was of crucial importance as the demands of transporting troops and war material were added to those of the world's largest trading nation. There were losses to civilian vessels throughout the war but these escalated in 1917 following the introduction of unrestricted submarine warfare by the German government.

In total 3,305 merchant ships and around 17,000 crew were lost in the First World War,

and of this number 12,000 casualties are commemorated, with other names being recorded on memorials in other cities.

The memorial was commissioned by the Imperial War Graves Commission from Sir Edwin Lutyens, their principal architect, who proposed one in a similar style to the one that he was working on to the Missing of the Somme at Thiepval, France. The original site proposed for the memorial was on the banks of the River Thames at Temple Steps.

However, the Royal Fine Arts Commission objected because it would have involved the demolition of another memorial and they would have preferred a site to the east of Tower Bridge. Lutyens and the Royal Fine Arts Commission could not agree so an alternative site was chosen at Tower Green.

After the Second World War the memorial was extended by Sir Edward Maufe with sculptures by Sir Charles Wheeler. This memorial commemorates 35,755 individuals with no known grave but the sea. This memorial is separately listed at Grade II*.

The Inscription

To the centre of the memorial is a square stepped attic and the principal inscription, which is in bronze, is to be found to the front – south facing – side of the central attic and reads – 1914-1918 TO THE GLORY OF GOD AND THE HONOUR OF TWELVE THOUSAND OF THE MERCHANT NAVY AND FISHING FLEETS WHO HAVE NO GRAVE BUT THE SEA. To each side there are elaborate bronze swagged wreaths and on the north side is carved 1914-1918.

20. 24th East Surrey Division, Battersea Park

Battersea Park (east end), Battersea, London SW11

Grade II*

Unveiled by Field Marshal Lord Plumer on 4th October 1924. Herbert Plumer had been a career soldier who commanded V Corps in France in 1915 and later in the same year commanded the Second Army. In November 1917, following an overwhelming victory over the Germans at the Battle of Messines, he was given command of the British Expeditionary Force in Italy. In 1918 Plumer refused the post of Chief of the Imperial General Staff and, instead, resumed command of the Second Army. In 1925 he was appointed first High Commissioner of the British Mandate for Palestine and was created Viscount Plumer in 1929. The memorial was dedicated by Cyril Garbutt, Bishop of Southwark who ultimately became Archbishop of York in 1942.

Designed and Sculpted by Eric Kennington (1888-1960) who was born in Chelsea, the son of portrait painter Thomas Kennington, and educated at St Paul's School and the Lambeth School of Art. When the First World War broke out, Kennington joined 13th Battalion London Regiment and fought on the Western Front before being wounded in an accident in January 1915. By 1917 Kennington had become a war artist attached to the Ministry of Information, and he was also an official war artist in World War Two. He was friendly with T. E. Lawrence – Lawrence of Arabia - and was one of his six pallbearers. Kennington became an associate member of the Royal Academy in 1951 and a full member in 1959.

Design Features:

The memorial to the 24th East Surrey Division is a simple, but unusual, sculpture of three soldiers in full kit with their legs entwined by a serpent on a three part column base. The style of sculpture was considered avant-garde when it was unveiled.

The Story behind The Memorial:

The regiment was raised from men who volunteered for Lord Kitchener's New Army. The memorial commemorates the over 10,000 men of the 24th Division who were killed, or "missing presumed dead", during the war. The soldier on the left of the group represents Robert Graves, the poet and author of the book *'Goodbye to all That'*

The Inscription

The base of the memorial bears the inscription – XXIV DIVISION FRANCE 1914-1919 – around the top, whilst the lower section has the badges of twenty military units which comprised the division.

21. War Memorial to the Children of Upper North Street School

Poplar Recreation Ground, East India Dock Road, Tower Hamlets, London E14   Grade II*

Unveiled on 23rd June 1919 by Major General Edward Ashmore, a career soldier who served initially with the Royal Horse Artillery before joining the Royal Flying Corps in January 1914. Although he was 40, he learnt to fly and held a number of largely administrative roles before becoming Commander of the London Air Defence Area in August 1917, a role that was created as a direct result of the air raid which had caused the deaths at Upper North Street School.

Designed by A.R. Adams, a local funeral director and prominent member of the East End community. The company Adams founded in 1900 is still trading.

Design Features:

The memorial takes the form of an angel in mourning with wings outstretched and hands clasped. The angel stands on a three-stage structure typical of an ornate 'Victorian' grave marker. The upper stage is a hooded shrine, with blind arches on each face supported by non-canonical Corinthian columns at each corner, with black stone shafts and white stone capitals and bases. The arch to the front face of the memorial is decorated with floral carvings in low relief, and the panel below it has a roundel, which encloses the seal of Poplar Borough Council. The middle section, of white stone is made up of three steps which support the shrine, and the bottom section comprises a large black base.

The Story behind The Memorial:

13th June 1917 saw the first attack by a squadron of German bombers over London. 14 German Gotha bombers flew from Belgium and attacked Margate, Shoeburyness and London. The attack on London caused 162 civilian deaths and 432 injured, including 18 children killed and 37 injured when a bomb went through two floors before exploding in a classroom of 60 infants at Upper North Street School. 16 of the children killed were aged five or six years. Two funds were set up, one to send the surviving children and bereaved mothers to Maidenhead to recuperate and a second to build a memorial. The memorial fund raised £1,455 9s 11d,which not only covered the £230 cost of the memorial but endowed a bed in the children's ward at Poplar Hospital and another at the Lord Mayor's home for crippled children in Alton, Hampshire.

The burial service was led by the Bishop of London, and over 600 wreaths were sent, as was a message from the King and Queen which was read out to the mourners.

The Inscription

The principal inscription is on the front of the memorial and reads: IN MEMORY OF 18 CHILDREN WHO WERE KILLED BY A BOMB DROPPED FROM A GERMAN AEROPLANE UPON THE L.C.C. SCHOOL UPPER NORTH STREET POPLAR ON THE 13th JUNE 1917. ALFRED H. WARREN O.B.E. MAYOR J BUTEUX SKEGGS, TOWN CLERK.

On the middle step of the middle section there are the words: ERECTED BY PUBLIC SUBSCRIPTION with A.R. ADAMS POPLAR below.

War Memorial to the children of Upper North Street School (left) previous page

Twickenham War Memorial (right) and its inscription (below) next page

The Inscription

On the south side of the pedestal there is a bronze relief plaque of the arms of the borough and, beneath, is the inscription: 1914 – 1918 TO THE GLORIOUS MEMORY OF THE MEN OF TWICKENHAM WHO FELL IN THE GREAT WAR THEIR NAME LIVETH EVERMORE AND TO THOSE WHO GAVE THEIR LIVES IN THE WAR OF 1939 – 1945.

22. Twickenham War Memorial

Cross Deep, Twickenham, London, TW1   Grade II*

Unveiled on 2nd November 1921 by Field Marshall Sir William Robertson. Robertson was a career soldier who achieved the unique distinction of rising from private soldier to the rank of Field Marshal. More biographical details can be found in the British Thomson-Houston War Memorial on page 110.

Sculpted by Mortimer John Brown (1874-1966) who was born in Staffordshire. After studies at Hanley School of Art and the National Art Training School from the mid-1890s, Brown studied at the Royal Academy Schools where he was awarded the Landseer scholarship and, in 1898, the British Institution Scholarship. Although his 1911 work *The Shepherd Boy* was purchased by the Chantrey Bequest and gifted to the Tate Gallery, his best-known piece of work is this memorial.

Design Features:

The memorial is in Radnor Gardens which was created from the grounds of Radnor House in 1903. The principal element of the memorial is a life-sized bronze statue of a soldier returning from war. The soldier, still in uniform, is striding out and smiling. In his right hand, he is waving his cap to those waiting to greet him whilst his rifle trails in his left hand. The soldier's helmet lies behind him, discarded as no longer required.

The statue stands on a pedestal with a moulded base and plinth made of Portland stone.

On the north, west and east sides of the plinth there are bronze reliefs depicting the military and civilian services during the war. The plaque which represents the Royal Air Force shows three airmen in hats and goggles standing in front of an aircraft propeller and wheel. The two airmen at the front are shaking hands. Two naval officers are represented on another plaque; they are on the bridge of a ship and while one looks through his binoculars the other officer points into the distance. There is the head of a sailor in the foreground. On the third plaque, there is a nurse and a woman in Voluntary Aid Detachment uniform with a vehicle in the background.

The Story behind The Memorial:

This memorial is unusual in two respects, firstly, that it represents a joyful homecoming as opposed to the more common attitude of sorrow or defiance and, secondly, that it illustrates a woman in uniform. Whilst women are represented on a number of memorials it is more often in the 'home front' role, caring for children or mourning lost sons/husbands yet this memorial shows a woman in uniform. The Voluntary Aid Detachment (VAD) had been formed in 1909 and by the outbreak of the First World War it numbered 74,000, two thirds of whom were women or girls, with most volunteers coming from the middle and upper classes. The military were initially unwilling to have then serve overseas fearing that the conditions and the sights they may see would prove too shocking for them. However, by 1918 there were 80,000 VAD members including 60,000 unpaid volunteers working in auxiliary hospitals, and others who were cooks and ambulance drivers.

The memorial is sometimes referred to as 'The Men of Twickenham Memorial'.

In 2011 the plaque representing the Royal Navy was stolen and the local authority commissioned Leander Architectural to produce a replacement working from photographs.

23. Kingston-upon-Thames War Memorial

Memorial Gardens Kingston upon Thames, KT1

Grade II*

Unveiled Unveiled on 11th November 1923 by Frederick George Penny, 1st Viscount Marchwood, who was MP for Kingston upon Thames.

Designed by Richard Reginald Goulden.

Design Features:

The memorial is situated within gated memorial gardens which were laid out on a former burial ground. It is topped by a life-size bronze figure of a naked man striding forwards with his left arm raised and holding a flaming cross. He carries a sword in his right arm, which shields two small children, one of whom is looking up at him, whilst the second hides behind the man's legs. The man has his foot on a serpent whilst he is using his sword to push back thick stems of thorn covered brambles.

The figures stand on a two-tiered granite pedestal with flanking walls, whilst the whole memorial is on a three-stepped base. The front of the flanking walls, together with the front and two sides of the base of the plinth, have bronze plaques which have the names of the 624 fallen in the First World War.

The Story behind The Memorial:

The preparatory work for a war memorial was started when the Borough Librarian of Kingston upon Thames started to collect the names of local casualties as they arrived. Goulden's design for the memorial mirrors his work on other memorials, of which he designed eleven after the First World War. The bronze for the memorial was cast at A B Burton's Foundry in Thames Ditton.

The memorial was conserved in 2006 with the assistance of a £3,000 grant from War Memorials Trust.

The Inscription

Around the base of the sculpture are the words: AT THE GOING DOWN OF THE SUN AND IN THE MORNING WE WILL REMEMBER THEM – these words are from Laurence Binyon's poem 'For the Fallen' written in 1914. On the front of the pedestal is the principal inscription: IN HONOUR OF THE MEN OF THIS TOWN WHO GAVE THEIR LIVES IN THE GREAT WARS 1914-1919 1939-1945.

24. Croydon War Memorial

Katharine Street, Croydon, CR0

Grade II*

Unveiled on 22nd October 1924 by Henry Cubitt, 2nd Baron Ashcombe, a former Conservative Member of Parliament, and Lord Lieutenant of Surrey from 1905 to 1939. Three of Ashcombe's six sons had been killed in the First World War.

Designed by James Burford

Sculpted by Raphael Montford (1868-1938) who was born in Kentish Town, London, where his father, Horace, was a sculptor who won a gold medal at the Royal Academy Schools in 1869. Montford was initially taught by his father and later at the Royal Academy Schools, where he also won the gold medal and travelling scholarship for sculpture. He undertook many public and private commissions, both in the UK and especially in Australia, to where he moved when he struggled to get work. Montford was President of the Victorian Artists Society from 1930 to 1932 and won the gold medal of the Royal Society of British Sculptors in 1934.

Design Features:

The memorial is a Portland stone pylon 29ft (9m) tall topped by a sarcophagus, and is incorporated into the balustrade of the Town Hall. At the top of the pylon is a bronze cross with the dates 1914 and 1918: 1939 and 1945 were added later. There are two bronze figures, one to each side of the pylon. To the left is a soldier who is putting a dressing on his injured arm, he already has a dressing around his head. He is sitting on his greatcoat, with his rifle behind him and a water bottle in his lap. There is a grenade at his feet and his puttees are covered in sacking. The figure to the other side of the pylon is a woman who is holding a child on her lap. She is also sitting on a coat and has her right arm extended towards the soldier with a letter in her hand. The woman's face is turned towards the soldier and her eyes are closed to indicate a connection between them. A wedding ring is clearly visible with its suggestion that the three figures make up a family group.

The Inscription

The pylon is inscribed: AND IN MEMORY OF THOSE WHO LOST THEIR LIVES IN WARS AND CONFLICTS SINCE. The base of the pylon is inscribed: A TRIBUTE TO THE MEN AND WOMEN OF CROYDON WHO DIED AND SUFFERED.

25. Bromley War Memorial
St Martin's Hill, Bromley, Greater London, BR2
Grade II*

Unveiled on 29th October 1922 by Major General Henry Horne. 1st Baron Horne was a career soldier who had been the only artillery officer to command an army during the First World War. The dedication was performed by John Harmer, Bishop of Rochester, who was previously Bishop of Adelaide in Australia.

Designed and Sculpted by Sydney March (1876-1968) whose biography can be found on Page 38.

Design Features:

The memorial, which is situated inside Bromley's Martins Hill Park, and is on a flat topped mound within a fenced and gated area, is a square obelisk of Portland stone on a two staged base with three steps. Three allegorical bronze figures are positioned around the base of the obelisk, representing Victory in the centre, flanked by Liberty and Peace. Victory holds a laurel wreath aloft, whilst Liberty carries a torch and Peace scatters flowers of remembrance. On the four sides of the base are bronze plaques with the names of the fallen.

The Inscription

The memorial bears the names of 769 servicemen who were killed in the First World War, together with 476 military and civilian victims of the Second World War. With the addition of the victims of the Second World War the memorial was rededicated in 1949 by Rev W H Murray-Walton, vicar of Bromley. Among the congregation was Harold Macmillan, who was MP for Bromley and Prime Minister from January 1957 to October 1963.

Civic Voice

Civic Voice is the national charity for the civic movement in England. We make places more attractive, enjoyable and distinctive. We promote civic pride.

One hundred years on from the First World War, and now that those people who were directly involved in the conflict are no longer with us, war memorials have become even more significant as reminders of the sacrifices made.

War memorials are some of the most tangible and poignant reminders we have of the enormous impact that wars have had on local communities across the country. The widespread erection of war memorials (especially after the First World War) is the largest known wave of publicly commissioned art and sculpture this land has ever seen. Estimates put the number of existing war memorials across the UK as high as 100,000.

In 2014, following a call from civic societies up and down the country who wanted to take action to commemorate the centenary, Civic Voice joined with Historic England, Imperial War Museums and War Memorials Trust to create the First World War Memorials Programme.

Throughout the centenary we want to ensure that war memorials are the fitting tributes that former members of our communities deserve. With government funding, the programme has been developed to help communities discover, care for, conserve and protect their local First World War memorials.

Our aim is to ensure that as many war memorials as possible are cherished, protected and conserved so that they stand for generations to come as a testament to the enduring impact that wars have had on local people. The programme is doing this in a number of different ways; by providing specialist conservation advice for war memorials; disbursing £2m in grant funding for repairs; providing practical conservation training to those carrying out works to war memorials; delivering public workshops to train up to 5000 volunteers; providing education materials and resources for schools; creating resources for the public to research war memorials on the internet; adding 2,500 war memorials to the National Heritage List for England, thereby giving them greater protection.

Civic Voice is helping local communities get involved by running a programme of training workshops about how to assess the condition of a war memorial. This is helping to identify memorials that need repair and conservation and which could benefit from grant funding. Civic Voice is also helping communities protect them for the future by training them how to apply to have a war memorial listed.

Anyone can get involved and you can find more information at *http://www.civicvoice. org.uk/campaigns/war-memorials-/* or by contacting *info@civicvoice.org.uk* or tel: *0121 792 8177*.

SOUTH EAST

1 Reigate and Redhill
2 Chatham
3 Maidstone
4 Faversham
5 Canterbury
6 Deal
Dover 7
8
9 Folkestone
10 Hythe
11 Burwash
12 Ditchling
13 Lewes
Worthing

CONTENTS

Map reference and Memorial Name   **Page**

1. Reigate & Redhill War Memorial

Shaw's Corner, Hatchlands Road, Redhill, Surrey, RH1   Grade II*

Unveiled on 5th August 1923 by Admiral the Rt. Hon 1st Earl Beatty. Beatty was a Royal Navy officer who commanded the 1st Battlecruiser Squadron at the Battle of Jutland in 1916, where he made the comment: *"There seems to be something wrong with our bloody ships today"* after two ships of his squadron exploded and sank.

Later in the First World War, Beatty was Commander-in-Chief of the Grand Fleet and he received the surrender of the German High Seas Fleet at the end of the war. Beatty went on to become First Sea Lord, a position that he held for 7 years and 9 months, and it was in that capacity that he unveiled the memorial.

Designed and Sculpted by Richard Reginald Goulden.

Design Features:

The memorial stands on a prominent site at Shaw's Corner, which is a former village green and stands at the junction of three roads. The memorial has a square-set tapering granite plinth with a two-stepped base. On top of the plinth is a bronze sculpture of a naked man carrying a small child, to represent future generations in his right arm, whilst his left arm holds aloft a flaming torch. The man is striding through thick, thorny brambles that are wrapped around him. There are no names on the memorial, although they are on a Roll of Honour in the Municipal Buildings.

The Story behind The Memorial:

Discussions about a war memorial started within a month of the Armistice in November 1918 in both Reigate and Redhill and, whilst there was general agreement that there should be a memorial, there was no agreement as to where it should be sited, nor what form the memorial should take. Eventually Shaw's Corner was chosen because it was a prominent position that was roughly half-way between Reigate and Redhill. The War Memorial Committee looked at a number of designs before agreeing on the one presented by Richard Goulden.

The Inscription

The inscription, which is in gold coloured, raised letters on the upper plinth initially said: IN MEMORY OF MEN OF REIGATE AND REDHILL WHO FOUGHT AND GAVE THEIR LIVES IN THE GREAT WAR 1914-1919 although after the Second World War this was changed to the present inscription: IN MEMORY OF MEN AND WOMEN OF THIS BOROUGH WHO GAVE THEIR LIVES IN THE TWO WORLD WARS 1914-1919 1939-1945.

On the other three sides of the plinth the words COURAGE, HONOUR and SELF-SACRIFICE are inscribed; one on each side.

The upper step of the base has a bronze relief panel set into its front face which reads: THE BRONZE REPRESENTS THE TRIUMPHANT STRUGGLE OF MANKIND AGAINST THE DIFFICULTIES THAT BESET HIM IN THE PATH OF LIFE. SHEILDING AND BEARING ONWARD THE CHILD, THE FIGURE HOLDS ALOFT THE SYMBOL OF SELF-SACRIFICE TO LIGHT THE WAY. THE FLAMING CROSS IS USED TO INDICATE THE SUFFERING ENDURED BY MEN IN THE WAR. FLAMES CONSUME THE FLESH. THE SPIRIT IS UNCONQUERABLE.

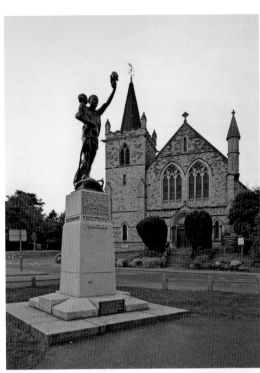

Reigate & Redhill War Memorial
(left) previous page

Chatham Naval War Memorial
(below) next page

2. Chatham Naval War Memorial

Great Lines, Chatham, Medway, ME7   **Grade I**

Unveiled on 26th April 1924 by HRH Edward, Prince of Wales. Edward, the future Edward VIII, who had been in the Grenadier Guards during the First World War and although never directly involved in fighting, because the War Office were worried that he may be captured, he did visit the front line as often as possible, which made him popular with former servicemen after the war.

Designed by Sir Robert Lorimer   **Sculpted by** Henry Poole

Design Features:
The memorial is situated up a steep path from the Town Hall Gardens on a site that overlooks the town. This large and impressive memorial consists of a tall Portland stone obelisk, topped with four ships prows and bronze figures to represent the four winds, and surmounted by a copper sphere to represent the Earth. The inspiration for the memorial came from a naval "leading mark", a powerful naval symbol, as it is guide to navigation for ships entering the safety of a port. The obelisk sits on a square base with corner projections, each of which has a lion couchant. Low down on each face of the obelisk is a naval badge of an anchor, set within a laurel wreath and surmounted by a Navy crown.

The Story behind The Memorial:
The Royal Navy played a crucially important role during the First World War with some 50,000 men and women paying the ultimate sacrifice. As well as conventional naval warfare, the Royal Navy provided a division that fought as infantry on the Western Front. After the end of the war, the Imperial War Graves Commission was keen to find a suitable war to memorialise those of the Royal Navy who had no known grave, and their solution was three identical memorials at Plymouth, Portsmouth and Chatham, the three principle manning ports. The memorial was extensively enlarged following the Second World War to include quadrant walls and a sunken garden. The walls are mounted with bronze plaques including the names of the naval personnel lost in the Second World War. These later additions were designed by Sir Edward Maufe with sculptures by Charles Wheeler.

The Inscription

Between the lions there are large bronze plaques. The plaque on the south, seaward face, bears the inscription: IN HONOUR OF THE NAVY AND TO THE ABIDING MEMORY OF THESE RANKS AND RATINGS OF THIS PORT WHO LAID DOWN THEIR LIVES IN THE DEFENCE OF THE EMPIRE AND HAVE NO OTHER GRAVE THAN THE SEA AND THEIR COMRADES OF AUSTRALIA   SOUTH AFRICA NEWFOUNDLAND INDIA PAKISTAN CEYLON FIJI GOLD COAST HONG KONG KENYA MALAYA NIGERIA SIERRA LEONE AND BURMA WHOSE NAMES ARE HERE RECORDED.

The plaques on the other faces show low relief impressions of naval actions during the First World War. Around the base of the column are bronze plaques with the names of 7,251 naval personnel killed in the First World War. The names are arranged alphabetically within the year of the death and their role in the Navy, these roles themselves also being listed alphabetically. The names include personnel from Australia and South Africa although other Empire/Commonwealth nations chose to make their own separate memorials.

3. The Queen's Own Royal West Kent Regiment Cenotaph

Brenchley Gardens, Maidstone, Kent, ME14

Grade II*

Unveiled on 30th July 1921 by Major General Sir Edmund Leach, a regular soldier who was Honorary Colonel of the regiment from 1904 to 1921. The memorial was dedicated by Randall Davidson the Archbishop of Canterbury in the presence of Lieutenant General Sir Edwin Alderson KCB, a veteran of the regiment, who had led the Canadian Expeditionary Force in France during the first part of the war.

Designed by Sir Edwin Lutyens and built by local builders Messrs G E Wallis and Sons Ltd.

Design Features:

The memorial, which is built of Portland Stone, is a two-thirds scale reproduction of Lutyen's cenotaph in Whitehall, London. It stands on a rectangular stone platform of three steps. At the top of the memorial there is a plain chest tomb with a moulded cover which carries a laurel wreath, and stands on a three-stage base which is on a tall shaft. The two narrow ends of the shaft have laurel wreaths, one of which is surrounded by 1919 and 1945 expressed in Roman numerals, and the other wreath has the dates 1914 1939 also expressed in Roman numerals.

The Story behind The Memorial:

Whilst Lutyens was agreeable to producing this memorial as a reduced version of his London Cenotaph, he always refused to agree that his Stone of Remembrance be reproduced in a reduced size. During the First World War some 40,000 men had served with the Queens Own Royal West Kent Regiment, of whom approximately 26,000 became casualties.

The Inscription

The north-east and south-east faces bear the inscription THE GLORIOUS DEAD OF THE QUEENS OWN ROYAL WEST KENT REGIMENT NUMBERING 6866 OF ALL RANKS ALSO NUMBERING 1663 OF ALL RANKS. The lower figure representing the men of the regiment who were killed in the Second World War.

4. Memorial to the Victims of the 1916 Faversham Munitions Explosion

Faversham Cemetery, Love Lane, Faversham, Kent ME18   Grade II*

Unveiled on 27th September 1917 by the Archbishop of Canterbury, the Most Reverend Randall Davidson.

Designer: Not recorded: the design is not complicated and would have been well within the capabilities of any local stone mason.

Design Features:

The mass grave is in the central part of the cemetery and consists of an enclosure framed by a low granite kerb with low piers and caps at regular intervals. There are flights of two steps upwards at each end of the memorial which lead onto the grassed area. These steps are flanked with piers which, at one stage, were topped by urns although these now appear to be missing. In the centre of the grave there is a large granite Celtic Cross on a three stepped base. The names of the victims are recorded in lead lettering on the coping stones of the low kerb. There is a rough hewn, free-standing, granite stone a short distance to the east of the memorial on which are recorded the names of the 35 victims who are buried elsewhere.

The Story behind The Memorial:

This memorial is unique in this guide in that it is predominately in memory of civilians killed in the First World War, and also killed in an accident rather than by enemy action. Faversham was the site of England's first gunpowder mill, which was established in the sixteenth century and was still an important area for munitions manufacturing during the First World War. Although extensive efforts were made to avoid fire on 2nd April 1916, one broke out in the Explosives Loading Company's site at Uplees. The cause of the fire remains uncertain, although an inquiry into the explosion, which reported on 17th April 1916, absolved the company from all blame.

15 tons of TNT and 150 tons of ammonium nitrate – one of the components of explosives – were stored in the building. The works fire brigade, aided by the fire brigade from an adjacent works, fought the fire bravely, and workers tried to remove boxes of TNT from the building, but at 2.20pm there were three massive explosions which killed at least 108 and injured 64. Windows in Southend-on-Sea, 15 miles away, were broken by the force of the explosion which was heard in Norwich and France.

Seventy-three victims were buried in the mass grave, although of these only 34 could be identified with the other bodies being recorded in the registry as 'a male person unknown'. 35 of those killed were buried elsewhere. All the members of the works fire brigade were killed as were four soldiers. The families of each of the victims received £300 compensation – this was at a time when a tram driver earned £1 per week.

This was the worst disaster, in terms of numbers killed, to befall the British explosives industry in 450 years.

The Inscription

The inscription is on the front of the three stepped base and reads – SACRED TO THE MEMORY OF THE MEN WHO DIED IN THE SERVICE OF THEIR COUNTRY 2ND APRIL 1916. 'FATHER IN THY GRACIOUS KEEPING LEAVE NOW THY SERVANTS SLEEPING'

Memorial to the Victims of the
1916 Faversham Munitions
Explosion (above) previous
page

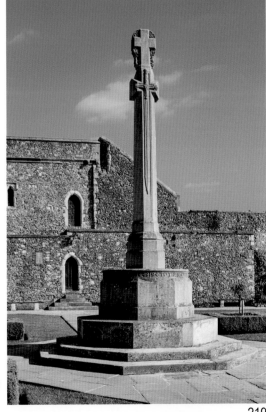

County of Kent Memorial Cross
(right) next page

5. County of Kent War Memorial Cross

Harris Memorial Garden, The Precinct, Canterbury Cathedral, Canterbury, Kent CT1

Grade II*

Unveiled on 4th August 1921 by Lady Camden, wife of 4th Lord Camden, the Lord Lieutenant of Kent, with the dedication performed by Randall Davidson, the Archbishop of Canterbury. An address was given by Admiral Sir H. Evan-Thomas, Commander-in-Chief, The Nore and Commander of the 5th Battle Squadron of the Grand Fleet during the First World War. Lord Harris, Chairman of the Memorial Committee, presented the memorial to the Dean of the Cathedral.

Designed by Sir Herbert Baker.

Design Features:

The memorial takes the form of a wheel-head cross that rises from a short-armed Latin cross on a tall octagonal shaft. The overall height of the memorial is 20ft (6m) and the design is known as an Ypres Cross, or Cross of Lorraine, although the design is different from what many would now recognise as the Cross of Lorraine. The circle of the wheel-head is decorated with roses and lilies to represent England and France and these trail down the shaft. On the east face of the Latin cross there is a warship with billowing sails, whilst a reversed broadsword is carved on the west face of the Latin cross and the shaft.

The cross shaft ends on a moulded foot which stands on an octagonal drum-like plinth which, in turn, stands on a three-stepped base. The whole memorial stands on an octagonal pavement in the centre of the Harris Memorial Garden. Paths lead to the memorial and divide the lawns into quadrants.

The Story behind The Memorial:

There was an initial discussion as to whether the county war memorial for Kent should be in Rochester, Maidstone or Canterbury until it was decided, in June 1920, that it should be sited on a former bowling green in Canterbury Cathedral Close within the city walls. The original plan included arcades to the north and south sides of the garden although these were later dropped.

The works, which were carried out by Mr George Browning, included the erection of the cross, ground-works within the garden and repairs to the nearby bastion in the city wall. Some of the works, which were paid for by public subscription, were not completed until after the dedication of the memorial.

During the Second World War the memorial was damaged in an air-raid, when it lost the uppermost cross-head along with pieces of stonework in the cross shaft, plinth and base. Repairs were carried out in the 1950s under the supervision of Harold Anderson FSA FRIBA, Surveyor to the Fabric of Canterbury Cathedral.

The Inscription

The simple inscription is carved in relief around the circular head of the plinth and reads: TO THE SACRED MEMORY OF THE SONS AND DAUGHTERS OF KENT WHO DIED IN THE GREAT WAR 1914-1919.

6. St George's Church Memorial Cross
High Street, Deal, CT14
Grade II*

Unveiled on 12th November 1916 by Bishop Taylor-Smith, who was Chaplain-General to the Forces. From 1896 to 1901 he was Honorary Chaplain to Queen Victoria and Bishop of Sierra Leone from 1897 to 1901. From 1901 to 1925 he was Chaplain-General to the Forces and saw the number of chaplains in the Army rise from 120 in 1914 to almost 3,500 in 1918.

Designer: No details of the designer survive. The cross is of a relatively straight-forward design that a local monumental stone mason could easily design and construct.

Design Features:

The memorial is 10ft (3m) tall and consists of a granite Celtic Cross at the top of a tapering shaft. The arms of the cross are decorated with interlaced patterns carved in

relief with a central boss that is surrounded by 12 small hemispheres. The front of the shaft is divided by horizontal bars into three sections, the uppermost of which is blank. The middle section bears the Tisdall family arms, whilst the lower section carries a bronze depiction of the Victoria Cross hanging from a laurel wreath. Within the area created by the wreath is a bronze of the reverse of the University of Cambridge's Chancellor's Medal for Classical Learning. The arms of Deal are carved in relief near the base of the rear of the shaft, which is set on a tapering plinth which, in turn is on a tapering step, whilst the whole rests on a square base.

The Story behind The Memorial:

This is a very early First World War memorial and was originally intended as a personal one to Rev. Tisdall's eldest son, Arthur, although his second son, John, was also added later, as were the names of 56 men from the parish who died. The names of the dead are recorded with rank, regiment or ship, and date of death. The Rev. Tisdall paid for the original memorial, although fundraising events were held by the congregation so that cutting and lettering for names could be added. In that way all the names from the parish were included, regardless of the ability of families to pay.

The memorial was cleaned and the letters re-enamelled in 1995 at the expense of the Old Boys Association of Bedford School which both Tisdall sons had attended. The memorial was re-dedicated on 18th June 1995.

The Inscription

On the rear of the shaft near the base there is the following inscription set in raised metal lettering: IN PROUD & LOVING MEMORY OF THE MEN WHO FROM THE PARISH & CONGREGATION OF ST GEORGE'S DEAL HAVE GIVEN THEIR LIVES FOR THEIR COUNTRY.

On the east of the plinth and also in raised metal letters an inscription reads: AD GLORIAM DEI *(the glory of God).* TO THE BRIGHT & BEAUTIFUL MEMORY OD ARTHUR WALDERNE ST CLAIR TISDALL, V.C. SUB LIEUT. R.N.V.R. SCHOLAR OF TRINITY COLLEGE (B.A. DOUBLE 1ST CL. HON.) & CHANCELLORS GOLD MEDALLIST IN THE UNIVERSITY OF CAMBRIDGE SON OF REV W. ST. C. TISDALL, D.D. VICAR OF ST GEORGE'S CHURCH, DEAL, & OF MARIAN (NEE GRAY) HIS WIFE BORN JULY 21, 1890, KILLED FIGHTING GALLANTLY IN THE ATTACK ON ACHI BABA, GALLIPOLI, MAY 6, 1915. *The inscription continues on the tapering step:* AWARDED THE VICTORIA CROSS BY HIS KING & COUNTRY IN RECOGNITION OF HIS MOST CONSPICUOUS BRAVERY AND DEVOTION TO DUTY IN RESCUING MANY WOUNDED OFFICERS & MEN UNDER VIOLENT & ACCURATE FIRE, DURING THE LANDING OF THE BRITISH TROOPS FROM THE S.S. "RIVER CLYDE" AT V BEACH GALLIPOLI APRIL 25. 1915.

On the north face: ALSO OF HIS BROTHER JOHN THEODORE ST. CLAIR TISDALL. LIEUT. 1ST THE KINGS (LIVERPOOL) REGT. SCHOLAR OF PETERHOUSE COLLEGE AND BELLSCHOLAR IN THE UNIVERSITY OF CAMBRIDGE BORN OCT. 9. 1893. KILLED GALLANTLY LEADING HIS COMPANY AT GUILLEMONT, FRANCE. AUG. 8. 1916.

All four faces carry names of parishioners and those from the congregation who died in the First World War.

DID YOU KNOW THAT?

The War Horse Memorial in Ascot in Berkshire is dedicated to the millions of UK, Allied and Commonwealth horses, mules and donkeys lost in the First World War. It pays tribute to the nobility, courage, unyielding loyalty and unmeasurable contribution these innocent animals played in giving us the freedom of democracy we all enjoy today. It signifies the last time the horse would be used on a mass scale in modern warfare.

THE WAR HORSE MEMORIAL
Strength in Adversity

It consists of a larger than life bronze horse standing on an inscribed Portland stone plinth. A nearby stone monolith has embedded computer technology, which describes on-going fundraising initiatives to support military and equine charities. The main beneficiaries are the Mane Chance Sanctuary and the Household Cavalry Foundation, which is the official charity for the Household Cavalry.

The four antecedent regiments of today's Household Cavalry (The 1st and 2nd Life Guards, the Royal Horse Guards (The Blues) and the 1st Royal Dragoons) and their modern successors in The Life Guards and The Blues & Royals have fought, as the Army's senior regiments, in every major British campaign since the seventeenth century.

The sculptor, Susan Leyland who was originally from Lancashire, describes the memorial as a horse standing motionless, with the only movement in the tail caught in gust of wind, to give a sign of life and hope for the future that their sacrifice was not in vain.

Charities sell different colour poppies. White symbolise peace without violence, and purple poppies are worn to honour animals killed in conflict. A fundraising Purple Poppy Day will be held on August 23rd each year.

7. The Dover Patrol Monument

Leathercoat Point, St Margaret's Bay, Dover, Kent, CT15

Grade II*

Unveiled by The Prince of Wales, the future Edward VIII, on 27th June 1921, whose brief biographical details can be found on page 75.

Designed by Sir Aston Webb (1849-1930) who was born in London, the son of a watercolourist. He established his own architectural practice in London in 1874, and from the early 1880s, started to work with Ingress Bell, with their first major commission being the Victoria Law Courts in Birmingham. Webb's best known works are the Victoria Memorial in front of Buckingham Palace, the façade to Buckingham Palace, the Victoria & Albert Museum's main building, Admiralty Arch and the Britannia Royal Naval College in Devon.

In 1883 Webb was admitted to the Royal Institution of British Architects and became a full member in 1903, receiving their Gold Medal in 1905 and serving as President from 1902 to 1904. Webb was knighted in 1904, appointed a Commander of the Order of the Bath in 1909 and appointed to the Royal Victorian Order in 1911, rising to Knight Grand Cross of the Order in 1925.

Design Features:

This large impressive, yet simple memorial, is made from stone ashlar blocks and is over 82ft (25m) tall. It takes the form of a square section obelisk standing on top of a tall stone plinth which flares out onto a square base. Centrally placed on three sides of the plinth are small temple-like surrounds, two of which act as frames to an incised panel. There is an unframed inscription on the fourth side of the plinth.

The monument is reached by steps and is within a grassed enclosure. There is a fence around the lawn comprising of a chain connected to concrete posts. Within this area are a large anchor and a muzzle-loading gun. All the above features are included in the listing.

The Story behind The Memorial:

The Dover Patrol was based in Dover and Dunkirk throughout the First World War with the primary function of preventing German shipping, chiefly submarines, from entering the English Channel, which meant that German U-Boats had to travel by the longer route around the north of Scotland.

The tasks and vessels of the Dover Patrol expanded during the war to include, in addition to the anti-submarine patrols, escorting merchant ships, hospital and troop ships, laying and sweeping for mines, bombarding German military positions in Belgium and blockading the port of Zeebrugge during the attack of 22nd/23rd April 1918. To accomplish this task the patrol was equipped with cruisers, monitors, destroyers, armed trawlers and drifters, paddle-wheeled minesweepers, armed yachts, motor launches, coastal motor boats, submarines, seaplanes, aircraft and airships. It is estimated that during the war some 125,000 ships passed through the area controlled by the Dover Patrol of which only 73 were lost to enemy action.

The Patrol suffered heavy losses, but its personnel received many decorations for bravery including six Victoria Crosses during the Zeebrugge Raid alone.

The monument was funded by public subscription, a committee having been formed in November 1918. The fund raised £45,000 which included a £1,000 donation from King Albert and Queen Elizabeth of the Belgians. The land on which the monument is built was donated by Granville Leveson-Gower, 3rd Earl Granville.

The monuments at Sangatte near Calais and in the John Paul Jones Park, Fort Hamilton, New York are identical to the one in Dover.

The Inscription

The inscription on the south-west face of the plinth reads: THIS STONE WAS LAID BY H.R.H. PRINCE ARTHUR OF CONNAUGHT, K.G. 19th NOVEMBER 1919 AND THE MEMORIAL WAS UNVEILED BY H.R.H. THE PRINCE OF WALES, K.G. 27th JUNE 1921.
On the north-west side the inscription is unframed: THIS MONUMENT TO THE DOVER PATROL WAS ERECTED IN THE YEARS 1920 & 1921 BY PUBLIC SUBSCRIPTION TOGETHER WITH THOSE AT CAP BLANC NEZ, FRANCE AND NEW YORK HARBOUR, AMERICA. THE NAMES OF THOSE WHO GAVE THEIR LIVES SERVING THEIR KING AND COUNTRY IN THE DOVER PATROL ARE RECORDED IN THE BOOK OF REMEMBRANCE IN THE TOWN HALL, DOVER, A COPY OF WHICH IS KEPT AT THE PRISH CHURCH, ST MARGARETS AT CLIFFE.
The south-east inscription reads: TO THE GLORY OF GOD AND IN EVERLASTING REMEMBRANCE OF THE DOVER PATROL 1914-1919 THEY DIED THAT WE MAY LIVE MAY WE BE WORTH OF THEIR SACRIFICE TO THE MEMORY OF THE OFFICERS AND MEN OF THE ROYAL NAVY AND MERCHANT NAVY WHO GAVE THEIR LIVES IN SHIPS SAILING UPON THE WATERS OF THE DOVER STRAIGHT 1939-1946.

8. The People of Dover War Memorial

Garden of Remembrance, Maison Dieu House, Biggin Street,

Dover, Kent, CT16

Grade II*

Unveiled on 5th November 1924 by Vice Admiral Sir Roger Keyes, 1st Baron Keyes. He joined the Royal Navy as a cadet and saw action in East Africa, China and in various theatres during the First World War until, in January 1918, he became Commander-in-Chief Dover and Commander of the Dover Patrol, in which capacity he planned and led the attacks on Zeebrugge and Ostend on 23rd April 1918.

At the time Keyes unveiled the memorial in 1924 he was Deputy Chief of the Naval Staff. The dedication of the memorial was made by the Archbishop of Canterbury.

Designed by Richard Goulden.

Design Features:

The memorial comprises a bronze figure on top of a Cornish grey granite pedestal that carries bronze reliefs on three sides and the principal inscription on the fourth. The pedestal is on a stepped plinth and base and is situated in a Garden of Remembrance outside Maison Dieu House.

The bronze sculpture is of a life-sized young boy who represents Youth; he is holding his arms upwards and has a flaming cross in his right hand, whilst at his feet is a ring of thorns. On the front face of the pedestal the arms of Dover are represented in bronze relief and there are bronze wreaths to the two sides of the pedestal while, on the back, there is an additional First World War plaque that was added in 1934, as well as the Second World War plaque which was added in 1949.

Low flanking walls carry a 14ft (4m) long roll of honour of those who died in the First World War. There is a 1ft 6ins (0.45m) tall plinth which is 15ft (4.5m) long with sunken integral flower holders.

The Story behind The Memorial:

A sub-committee of Dover Town Council met in May 1920 to consider various options for an outdoor war memorial. After a year of debate, it was resolved to create a shrine at the Maison Dieu House to include a Book of Remembrance. Some £300 had been raised by public subscription by this stage and the Town Clerk started to compile a list of names to be included in the book. Two Dover artists, amongst others, were asked to submit designs for a suitable shrine, one of them was Richard Goulden, who said that he would not charge for the design.

It was not until February 1924 that a public meeting was called to consider the designs that had been submitted. There was unhappiness expressed at this meeting that the delay in creating a memorial was unacceptable, and there was pressure to consider the building of a maternity home as something that the town needed and that could also act as a memorial. This was rejected because it was thought that there was no way that sufficient funds could be raised. In June 1924 Goulden submitted a model of the memorial that was subsequently built and the committee accepted this, because they were coming under increasing pressure over the perceived delay in building a memorial, and some people were asking for their subscriptions to be returned.

The memorial was completed at a cost of £1,200 although it would not be until October 1925, a year after the work was completed, that the full amount was raised.

A further panel with 70 names missing from the original panels was added in the 1930s and in 1949 a re-dedication service was held following the addition of the names of those who died in the Second World War.

The Inscription

The principal inscription, in applied bronze lettering, is on the front face of the pedestal: TO THE GLORIOUS MEMORY OF THE PEOPLE OF DOVER WHO GAVE THEIR LIVES FOR THEIR COUNTRY IN THE GREAT WARS 1914-1919 – 1939-1945.
Under the relief of the arms of Dover is the inscription: VILLE ET PORTUS DOVOR (the town and port of Dover) – the motto of the town.

There is a further dedication on a stone adjacent to the memorial: THIS MEMORIAL WAS ERECTED BY PUBLIC SUBSCRIPTION FUNDS COLLECTED FOR DOVER PRISONERS OF WAR ALSO GIVEN AS A THANK OFFERING FOR THOSE WHO RETURNED SAFELY.

9. Folkestone War Memorial

Road of Remembrance, Folkestone, Shepway, Kent, CT20
Grade II*

Unveiled by Jacob Pleydell-Bouverie, 6th Earl of Radnor on 2nd December 1922. The Earl had long connections with Folkestone, having been Viscount Folkestone from 1889 to 1900 when he inherited his title and, in 1901, he was the elected Mayor of Folkestone. Having been a Member of Parliament, the 6th Earl saw active service in South Africa during the Boer War and commanded the 4th Battalion the Wiltshire Regiment. During the First World War he was Brigadier-General of the Dehra Dun Brigade in India, and from 1918 he was Director of Agricultural Production for the British Expeditionary Force. The dedication was by Rev, Canon Tindall, after which floral tributes were laid by the Mayor of Folkestone, Colonel W J Dugan on behalf of the Shorncliffe Garrison, by the Mayor of Calais and the Vice-Consuls of Belgium and Italy.

Sculpted by Ferdinand Victor Blundstone (1882-1951) although the name of the designer of the plinth does not appear to have been recorded. Although born in Switzerland, Blundstone's family lived in Manchester, where his father was an India rubber merchant. Blundstone studied at the South London Technical Art School and Royal Academy Schools, where he won the Landseer Scholarship. As well as The Plimsoll Line Memorial in London, and the sculptures on the Tyne Cot Memorial in Belgium, Blundstone also designed war memorials and other memorials in the United Kingdom, Canada and New Zealand.

Design Features:

The memorial stands, facing the sea, on a roundabout at the junction of The Leas, West Terrace and the Road of Remembrance.

A central pedestal of white Cornish granite 25ft (8m) high and 26ft (78m) wide with shallow curved flanking walls to either side comprise the base of the memorial. On top of the pedestal is a bronze female figure, who wears a robe from the waist down and holds a cross in her left hand, to symbolise sacrifice, and a laurel wreath, to represent victory, in her right hand. Flying at half mast from the shaft of the cross is a Union Flag. The figure faces towards the battlefields of Flanders.

The memorial is surrounded by a low stone wall, to the front of which is a pair of bronze gates. This wall was added to the memorial following the Second World War to commemorate those from the town who died during that conflict.

The Story behind The Memorial:

Folkestone war memorial was raised not only in memory of the men from the town killed during the First World War, but of the thousands of soldiers from across the Empire who passed through the town on their way to the battlefields of France. Folkestone Harbour Station gave direct access to the cross-channel ships, however many soldiers also marched through the town and passed the present position of the memorial, before continuing down the road which was re-named, Road of Remembrance, at the end of the First World War.

228

The Inscription

The pedestal and the bronze gates carry the inscription: MAY THEIR DEEDS BE HELD IN REVERENCE. On the base of the pedestal, between the flanking walls, is a cast bronze panel which depicts, in bas relief, soldiers marching towards Folkestone Harbour and below that is the following dedication: THANKS BE TO GOD WHO GIVETH US THE VICTORY IN GRATEFUL MEMORY OF THE BRAVE MEN FROM FOLKESTONE, AND THE MANY THOUSANDS FROM ALL PARTS OF THE EMPIRE WHO PASSED THIS SPOT ON THEIR WAY TO FIGHT IN THE GREAT WAR (1914-1918) FOR RIGHTEOUSNESS AND FREEDOM, AND ESPECIALLY THOSE OF THIS TOWN WHO MADE THE SUPREME SACRIFICE, AND WHOSE NAMES ARE HERE RECORDED, THIS MEMORIAL IS HUMBLY DEDICATED. The flanking walls also have bronze plaques on which are inscribed the names of the 578 men from Folkestone who died.

10. Hythe War Memorial

The Grove, Prospect Road, Hythe, Kent, CT21
Grade II*

Unveiled on 16th July 1921 by Willian Lygon, 7th Earl Beauchamp, Lord Warden of the Cinque Ports, a post that dates from at least the twelfth century.

Designed and Sculpted by Gilbert Bayes (1872-1953). who was born in London where his father was an artist. As a student under Sir George Frampton and Harry Bates he became associated with the British New Sculpture movement, which focused on architectural sculpture. He worked on a number of war memorials, on Broadcasting House in Portland Place and a frieze at the former Saville Theatre, Shaftsbury Avenue, London. Bayes was President of the Royal British Society of Sculptors from 1939 to 1944.

Design Features:

The Memorial is situated in a small garden of remembrance besides the Grand Military Canal. It comprises a pillar of white marble, square in section, with faces carved in bas-relief to depict twelve servicemen from different forces and of ranks. The corners of the pillar are rounded and carved with laurel garlands. On the top of the pillar is a marble orb, with a stylised depiction of the sea made from blue mosaic complete with carved fish. On top of the orb is a bronze figure of winged Victory who holds, over her head, a medieval ship.

The memorial stands on a square marble base in the centre of what was originally designed to be a shallow circular pool, but is now planted as a flower bed. The base of the pillar used to have bronze lion-head spouts that fed water into the pool, although these are no longer in place. Around the flower bed is a wide stone pavement.

Behind the memorial is a low, curved, stone wall with the inscription and ceramic panels which have the names of the 154 from the town who died in the First World War. When first built, the wall terminated with a pier at each end and these piers now carry plaques to those who fell in subsequent wars. The wall has been extended to both sides following the curve of the original before straightening out to form short wings which end in a further set of piers.

The Inscription

The inscription is on the stone wall behind the memorial and states, simply: THESE DIED THAT WE MAY LIVE.

11. Burwash War Memorial
High Street, Burwash, Rother, East Sussex, TN19
Grade II*

Unveiled on 24th October 1920 by General Lord Horne, whose boigraphy can be found on page 142.

Designed by Sir Charles Nicholson.

Design Features:

The memorial is a hexagonal Eleanor Cross, consisting of three stages on a plinth with a double hexagonal base. The top stage has an open 'lanterne des morts' (lantern of the dead) with round-headed openings and a crenelated moulded cornice, which is topped by a cross. The middle stage has chamfered panels with shields on each face representing the Royal Navy, Royal Air Force, Royal Artillery, Cross of St George, Peace and Victory and the Arms of Sussex. The lower stage has a crenelated string-course, below which on one side is a small ogee arch with a lockable wooden opening, allowing access to the lantern mechanism. The other sides are inscribed with the names of the men from Burwash who died during the two World Wars: sixty-three in the First World War and fourteen in the Second World War.

The Story behind The Memorial:

A Burwash War Memorial Committee was established in 1917, which included the author Rudyard Kipling who lived in the parish. Designs were submitted by the architects Sir Herbert Baker and Sir Charles Nicholson. Nicholson's Eleanor Cross design was chosen, in part, because Kipling was particularly interested in lanterns commemorating the dead which he had seen in France. Kipling composed the words inscribed on the memorial and contributed to the £696 3s 5d cost of the memorial.

Kipling's 18 year old son, Lt John Kipling of the Irish Guards, was reported missing in September 1915 during the Battle of Loos, just six weeks after his 18th birthday. John Kipling's body was not found and Rudyard Kipling spent several years visiting the battlefields and meeting with comrades of his son in an attempt to find out what happened and to locate his grave. Lt John Kipling's grave was, finally, identified in 1992 and he is one of the sixty-three Burwash men commemorated on the memorial.

A unique custom is that the lantern at the top of the memorial is lit to commemorate the anniversary of the death of each Burwash man who is recorded on the monument. This was followed from 1920 onwards, except during the Second World War to comply with blackout regulations.

The Inscription

The inscription at the top of the lower stage reads REMEMBER THE MEN OF BURWASH WHO DIED FOR THEIR COUNTRY AD 1914-1919 whilst at the bottom of the lower stage is the inscription THEIR NAME LIVETH FOR EVERMORE with the dates 1939-1945 and a cross inscribed on one side of the plinth.

Two different aspects of The Burwash Memorial (previous page)

12. Ditchling War Memorial

Junction of West Street and Lodge Hill Lane, Ditchling,
Lewes, East Sussex BN6
Grade II*

Unveiled on 21st August 1919 by Colonel Attree (who had lost his only son in the war) and the dedication was made by Canon J J Mallaby from nearby Keymer, the Treasurer of Chichester Cathedral.

Designed by Eric Gill

Sculpted by Gill's principal assistant, Joseph Cribb.

Design Features:

The memorial is constructed from Portland stone, encompassing a tall pillar, 8ft (2.6m) high, which tapers towards the top. It stands on a plinth that was designed as a seat, which stands on a base with moulded edges.

The Story behind The Memorial:

The memorial was commissioned by the village, which had formed a war memorial committee, and who were determined to get members of the local flourishing arts and crafts scene involved. Eric Gill had moved to Ditchling in 1907 and he was asked to oversee the project along with his assistant Joseph Cribb.

Local people helped to level the site and the committee wanted to make the setting of the memorial 'simple, natural and homely', and they hoped that children would play on the green, and enable people to sit on the memorial seat around the base.

The Inscription

At the top of the east face of the pillar is a simple carved cross with an inscription underneath, which reads: - REMEMBER / (NAMES)/ 1914-1918. The south face also has the same simple carved cross and inscription which reads REMEMBER/ (NAMES)/ 1939-1945. Around the plinth the inscription reads GREATER LOVE HATH NO / MAN THAN THIS THAT A/ MAN LAY DOWN HIS LIFE/ FOR HIS FRIENDS. There are 20 First World War names on the memorial, and after the Second World War, 13 names from that conflict were added.

13. Lewes War Memorial

Junction of High Street and Market Street, Lewes, East Sussex, BN7

Grade II*

Unveiled on 9th September 1922 by Major General Sir Henry Crichton Sclater. Sclater was a career soldier having been commissioned into the Royal Artillery in 1875 and seeing service, as a staff officer, in the Nile expedition 1884-5 and the Second Boer War 1899-1902. After the Boer War, he became Director of Artillery at the War Office, before taking up commands in India. From 1914 to 1916 Sclater was Adjutant-General to the Forces and a member of the Army Council, and from 1916 to 1919 he was General Officer Commanding-in-Chief for Southern Command. Sclater was a major landowner in East Sussex. The dedication of the memorial was by the Bishop of Lewes.

Sculptor: Vernon March (1891-1930) was born in Hull, the ninth of nine children, and the family moved to London. At the age of 16 he became one of the youngest exhibitors at the Royal Academy of Arts, London, where he displayed the sculpture -'Psyche'- which was purchased on the third day. Vernon's older brother, Sydney, designed and sculpted the Bromley War Memorial, and more information about the March family appears on page 38..

Vernon March died of pneumonia in 1930 at the age of 38.

Design Features:

The memorial is made from Portland stone with a bronze figure representing Victory. The dramatic bronze statue faces towards Flanders and stands on a globe which, in turn, sits on a truncated stone obelisk which is inscribed with the word LIBERTY. Victory is soaring and in her right hand which is raised she holds a laurel wreath.

The plinth is cruciform in shape with quadrants of steps between the piers. On the west face there is a seated bronze, winged, figure holding a torch, which represents Liberty, while on the east face another seated figure, also winged, represents Peace. This latter figure has a dove on her left shoulder and her right arm rests on a wreathed bronze shield.

234

The Story behind The Memorial:

A request for designs for a war memorial was initiated on 1st August 1919 and Vernon March's design was chosen on 19th September in the same year, a remarkably short consultation period. The memorial was built quickly, although to the embarrassment of the town and its Council, the invoice was not fully paid until 1924. Although the quotation from Churchill was added in 1950 it was not until 1st March 1981 that the memorial was rededicated, after the addition of the names of those who died in the Second World War.

The Inscription

The principal inscription is on a wreathed bronze shield on the south east angle and reads: IN MEMORY OF THE MEN OF LEWES WHO DIED FOR THEIR COUNTRY AND FOR MANKIND IN THE GREAT WAR 1914 1918. The other diagonals have matching shields which carry the names of 251 men from Lewes who died in the First World War. The inscription THIS WAS THEIR FINEST HOUR was added to the obelisk after the Second World War as was the inscription: LIKEWISE REMEMBER THOSE OF THIS TOWN WHO GAVE THEIR LIVES IN THE WAR 1939-1945. Plaques on the north and south faces of the memorial carry the names of the 126 people from the town who died in the Second World War.

14. Worthing War Memorial
The corner of Chapel Road and Stoke Abbott Road Worthing BN11
Grade II

Unveiled Unveiled on 11th April 1921, when around 7,000 people attended, including local business people who had closed for the day. The memorial was unveiled by Field Marshall Sir William Robertson with a military Guard of Honour provided by the Horsham (West Sussex) based 4th Battalion of the Royal Sussex Regiment. The unveiling commenced at 3pm, allowing time for Sir William to return to London by train.

The memorial was accepted on behalf of Worthing by the Mayor of Worthing, Alderman Mrs Chapman, J.P. The Regular Artillery Battery at Brighton provided two cornet players to sound The Last Post. with their Lieutenant asking for 6/10d to cover their expenses.

Designed by Whitehead and Sons Ltd of London, who were commissioned to make the bronze figure for £500. The company would not specify the name of the artist within their design department, as they believed it to be a collective endeavour.

The pedestal was provided by Monumental Mason and Sculptors in North Street, Worthing for a cost of £400.

Design Features:

A Portland stone plinth sits beneath a soldier made from bronze, holding a rifle in his left hand and his helmet aloft with his right hand, and the base is covered with the debris of war.

The plinth has a low chain around its base with a wreath at the top of each face. The soldier is the same figure that is used on memorials in Chertsey, Ebbw Vale, Truro and the King Edward Street Post Office in London.

The Story behind The Memorial:

In October 1919, after the local council abandoned a fund-raising scheme to build a memorial, the Worthing Gazette (today the Worthing Herald) set up the Worthing War Memorial Gazette Shilling Fund, and registered it as an official War Charity.

By November 1920 enough money had been raised to meet the anticipated cost of £1,000 for the memorial, and the council could start planning the build.

236

The agreed location for the memorial was in the garden of Tudor Lodge, with the council having purchased the property in June 1920 as temporary council offices. The choice of location was generally applauded by donors to the fund-raising scheme.

Whilst the bronze statute was designed and made in London, it was decided that the pedestal should be supplied by a local trader, who was based just a few hundred yards from where the memorial was to be built.

After settling all other administration fees, and with £16 8s 2d remaining in The Shilling Fund, it was agreed to donate it to Worthing Hospital towards its Maternity Extension fund.

The memorial was moved slightly in 1933, when Worthing built their new Town Hall in Chapel Road.

The Inscription

The surnames and initials of over 660 local men who had died in the First World War cover all four sides of the of the pedestal column.
At the top of its base, and in the northerly direction to which the soldier faces, it reads OUR GLORIOUS DEAD 1914 – 1918 DUTY NOBLY DONE
Below this reads ALSO IN MEMORY OF THOSE WHO FELL IN THE WAR 1939 – 1945. With the other three sides carries names of those fallen during this conflict.
The top of the base to the back of the soldier reads THIS MEMORIAL WAS ERECTED BY PUBLIC CONSCRIPTION RAISED THROUGH THE WORTHING GAZETTE. IT WAS UNVEILED BY Field-Marshall Sir William Robertson B.A.R.T., G.C.B ON 11TH APRIL 1921.
On another facing of the base, there is also reference to OTHER CONFLICTS, bearing the names of 3 men.

War Memorials Trust

The Charity that helps protect and conserve War Memorials

England's estimated 85,000 war memorials take on a huge variety of forms and styles reflecting each community's response to loss and their experience of conflict. The diversity is something to cherish and recognition of those war memorials of the highest quality through the listing processes is

wonderful protection to help their long-term preservation. This book offers a chance to explore some of these memorials and find out what makes them so special.

Often people assume that just being a war memorial makes something protected. This is not the case. War memorials have no specific legal protection outside of planning legislation, but rely on communities and individuals to look after them. At times moral pressure is the strongest form of protection as people's emotional response to their war memorials can help preserve them.

As the charity that helps protect and conserve war memorials across the UK, War Memorials Trust deals on a daily basis with concerns about war memorials.

The Trust offers a free-of-charge advice service to anyone with a war memorial enquiry and its website has an array of information for those looking to find out more. Often those dealing with war memorials may be unfamiliar not just with potential legal protections but also how to deal with historic structures or objects, the materials from which they are constructed and the implications of those considerations on appropriate maintenance.

Underpinning all War Memorials Trust's work is best conservation practice. Its advice and guidance is based on promoting the best-known ways to manage historic structures and objects to preserve this vital part of our shared heritage. Sometimes works are proposed to war memorials with the best of intentions but the methods suggested will cause irreversible harm. War Memorials Trust seeks to support the custodians of our war memorials across the country to avoid such situations.

Alongside its advice, the Trust manages grant schemes that facilitate repair and conservation projects. During the centenary of World War I the charity distributed an additional, one-off £2million in government funding for grants through the First World War Memorials Programme alongside the funding its raises from public donations. The centenary sparked an increased interest in our war memorials; stimulated before that date by genealogical research. Many more communities sought to address the condition of their war memorials ensuring a significant increase in grants awarded ranging from £100 to £100,000.

Many of those memorials helped in this period have been listed war memorials including the Grade I listed Sledmere Eleanor Cross in East Yorkshire (right) and Alcester War Memorial Town Hall in Warwickshire as well as the Grade II* Crich Stand lighthouse in Derbyshire.

The centenary also saw the launch of War Memorials Online, a website seeking to create a greater understanding of the condition of war memorials across the UK.

Anyone can register online and start updating information, sharing photographs and, most importantly, adding condition information on war memorials. Through this, those war memorials in greatest need can be identified and efforts made to help repair and conserve them.

War Memorials Trust is a registered charity that relies on voluntary donations and the subscriptions of its members to protect and conserve war memorials. Anyone interested in supporting its work is encouraged to get involved and make their contribution to protecting and conserving the UK's war memorial heritage.

To help create a picture of the condition of war memorials across the UK make your contribution to War Memorials Online. You can upload information, photographs and provide a condition update at www.warmemorialsonline.org.uk.

To find out about grants, donate or join the charity or find out more about our volunteering and educational activities visit www.warmemorials.org.

Frances Moreton

Director

War Memorials Trust

SOUTH

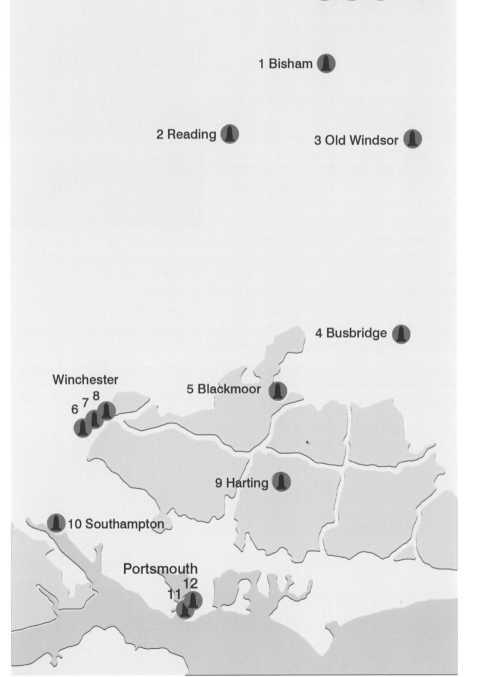

1 Bisham

2 Reading

3 Old Windsor

4 Busbridge

Winchester

6 7 8

5 Blackmoor

9 Harting

10 Southampton

Portsmouth

11 12

CONTENTS

Map reference and Memorial Name   **Page**

1. Bisham War Memorial

Junction of Marlow Road and Temple Lane, Bisham, Berkshire, SL7

Grade II*

Unveiled on 18th June 1919 by the Vicar of Bisham and the Bishop of Buckingham after an evening service in All Saints Church.

Designed and Sculpted by Eric Gill.

Design Features:

This Portland stone memorial consists of a tapering and chamfered shaft which is almost round at the bottom with a calvary cross at the top.

The shaft stands on a plain, square base. Whilst there is a canopy over the figure of Christ this is not a 'traditional' suffering Christ; this depiction shows a strong and triumphant Romanesque figure.

The Story behind The Memorial:

Lady Maisie Kelly was the main moving force in the creation of this memorial, which was initially to be dedicated to her brother, Frederick Septimus Kelly who had been killed on the Somme aged 35. Kelly was a musician and composer who had rowed for Britain in the 1908 Olympic Games. He was a Lieutenant-Commander in the Royal Naval Volunteer Reserve, although fighting as an infantryman because the Royal Navy initially had so many men in their reserve forces that they did not have enough positions on ships for them, so two divisions were sent to fight as infantry.

Lady Kelly subsequently agreed to include the names of the 14 men from Bisham who had died in the First World War, and it was she who commissioned Eric Gill to design the memorial.

The re-dedication to include the names of those from the area who died in the Second World War was in 1950.

In 1961 an Army crane accidentally demolished the memorial but it was fully restored.

The Inscription

Above the figure of Christ is inscribed INRI [an abbreviation of the Latin for Jesus of Nazareth King of the Jews]. The inscription on the front face of the shaft reads: JESU MY STRENGTH AND MY REDEEMER. On the right of the shaft the inscription is: REMEMBER F S KELLY DSC BISHAM GRANGE + NOV. 13.1916 REMEMBER LIKEWISE HIS COMRADES IN ARMS OF THIS COUNTRYSIDE with this inscription are the names of local men in date order of their deaths. The inscription of the left side of the shaft reads: ERECTED IN MEMORY OF A MOST BELOVED BROTHER LIEUT. COMMDR. FREDERICK SEPTIMUS KELLY DSC HOOD BATTLN. RYL. NAVAL DIVN. WHO FELL AT THE TAKING OF BEAUCOURT SUR ANCRE AFTER SERVING THROUGHOUT THE GALLIPOLI CAMPAIGN REMEMBER ALSO - seven names - in date order of those from the local community who died in the Second World War. On the base of the memorial is the inscription: HERE WAS A ROYAL FELOWSHIP OF DEATH – a quotation from Shakespeare's Henry V.

Bisham War Memorial
(left) previous page

Beaumont College
War Memorial (below)
next page

2. Beaumont College
Burfield Old Road, Windsor, Berkshire, SL4
Grade II*

Unveiled on 13th November 1921 by General Sir George MacDonough, a former pupil of the school, who had been a staff officer at the start of the First World War and was General Sir John French's Chief Intelligence officer. Later in the war, MacDonough was to become Director of Military Intelligence despite facing prejudice because of his Catholic faith and a tendency to extreme shyness.

Designed by Sir Giles Gilbert Scott and his younger brother, Major Adrian Gilbert Scott MC. Adrian (1882-1963). He was an ecclesiastical architect and worked with his brother on a number of projects, including the Liverpool Anglican Cathedral.

Sculpted by Miss Francis Bessie Burlison (1875-1974), who was born in London, where her father made stained glass windows. She was originally educated as a governess, but later attended the Slade School of Fine Art. She first exhibited with The Society of Lady Artists in 1898.

Design Features:

The memorial, rising to some 50ft (15m), consists of an open-air altar and calvary. The altar tops a four stepped podium and includes seays at the side for Mass celebrants. Above the altar is a large arched opening in which there is a stone cross bearing a bronze life-sized figure of Christ. The memorial carries bronze panels with the names of the 132 former pupils who paid the ultimate price in the First World War, together with an additional plaque which was added in 1948 with names of the 90 who died in the Second World War.

The Story behind The Memorial:

Beaumont College had been a Jesuit public school for almost 100 years at the time of the First World War and both Giles Gilbert Scott and his brother Adrian, who collaborated on the design, were former pupils. Cardinal Bourne the Archbishop of Westminster performed the dedication of the memorial. The 1948 re-dedication, when the Second World War plaques were added, was conducted by Bishop Chichester, Headmaster and Rector of Beaumont. The majority of those named on the Second World War panel served in the Royal Air Force and include five Americans, three who served with Special Operations Executive and the French Resistance. The school closed in 1967 and the building is now an hotel and conference centre known as the De Vere Beaumont Estate. Former pupils of Beaumont College attend a service at the memorial each year on Remembrance Sunday.

The Inscription

There is a Latin inscription on the memorial – REQVIEM AETERNAM DONNA EIS DIMINE – "Lord grant them eternal peace". The names on the plaques include a father and son and seven sets of brothers, as well as six French soldiers and two Americans, one of whom, Harry Butters RFA, was the first of many Americans who joined the British Army before the United States became involved in the war.

3. The Royal Berkshire Regiment Cenotaph

Brook Barracks, Oxford Road, Reading, RG30

Grade II*

Unveiled on 13th September 1921 by Major-General ET Dickson, Colonel of the Royal Berkshire Regiment, who had been a professional soldier and served as Inspector of Infantry from 1914 to 1916.

Designed by Sir Edwin Lutyens.

Sculpted by Eric R. Broadbent who carried out a lot of work on Lutyens designs, and whose brief biographical details appear in the Royal Naval Division Memorial on page 186.

Design Features:

The design of the memorial is a half-size copy of Lutyens' Cenotaph in London. Although Lutyens always refused to allow his design for the Stone of Sacrifice to be constructed other than at full scale, he did allow this memorial to be reduced to half size at several sites. Unlike the Cenotaph in Whitehall, this memorial includes an urn on the top, which is the same style as the one on the gate piers of the Arch of Remembrance he designed in Leicester. This memorial also includes a painted stone flag on each of the two longer faces.

The memorial stands on a rectangular stone three stepped platform. The stone urn stands on four short pillars on top of the tomb chest, which in turn sits on a tapering stone shaft. At either end of the shaft are carved stone bosses with suspended laurels, whilst on each side of the memorial are carved and painted stone flags on flagpoles. Around the top of each of the flagpoles is a laurel wreath. The flag on the west side of the memorial is the King's Colour, whilst on the opposite side is the regimental colour.

The Story behind The Memorial:

The original estimate of the cost of the memorial, which was built by Messrs GE Wallis and Sons Ltd of London and Maidstone, was £2,500 although the actual cost exceeded this by £500, which was raised by a further collection from past and present members of the regiment. The memorial is not on its original site having been moved a few yards in 1932

The Inscription

A niche on the north side of the memorial contains the names of the fallen, along with a laurel wreath above which is the inscription: MCMXIV + MCMXVIII and below which is the inscription: TO THE MEMORY OF OFFICERS WARRANT OFFICERS NON COMMISSIONED OFFICERS AND MEN OF THE ROYAL BERKSHIRE REGIMENT. Below the corresponding wreath on the opposite side is the inscription: THIS MEMORIAL WAS ERECTED BY PAST AND PRESENT OFFICERS AND MEN OF THE ROYAL BERKSHIRE REGIMENT AND THEIR RELATIVES IN MEMORY OF THE 353 OFFICERS AND 6375 OTHER RANKS OF THE REGIMENT WHO FELL IN THE GREAT WAR 1914-1918 RE-DEDICATED TO THE MEMORY OF THE 93 OFFICERS AND 974 OTHER RANKS OF THE REGIMENT WHO FELL IN THE SECOND WORLD WAR 1939-1945.

The Royal Berkshire Regiment Cenotaph
previous page

Break of Day in the Trenches

Private Isaac Rosenberg
(Died 1st April 1918. Age 27)

"I've been forbidden to send poems home,
as the censor won't be bothered
with going through such rubbish"

4. Busbridge War Memorial
Churchyard of St John the Baptist, Brighton Road, Busbridge, GU7
Grade II*

Unveiled on 23rd July 1922 by General Sir George Monro 1st Baronet, who was a regular soldier and fought in the Second Boer War.

At the start of the First World War he was General Officer Commanding 2nd Division, and by July 1915 he had been promoted to General-Officer-Commanding Third Army. In 1916 he was Commander First British Army in France, before being made Commander-in-Chief, India, which included responsibility for the Mesopotamia campaign. Munro was to become Governor of Gibraltar in 1923.

Designed by Sir Edwin Lutyens.

Design Features:

The memorial is Lutyens' simple slender, tapering 'war cross design', 23ft (7m) tall, a lozenge shaped shaft and short cross arms. The shaft is linked to the base by stop chamfers and cyma moulding, and it stands on a base of four stepped rectangular blocks of unequal heights which, themselves, stand on a square platform of three low steps. The memorial is in the north-west corner of the parish churchyard, in a prominent position, where it overlooks the junction of Brighton Road and Hambledon Road.

The Story behind The Memorial:

Lutyens designed 15 'war crosses' which are all very similar in design; the first to be erected was Miserden in Gloucestershire in 1920 and the last was in 1925 in York.

Lutyens had a connection with Busbridge through Gertrude Jekyll, the Scottish garden designer and artist, who was both a friend and business collaborator. Lutyens and Jekyll worked together on a number of house and garden designs, and he had had designed Jekyll's house on the outskirts of Busbridge, together with memorials in the graveyard of St John the Baptist to members of Gertrude Jekyll's family. The memorial does not have names of those killed in either World War, with the names being recorded on a plaque in the church.

The Inscription

On the largest block on the base in incised: MCMXIV MCMXIX (1914-1919) THEY COUNTED NOT THEIR LIVES DEAR UNTO THEMSELVES to which MCMXXXIX MCMXXXXV (1939-1945) was added later.

5. Blackmoor War Memorial Cloister, Cross and Fountain

Blackmoor Road, Blackmoor, Hampshire, GU33　　　　**Grade II***

Unveiled in 1920　　　　　　　　**Designed by** Sir Herbert Baker.

Sculpted by Sir Charles Wheeler (1892-1974), who was born in Staffordshire, and studied at Wolverhampton College of Art between 1908 and 1912, when he won a scholarship to the Royal College of Art.　Wheeler was unfit for military service during the First World War and, instead, was involved in the modelling of artificial limbs for amputees. Wheeler's major works included the doors at the Bank of England in London, as well as several other works for Sir Herbert Baker. Wheeler was a Fellow of the Royal Academy from 1940, and was the first sculptor to hold the presidency of that body, which he did from 1956 to 1966.

Design Features:

The memorial is between the school and school house, and the Church of St Matthew on the north side of the road through Blackmoor. The building takes the form of a three-sided arcaded cloister open to the south. It is constructed from a heavy timber frame with a Bargate stone wall to the rear. The roof comprises Horsham slates and each side ends with a gable.

A Celtic Cross stands at the centre of the garden. The cross rises from a moulded collar which is on top of an octagonal shaft. The moulded foot of the cross shaft is encircled by low-relief carvings and stands on an octagonal plinth which, in turn, stands on a three-stepped octagonal base.

Bronze plaques are fixed to the rear (north) wall of the cloister. The western-most and eastern-most plaques are square, whilst the two plaques either side of the central fountain have semi-circular heads. The 'War' plaque is ornamented with a leafless tree, whilst the 'Peace' plaque is ornamented with a tree in full leaf with blossoms. In the centre of the north wall a niche houses the fountain, with a rose encircled by a laurel wreath cast in low relief above the dedication to the men of the village, and a small lion's head for the water spout.

The walkway in the cloister is paved in stone and there is a low bench to the rear wall, which is broken only by the semi-circular drain for the fountain.

The Story behind The Memorial:

The memorial was commissioned by Lord and Lady Selbourne in memory of their son, the Honourable Robert Stafford Arthur Palmer, who was a Captain in the Hampshire Regiment and was killed in action in Mesopotamia in January 1916. Lord Selbourne was a Liberal politician who had previously held office as First Lord of the Admiralty and High Commissioner to South Africa. From May 1915 to July 1916 he was President of the Board of Agriculture. As well as Captain Palmer, the memorial commemorates the local men killed in the First World War and, subsequently, the Second World War. The inclusion of a fountain was intended to encourage children from the adjacent school to go to the memorial so that their "… daily presence was to provide animation and lively activity, uniting the dead and the living future of the village." The memorial received a grant from War Memorials Trust in 2009 and was re-dedicated in 2010.

The Inscription

The inscription around the circular head of the cross reads: TRULY THERE IS A GOD THAT JUDGETH THE EARTH.

The inscriptions on the various plaques are as follows:

(North, far left) REMEMBER CHILDREN THE GLORY AND THE SADNESS OF WAR THE COURAGE OF THE MEN & THE SORROW AND SUFFERING OF ALL THE PEOPLE

(North, left) + WAR + IN THE HAND OF THE LORD THERE IS A CUP & THE WINE IS RED IT IS FULL MIXED AND HE POURETH OUT OF THE SAME + AS FOR THE DREGS THEREOF ALL THE UNGODLY OF THE EARTH SHALL DRINK THEM AND LAP THEM UP

(North, fountain) CHILDREN REMEMBER THE NAMES OF THE MEN FROM THIS VILLAGE WHO FEARLESSLY GAVE THEIR LIVES FOR THEIR COUNTRY IN THE WAR OF 1914-1918 – the names of the 36 men from the village who died in the First World War are included on this plaque.

(North, right) + PEACE + BLESSED ARE THE PEACE MAKERS FOR THEY SHALL BE CALLED THE CHILDREN OF GOD. ACCOUNT NOW BY SELF WITH GOD BE AT PEACE THEREBY GOOD SHALL COME UNTO THEE THERE IS NO PEACE SAITH MY GOD TO THE WICKED

(North, far right) IN MEMORY OF ROBERT STAFFORD ARTHUR PALMER KILLED IN BATTLE HIS PARENTS HAVE CAUSED THIS CLOISTER AND FOUNTAIN TO BE MADE

(East) 1939-1945 ALSO IN SACRED MEMORY OF THOSE MEN FROM BLACKMOOR WHO GAVE THEIR LIVES IN THE SECOND WORLD WAR GREATER LOVE HATH NO MAN THAN THIS – the names of 8 men from the village who died in the Second World War are included on this plaque.

(West) This plaque was added in 2010 when a further 6 names from the First World War and a further 4 from the Second World War were added to the memorial IN SACRED MEMORY/ OF THOSE MEN FROM THIS PARISH WHO ALSO GAVE THEIR LIVES IN TWO WORLD WARS 1914 – 1918 1939 – 1945 WE WILL REMEMBER THEM.

6. The Hampshire, Isle of Wight and Winchester War Memorial

The Close, Great Minster Street, Winchester, Hampshire, SO23

Grade II*

Unveiled on 31st October 1921 by Major-General Seely M.P. who was Lord Lieutenant of Hampshire, who owned substantial land on the Isle of Wight and in London. He was a career soldier and a politician, who was elected initially for the Conservative Party and later as a Liberal. Having seen service in the Second Boer War, he remained a Yeomanry officer, and was recalled to service at the outbreak of the First World War. Seely was Secretary of State for War from 1912 to 1914, but returned to active service in France for virtually the whole of the war until he was gassed in 1918. He was the only member of the government, other than his good friend Winston Churchill, to see active service during the war, and his nickname in the Army was 'Galloping Jack', for leading a cavalry charge in France in March 1918 at the head of a thousand Canadian cavalrymen. Upon returning to London in 1918, he became Parliamentary Secretary to the then Minister of Munitions – Winston Churchill. Seely had lost his eldest son during the war. The dedication was carried out by the Dean of Winchester.

Designed by Sir Herbert Baker.

Design Features:

The memorial stands outside the west end of Winchester Cathedral, and comprises a tall memorial wheel-head cross, which rises from a moulded collar on an octagonal cross shaft. The circle of the wheel-head is decorated with roses and lilies to represent England and France, and this imagery trails down the Latin cross and onto the shaft. The cross shaft ends in a moulded foot and around the top of which are a series of coats of arms – Winchester City, the Hampshire Regiment, Hampshire County Council and the Isle of Wight. The west face of the bottom of the cross shaft is inscribed 1914 + 1919 whilst on the east face there is the inscription 1939 + 1945.

The cross shaft stands on octagonal base with two stages, and the top stage takes the form of an octagonal drum with a shallow circular head. The lower stage of the base carries the structure from the highest step to the level of the forecourt below. From either side of the inscription on the lower stage are blocks of four stages dying back to the uppermost stage, which extends from the base into the forecourt. Each of these blocks carries a large bronze wreath and decorations of small roses. The surface in front of the memorial incorporates the Ypres Cloth Hall stone which is carved with the Cross of Lorraine and Ypres. This stone had been brought back to Hampshire, and was part of the original Cloth Hall in Ypres, which had been completely destroyed in the fighting.

The Story behind The Memorial:

On 29th July 1918, several months before the end of the war, a meeting chaired by the Earl of Selborne approved plans for a war memorial for Hampshire and the Isle of Wight. The agreed design was a gatehouse accompanied with either a Celtic cross or menhir on the edge of the cathedral precincts. The plans for this memorial had already been drawn up by Sir Herbert Baker. The projected cost of the memorial was £20,000 and an appeal was launched to raise this sum. However, there was determined local resistance to the proposed site of the memorial and the plan was eventually dropped.

A meeting on 17th September 1920 approved a plan for a gateway and cross at the northern entrance to the cathedral. However, fund-raising did not raise sufficient money and the plan was scaled back to just the cross, which was to be built on the original site.

Sir Herbert Baker, in his capacity as one of the principal architects for the Imperial War Graves Commission, proposed that all military cemeteries should include a cross. Whilst this was agreed, a design by Sir Reginald Blomfield proved to be the universal choice over the one designed by Sir Herbert Baker. The cross used for this memorial is Baker's design, which he also incorporated into a number of other memorials.

The Inscription

Around the head of the upper of the two stages of the base is inscribed: 1914 1919 HE SHALL DELIVER THEIR SOULS FROM FALSEHOOD AND WRONG: AND DEAR SHALL THEIR BLOOD BE IN HIS SIGHT which is carved in relief. There are further inscriptions to the faces of this upper stage, on the west face: TO THE GLORY OF GOD AND IN PROUD AND GRATEFUL MEMORY OF FOUR HUNDRED AND SIXTY CITIZENS OF WINCHESTER WHO UPHELD UNDER KING GEORGE V THE TRADITIONS OF SERVICE AND SACRIFICE HANDED DOWN FROM THE DAYS OF KING ALFRED. On the east face the inscription reads: TO THE GLORY OF GOD AND IN PROUD AND GRATEFUL MEMORY OF THE UNCOUNTED HOST FROM HAMPSHIRE AND THE ISLE OF WIGHT WHO DIED FOR ENGLAND IN THE GREAT WAR WHEN SERVING IN THE NAVY THE MERCANTILE MARINE THE ARMY AND THE AIR FORCE BE MINDFUL OF THEM O LORD AND GRANT TO THEIR CHILDREN THE SAME FAITHFULNESS.

A Second World War inscription has been added to the base of this stage and this reads: AND OF THOSE WHO SO FREELY GAVE THEIR LIVES 1939-1945 REMEMBER ALSO THEIR SONS AND DAUGHTERS WHO DIED 1939-1945.

On the east side of the lower stage of the base there are dedications to the Hampshire Regiment: 1914-1919 TO SEVEN THOUSAND FIVE HUNDRED AND FORTY-ONE OF THE REGULAR, MILITIA, TERRITORIAL & SERVICE BATTALIONS OF THE HAMPSHIRE REGIMENT WHO DIED IN FLANDERS FRANCE ITALY RUSSIA, MACEDONIA PALESTINE EGYPT MESOPOTAMIA PERSIA INDIA AND SERBIA THE DARDANELLES OR WERE LOST AT SEA IN THE MEDITERRANEAN 1939-1945 TWO THOUSAND & NINETY FOUR DIED ON LAND SEA AND IN THE AIR.

There are further inscriptions to the blocks to the side of the lower section of the base:
(East face) TO SEVENTY FOUR OF THE HAMPSHIRE YEOMANRY CARABINIERS
(North face) TO THREE HUNDRED AND EIGHTY SIX OF THE ROYAL ENGINEERS AND THE HAMPSHIRE ROYAL ARTILLERY
Inscriptions on the north-east block read:
(South face) TO FORTY EIGHT OF THE ROYAL ARMY MEDICAL CORPS AND THE HAMPSHIRE ROYAL ARMY SERVICE CORPS
(East face) TO SEVEN HUNDRED AND THIRTY SEVEN OF HMS HAMPSHIRE SUNK BY A MINE OFF THE ORKNEY/ ISLANDS JUNE 5TH 1916

The Hampshire, Isle of Wight and Winchester War Memorial (left) previous pages.

King's Royal Rifle Corps War Memorial (right) and its Inscription (below) next page.

The Inscription

On the front (south) side of the pedestal is a version of the regimental badge, a Maltese Cross, on the top arm of which is a tablet inscribed: PENINSULA, surmounted by a King's crown. In the centre of the cross is a circle inscribed: THE KING'S ROYAL RIFLE CORPS. Within the circle is a stringed bugle and the figure '60'. Below the bottom arm of the cross is a tablet which is inscribed: CELER ET AUDAX [Swift and Bold]. Beneath the badge is the inscription: TO THE GLORY OF GOD AND IN MEMORY OF THE OFFICERS WARRANT OFFICERS NON-COMMISSIONED OFFICERS AND RIFLEMEN OF THE KING'S ROYAL RIFLE CORPS WHO GAVE THEIR LIVES FOR THEIR KING AND COUNTRY IN THE GREAT WAR 1914-1918 AND 1939–1945.

7. King's Royal Rifle Corps War Memorial, Winchester

Winchester Cathedral, Cathedral Close, Winchester, Hampshire, SO23

Grade II*

Unveiled on 26th May 1922 by Prince Henry, the third son of George V and Queen Mary and, himself, an officer in the King's Royal Rifle Corps. Prince Henry was accompanied by Princes Beatrice, Queen Victoria's youngest daughter and his sister Princess Mary, who had initiated the well-known Christmas present to all service personnel in 1914.

The dedication was carried out by Bishop Wood, Bishop of Winchester. The Cathedral choir was supplemented by choristers from Westminster Abbey and Christ Church, Oxford. 1,500 relatives of those from the regiment killed in the war were present, as well as representatives from each of the battalions of the Corps that had served in the war. There was also a contingent from the American Legion, acknowledging the fact that that the unit was originally formed in America.

Sculpted by John Tweed (1869-1933) who was born in Glasgow, where he studied at the Glasgow School of Art before moving to London in 1890 where he studied at the South London Technical Art School and the Royal Academy Schools.

Tweed was commissioned in 1901 to complete the portrait of the First Duke of Wellington in St Paul's Cathedral after the death of Alfred Stevens. He produced a number of war memorials after the First World War as well as this one, including the Rifle Brigade Memorial (viz page 170) and the statue of Kitchener on Horse Guards. Tweed was a close friend of Rodin and The V & A called him the 'British Rodin'.

Design Features:

The memorial comprises a Portland stone base with a single bronze figure and stands on a wide square base. The figure is of a rifleman of the King's Royal Rifle Corps in full service dress complete with knapsack, ammunition pouches and helmet, holding the barrel of his Lee-Enfield rifle in his right hand, with the butt resting on the ground.

He stands with his left leg forward, left fist clenched, and head facing frontward, as if to survey the terrain ahead of him.

The Story behind The Memorial:

The King's Royal Rifle Corps can trace its history back to the Seven Years War (1756-1763), when it was formed in Colonial America as the Royal American Regiment and trained to fight in a more mobile and open formation than the standard British infantry of the time.

For a period, the regiment was the 60th Regiment of Foot and it became known as the King's Royal Rifle Corps in 1830 when King George IV came to the throne. During the First World War the regiment had 22 battalions and served on the Western Front as well as in Macedonia and Italy. The regiment won seven Victoria Crosses and lost a total of 12, 840 men.

8. The War Cloister, Winchester College

Winchester College, College Street, Winchester, Hampshire, SO23

Grade I

Unveiled on 31st May 1924 by Prince Arthur, whose biographical details can be found on page 178 in the Royal Artillery Memorial. Relatives of the fallen and dignitaries attended, along with a guard of honour of the Winchester College Officer Training Corps and the band of the Coldstream Guards. The unveiling and dedications were pronounced by Bishop Talbot of Winchester followed by an address by Sir Edward Grey, Foreign Secretary 1905-1916.

Designed by Sir Herbert Baker

Sculpted by by Alfred Turner 1874-1940) Turner was the son of C.E. Halsey-Turner who was himself, a sculptor. Turner studied at the South London Technical Art School in Lambeth and at the Royal Academy Schools from 1895. He taught sculpture at the Central School of Arts and Crafts in London from 1907 and produced statues for private and corporate clients as well as undertaking relief work and being involved with the design of a number of war memorials. Turner was an Associate of the Royal Academy from 1922 and a full member from 1931, as well as being one of the early members of the Royal Society of British Sculptors, being a Fellow from 1923 until his death in 1940. His daughter, Winifred was also a distinguished sculptor.

Carvings by Charles Wheeler (1892-1974) whose biographical details can be found on page 234 in the Blackmoor War Memorial.

Inscription designed by R M Y Gleadowe, Art Master of Winchester College

Emblem designed by George K Gray (1880-1943) an artist who is best remembered for his designs of coinage and stained glass windows. Having studied at the Bath School of Art and the Royal College of Art, Gray served with the Artists Rifles and a camouflage unit of the Royal Engineers.

254

Garden designed by Gertrude Jekyll (1843-1932) an horticulturist and garden designer, who created over 400 gardens in the UK, Europe and the United States.

She was a prolific writer, writing over 1,000 articles and 15 books, and was one of the leading lights of the Arts and Crafts Movement, working on many house and garden designs with Sir Edwin Lutyens.

Design Features:

The memorial takes the form of a quadrangular cloister with a main entrance to the east and additional entrances at the south and south-west. There is a memorial cross sited in the garden at the centre of the cloister. The cloister building is constructed from knapped flint and Portland stone ashlar, with an oak roof covered by Purbeck stone slate. The name tablets are made from Derbyshire Hopton Wood stone, whilst the floor is laid with slabs of South African granite, Australian syenite, Canadian marble and Indian black marble.

The main entrance comprises a round-headed arch, which contains wrought-iron gates that are decorated with angels and sounding trumpets and set under a gable. A niche containing a carving of St Mary, the Patron Saint of the college, by Charles Wheeler is positioned above the arch: she stands beneath a crown and holds the Child Jesus upright in her hands.

Internally, there is a cloister arcade formed of Portland stone round-headed arches, supported on pairs of Tuscan columns and several pilasters, with gabled buttresses facing the garth. A low-chamfered stone wall or bench runs between the columns. The cloister walkway is covered by an open crown-post roof constructed of oak with tie beams supported by arched braces resting on corbels. A round-headed arched doorway at the south end of the west wall leads out to the South Africa (Boer War memorial) Gateway and Kingsgate Street.

A further arched doorway at the centre of the south wall leads to the college buildings on this side of the cloister. At each end of the east and the west cloister walks are shallow apses beneath finely-jointed ashlar hemi-domes. These four corners are dedicated to three Dominions of the British Empire, and to India.

Under each hemi-dome is a circular slab, each of which is inlaid with a national emblem in brass. In addition, there are four small gift-stones from Ypres set into the stone floor of the walkway next to Meads Gate.

The badges of 120 regiments in which Old Wykehamists served are emblazed on the corbels and tie beams of the roof and the walls of the cloister walk, which were designed by George K Gray and painted by Lawrence Turner. On the oak timbers of the roof, over the arches, are wooden angels carrying gilded symbols: a Jerusalem Cross, the double cross of Ypres, the Wooden Cross, and the War Graves cross.

There are four badges of regiments closely associated with Winchester: The Rifle Brigade, King's Royal Rifles, Hampshire Regiment, and the Royal Artillery. The spandrels of the arches surrounding the cloister garth are also carved in low relief with: the arms and badges of the four home nations; the town of Winchester; the county of Hampshire; Oxford and Cambridge; the military colleges; the Navy, Merchant Service and Royal Air Force; and notable Wykehamists who held high service during the war. The Royal Arms are positioned in front of the entrance arch to unite them all.

The Story behind The Memorial:

This memorial is the largest known private war memorial in Europe. A total of 2488 members of the Winchester College community served in the armed forces during the First World War, including teaching staff, Quiristers (choirboys), and pupils (known as Wykehamists). It is recorded that 513 died, including the Prime Minister's son, Raymond Asquith (1878-1916), who was killed during the Battle of the Somme.

As early as October 1915 a proposal for a war memorial in the form of a school hall was being discussed and, a year later, this idea had transformed into a large central gate flanked by two halls, providing space for a war museum, a new masters' common room, a new class room and a war memorial cloister. The architect Sir Herbert Baker, who had two sons at Winchester College, was commissioned to design the memorial and submitted his initial proposals in April 1918. In 1921 the larger scheme was abandoned due to lack of funds and it was decided that the memorial would be formed of the War Cloister alone. The cloister was to serve as a via sacra - a sacred way to the school precincts - and would be in addition to the colleges' three other memorials to Wykehamists who died during the Crimean War (1853-56), the Boer War (1899-1902) and to Major-General Sir Herbert Stewart (1843-1885). In addition, a new stone altar was erected in the chapel, the reredos was reconstructed, four memorial volumes printed, and provision made for the education of sons of Wykehamists who died during the war.

The foundation stone of the War Cloister was laid by Sir Edward Grey, the former Foreign Secretary and an old Wykehamist, in a ceremony on Saturday 15th July 1922. It took two years to construct and cost £65,000. A garden designed by the celebrated garden designer, Gertrude Jekyll was laid out within the cloister garth, which comprised of borders of flowers, in which roses and white lilies prevailed, set around four grass lawns (the borders were replanted in the 1960s and 2014). A memorial cross, flanked by crusaders, was erected at the centre of the garth to the design of the sculptor Alfred Turner RA.

The War Cloister became integrated into college life, and a tradition was adopted whereby pupils and staff would raise their hats upon entering the cloister in reverence and memory of those that died. After the Second World War, the names of old Wykehamists that lost their lives during the conflict were inscribed on panels attached to the insides of the pillars of the cloister, facing those commemorated in the Great War. The War Cloister was re-dedicated by Bishop Haigh of Winchester on 14th November 1948.

The Inscription

On either side of the main entrance are Latin inscriptions which commemorate the laying of the foundation stone and the opening of the War Cloister. In the north wall, close to the north-east angle, is a Craftsmen's Stone, which is inscribed with the craftsmen's names in Latin. The last sentence is translated: NOT FOR THEE, BUT FOR GOD AND THE DEAD

The cloister walk is encircled by a description in Lombardic style with lettering by R M Y Gleadowe, the art master of the college, and it reads THANKS BE TO GOD FOR THE SERVICE OF THESE FIVE HUNDRED WYKEHAMISTS, WHO WERE FOUND FAITHFUL UNTO DEATH AMID THE MANIFOLD CHANCES OF THE GREAT WAR. IN THE DAY OF BATTLE THEY FORGAT NOT GOD, WHO CREATED THEM TO DO HIS WILL, NOR THEIR COUNTRY, THE STRONGHOLD OF FREEDOM, NOR THEIR SCHOOL, THE MOTHER OF GODLINESS AND DISCIPLINE. STRONG IN

THIS THREEFOLD FAITH THEY WENT FORTH FROM HOME AND KINDRED TO THE BATTLEFIELDS OF THE WORLD AND, TREADING THE PATH OF DUTY AND SACRIFICE, LAID DOWN THEIR LIVES FOR MANKIND. THOU, THEREFORE, FOR WHOM THEY DIED, SEEK NOT THINE OWN, BUT SERVE AS THEY SERVED, AND IN PEACE OR IN WAR BEAR THYSELF EVER AS CHRIST'S SOLDIER, GENTLE IN ALL THINGS, VALIANT IN ACTION, STEADFAST IN ADVERSITY.

On each side of the cloister are groups of name tablets of Derbyshire Hopton Wood stone attached to the walls, which contain the names of the fallen of the First World War. The tablets are set in moulded surrounds with the names of the relevant battles or campaigns at the centre, beneath carved bas-reliefs. These are headed: ON THE SEAS; FRANCE FLANDERS (four panels); GALLIPOLI/ MACEDONIA/ ITALY/ MURMANSK/ARCHANGEL (one panel); EGYPT/ PALESTINE/ MESOPOTAMIA (one panel); TSING-TAU/ SIBERIA/ N.W. FRONTIER INDIA/ BALUCHISTAN/ PERSIA/ ADEN/ E.AFRICA/ S.W.AFRICA/ CAMEROONS (one panel). The name tablets are headed CAME TO WINCHESTER, followed by the year and names, commencing in 1868. The penultimate panel, ending in 1913, continues with DIED SINCE THE WAR in italics, followed by five names. The last tablet is headed ASSISTANT MASTER, followed by one name, and then QUIRISTERS, followed by six names.

The fallen of the Second World War are commemorated by twelve name tablets attached to the inside pilasters of the cloister arcade, with an inscription in the Celtic cross beneath the precursory panel. The name tablets are headed with years only, starting with 1913, and followed by names. On the last tablet, the last year – 1938 - is followed by ASSISTANT MASTER (one name), QUIRISTERS (three names) and REPORTED SINCE THE WAR (six names).

In the centre of the garden is a Celtic Cross by Alfred Turner, which is on the top of an octagonal stone column, with a moulded base resting on a two-tier octagonal plinth and two-tiered stepped base. On the top-tier of the plinth is a Latin inscription, which is translated as: BE FAITHFUL UNTIL DEATH AND I WILL GIVE THEE A CROWN OF LIFE.

9. Harting War Memorial

St Mary & St Gabriel Churchyard, Junction of The Street and Cow Lane,
Harting, West Sussex, GU31   Grade II*

Unveiled on 3rd July 1921 by the Venerable Archdeacon of Chichester.

Designed and Sculpted by Eric Gill, assisted by Desmond Chute who studied at The Slade and who looked upon Gill as a brother. In 1927 Chute became a Catholic priest.

Design Features:

The memorial sits on a single-stepped base on top of which is a plinth and a tall, tapering, slim cross some 20ft (6m) tall. The upper parts of both the shaft and the cross head are chamfered at the corners. The lower part of the cross shaft has low relief elongated cartouches which contain the inscriptions.

On two sides these cartouches incorporate small circular cartouches at the top. Below the cartouches on all four sides are smaller arched panels, on which are found relief carvings of Saint George, Saint Patrick, Saint Andrew and Saint David.

Saint George is in a typical pose, on a rearing horse as he seeks to spear a dragon with talons and a long tongue. Saint Patrick has a more religious air, haloed and in fine robes, he stands with a crosier in his left hand, while his right hand is raised in a blessing.

A haloed Saint Andrew is depicted standing in a boat that has a Scottish flag for a sail; he is shown raising both arms, while a haloed fisherman throws his net into a sea full of fishes. Saint David, like Saint Patrick, holds a crosier in his left hand, but he also holds a cross in his right hand as a congregation gathers to pray with him.

The Story behind The Memorial:

The memorial was commissioned by Rev A J Roberts of South Harting in March 1919. It had been Gill's original intention that the reliefs on the four panels were to represent the Nativity, the Crucifixion, the Entombment and the Resurrection, before his final design of the four patron saints.

Gill was a Roman Catholic and perhaps his original design lent more towards Catholicism than Anglicanism. The total cost of the memorial was £434 8s 11d.

The Inscription

The principal inscription is on the same side as the image of Saint Patrick and reads:
AND THUS THEY DIED LEAVING THEIR DEATHS FOR AN EXAMPLE OF A NOBLE COURAGE AND A MEMORIAL OF VIRTUENOT ONLY UNTO YOUNG MEN BUT UNTO ALL THEIR NATION – II MACC.VI.31.

Two other faces have the names of those from the area who died in the two world wars. One face is inscribed: REMEMBER THESE MEN WHO GAVE THEIR LIVES IN THE WAR OF 1914 TO 1919 and another face is inscribed AND IN 1939-1945.

Dulce et Decorum Est

Lt. Wilfred Owen (Died 4th November 1918. Age 23)

"I have not seen any dead. I have done worse. By the dank air I have perceived it, and in the darkness felt…."

Bent double, like old beggars under sacks,
Knock kneed, coughing like hags, we cursed through sludge,
Till on the haunting flares we turned our backs
And towards our distant rest we began to trudge.
Men marched asleep. Many had lost their boots
But limped on, blood shod. All went lame; all blind;
Drunk with fatigue; deaf even to the hoots
Of tired, outstripped Five-Nines that dropped behind.

The torn fields of France
What do you see in our eyes
At the shrieking iron and flame
Hurled through still heavens?
Poppies whose roots are in man's veins

Drop, and are ever dropping:
But mine in my ear is safe –
Just a little white with the dust.

10. Southampton Cenotaph

Watts Park, Above Bar Street, Southampton SO14

Grade I

Unveiled by Major General JEB Seely, in his capacity as Lord Lieutenant of Hampshire, on 6th November 1920. His Biographical details can be found on page 250 in the Southampton Cenotaph. The dedication of the memorial was carried out by the Right Reverend Edward Stuart, Bishop of Winchester.

Designed by Sir Edwin Lutyens.

Design Features:

The memorial is in the form of a cenotaph, comprising a five-tier tapering stone pylon topped by a stone sarcophagus, on which lies an effigy of a dead soldier. To the west side of the pylon is a Stone of Remembrance, whilst to the north and south sides are two shorter single pier pillars topped with fir cones. Fir cones are a symbol of eternity and the pillars are linked to the pylon by a wall and a seat. The pedestal of the pylon has recessed panels on the north and south sides, which carry the names of 1,793 people killed in the First World War. An additional Roll of Honour was added to the shoulder of the pylon in 1921 with 203 names, and an additional name was added in 1922.

There are various sculpted details included on the central pylon, the eastern face of which carries a Cross of Sacrifice, whilst the east and west faces of the third tier bears the arms of the City of Southampton. Lions are depicted on the shoulders of the north and south sides of the fourth tier, and just below the sarcophagus are wreaths which enclose emblems of the Army, Navy, Merchant Marine and Air Force.

In 2011 eight glass panels set in Portland stone were added to the memorial – four to each side – because the weather was beginning to erode the names on the main memorial. These panels contain the names of those who fell in the First and Second World Wars, the Malayan Emergency, the Korean War and the Mau Mau Uprising.

The Story behind The Memorial:

A public meeting held in Southampton shortly after the end of the First World War resolved that a war memorial be created to perpetuate the memory of those who had died in the Great War. The Lord Mayor, Alderman Sidney J Kimber, was appointed both Chairman and Treasurer of a committee, and it was decided that "The people of Southampton would like to point to some really fine outstanding memorial in the best position of the town, always to remind them of the sacrifices made for them and others."

Lutyens was engaged at the suggestion of a local architect and immediately rejected the site on Asylum Green which had initially been suggested by the city. Lutyens instead, suggested Watts Park and designed a Stone of Remembrance flanked by arches at the eastern and western entrances to the park. This design was rejected by the committee because it was thought that the cost may exceed the £10,000 budget. Lutyens redrew his plans for a more modest memorial which was approved in September 1919. Tenders were sought and Messrs Holloway Bros of Westminster submitted a price of £8,500 in December 1919.

The memorial includes the names of a number of women who had died while serving with the Merchant Navy and Queen Marys Army Auxiliary Corps.

The public collection towards the cost of the memorial raised £9,485 17s 3d. After deducting all costs a balance of £101 18s 11d remained, which was donated to the Hampshire County and Isle of Wight War Memorial Fund.

The Inscription

OUR GLORIOUS DEAD is carved into the lower tier on the eastern face of the pylon whist THEIR NAME LIVETH FOR EVERMORE is inscribed into the west face of the Stone of Remembrance.

11. City of Portsmouth War Memorial

Guildhall Square, Portsmouth PO1   **Grade II***

Unveiled on 19th October 1921 Prince Arthur, Duke of Connaught, whose biographical details can be found on page 178 in the Royal Artillery Memorial. It is estimated that over 30,000 people attended the unveiling ceremony.

Designed by James Glen Sivewright Gibson (1861-1951), who was born in Arbroath and served his articles with a firm of architects in Dundee, before becoming a draughtsman with a firm of engineers. He moved to London where he worked with a number of practices, before starting his own practice in 1889. In the same year he was admitted, by examination, as an Associate of the Royal Institute of British Architects. In 1909 Gibson took his two senior assistants, Frank Skipwith and Walter Symington Athol Gordon, into partnership. Skipwith was sadly killed during the First World War and the partnership continued as Messrs Gibson and Gordon.

Sculpted by Charles Sargeant Jagger, whose biographical details can be found on page 64 in the Hoylake and West Kirby War Memorial.

Design Features:

The memorial consists of a semi-circular screen which encloses a sunken area: to the inside of this screen, slightly curved bronze plaques are fixed, which have the names of around 4,500 men from Portsmouth who died during the First World War. Those who served in the Army are to the north, those who served in the Navy are to the south, with the names of women who died in the centre. Within the semi-circular screen there are two round-arched openings, each of which has a wrought-iron gate. The northern arch leads to a passage which goes under the railway and into Victoria Park, while the southern arch leads to Guildhall Square. The screen ends, at both extremities, in a rusticated niche with flanking piers; within each of the niches there is a bronze painted urn above a stone seat. Above the niches are shields, flanked with oak and laurel branches with weapons bristling around them: these carvings are surrounded by acanthus leaves and topped by crowns.

In the centre of the semi-circle three stone steps lead to a substantial pier, that is decorated by relief carvings of the war on land and at sea, including marching soldiers and a naval gun crew in action, above which there is a Greek-key cornice. The pier is topped by a large sarcophagus.

The front of the memorial is partly enclosed by a low balustrade, which is no longer symmetrical, following alterations to the memorial in the 1970s. The entrance to the memorial is marked by two stone pedestals: the south plinth has a sculptured figure of a sailor firing a Lewis Gun; the north plinth has a figure of a soldier firing a Vickers machine gun. A stone tablet was attached to the north plinth in 2003 to remember more recent sacrifices.

The Story behind The Memorial:

Whilst plans for a city war memorial began soon after the end of the First World War, it was not until 1920 that an appeal was made for public contributions to the cost. There is a list in Portsmouth Central Library of the donors and how much they contributed.

The names on the memorial are those nominated by people of the city with the criteria for inclusion being "That the man was born in Portsmouth, or that he resided in Portsmouth when the war began, or that his home was in Portsmouth when the war began."

Whilst it was emphasised that "Not a single name should be omitted" the fact that around 6,000 men from Portsmouth died whereas there are approximately 4,500 names on the memorial suggests many omissions. Indeed the writer's great grandfather was resident in Portsmouth at the start of the First World War, although his death is recorded on the war memorial in Morecambe, Lancashire which is where his mother lived.

During the 1970s Guildhall Square was redeveloped, and both the size and shape of the memorial were changed. It was not until 2005 that a separate war memorial to commemorate those citizens of Portsmouth killed in the Second World War was unveiled.

The Inscription

In the architrave above the plaques there is the simple inscription; THEIR NAME LIVETH FOR EVERMORE. A plaque on the cenotaph reads: THIS MEMORIAL WAS ERECTED BY THE PEOPLE OF PORTSMOUTH IN PROUD AND LOVING MEMORY OF THOSE WHO IN THE GLORIOUS MORNING OF THEIR DAYS FOR ENGLAND'S SAKE LOST ALL BUT ENGLAND'S PRAISE. MAY LIGHT PERPETUAL SHINE UPON THEM. There are two further inscriptions on the memorial on the plinths that carry the statues of the machine gunners. On the plinth with the sailor the inscription reads: THIS WAR MEMORIAL WAS UNVEILED BY FIELD-MARSHALL HIS ROYAL HIGHNESS THE DUKE OF CONNAUGHT K.G. ON THE 19TH OCTOBER 1921 whilst on the plinth with the army machine gunner the inscription is: THIS MEMORIAL WAS ERECTED BY PUBLIC SUBSCRIPTION IN HONOUR OF PORTSMOUTH'S SONS WHO FELL IN THE GREAT WAR 1914-1918 COUNCILLOR JOHN TIMPSON K.S.T. J.P. MAYOR 1918-1921. The stone added to the north plinth in 2003 has the following inscription: TO HONOUR ALL THOSE WHO DIED SERVING THEIR COUNTRY IN TIMES OF PEACE OR CONFLICT "WE WILL REMEMBER". A low stone wall behind the cenotaph is inscribed with the words: IN MEMORY OF THOSE WHO LOST THEIR LIVES IN WORLD WAR II 1939-1945.

263

12. Portsmouth Naval War Memorial
Southsea Common, Clarence Esplanade, Portsmouth, PO5
Grade I

Unveiled on 15th October 1924 by The Duke of York, the future King George VI. Despite his poor health, the Duke of York had a lengthy connection with the Royal Navy, having attended the Royal Navy College, Osborne from 1909 and the Royal Naval College Dartmouth from 1911. The Duke of York was mentioned in despatches as a turret officer on board HMS Collingwood at the Battle of Jutland.

Designed by Sir Robert Lorimer.

Sculpted by Henry Poole.

Design Features:

The memorial is situated in a prominent position on Southsea Common overlooking the sea. It is a large and impressive memorial, consisting of a tall Portland stone obelisk topped with four ships prows, bronze figures to represent the four winds, and is surmounted by a copper sphere to represent the Earth. The inspiration for the memorial came from a naval "leading mark", a powerful naval symbol, as it is a guide to navigation for ships entering the safety of a port. The obelisk sits on a square base with corner projections, each of which has a lion couchant. Low down on each face of the obelisk is a naval badge of an anchor set within a laurel wreath, surmounted by a Royal Navy crown.

Between the lions there are large bronze plaques. The plaques on the faces that do not have an inscription show low relief impressions of naval actions during the First World War. Around the base of the column are bronze plaques with the names of 7,251 naval personnel killed in the First World War. The names are arranged alphabetically within the year of the death and their role in the Navy, these roles themselves also being listed alphabetically.

264

The names include personnel from Australia and South Africa, although other Empire and Commonwealth nations chose to make their own separate memorials.

The memorial was extensively enlarged following the Second World War to include quadrant walls and a sunken garden. The walls are mounted with bronze plaques including the names of the naval personnel lost in the Second World War. These later additions were designed by Sir Edward Maufe with sculptures by Charles Wheeler.

The Story behind The Memorial:

The Royal Navy played a crucially important role during the First World War, with some 50,000 men and women paying the ultimate sacrifice. As well as conventional naval warfare, the Royal Navy provided a division that fought as infantry on the Western Front. After the end of the war, the Imperial War Graves Commission was keen to find a suitable way to memorialise those of the Royal Navy who had no known grave, and their solution was three identical memorials at Plymouth, Portsmouth and Chatham, as these were the three principle manning ports.

The Inscription

The plaque on the south, seaward, face bears the following inscription: IN HONOUR OF THE NAVY AND TO THE ABIDING MEMORY OF THESE RANKS AND RATINGS OF THIS PORT WHO LAID DOWN THEIR LIVES IN THE DEFENCE OF THE EMPIRE AND HAVE NO OTHER GRAVE THAN THE SEA AND THEIR COMRADES OF AUSTRALIA SOUTH AFRICA NEWFOUNDLAND INDIA PAKISTAN CEYLON FIJI GOLD COAST HONG KONG KENYA MALAYA NIGERIA SIERRA LEONE AND BURMA WHOSE NAMES ARE HERE RECORDED.

265

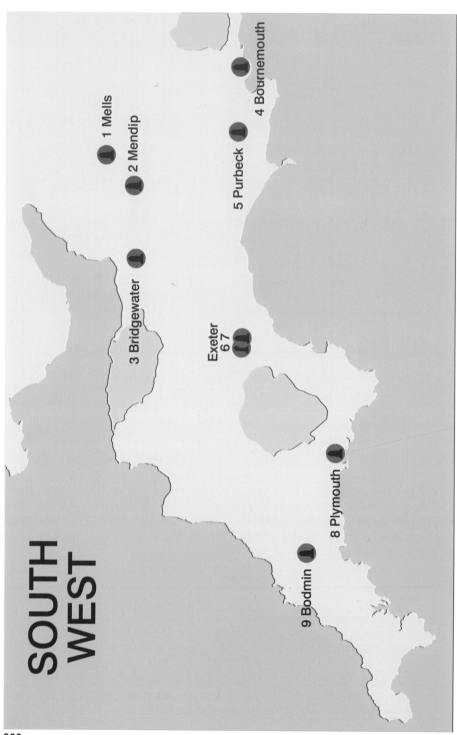

SOUTH WEST

1 Mells
2 Mendip
3 Bridgewater
4 Bournemouth
5 Purbeck
Exeter
6 7
8 Plymouth
9 Bodmin

CONTENTS

1. Mells War Memorial

Junction of Sellwood Street and Fairview, Mells, Somerset, BA11

Grade II*

Unveiled on 26th June 1921 by Brigadier General Arthur Asquith DSO**. H H Asquith was the Prime Minister at the outbreak of the First World War, and Arthur Asquith was his youngest son. H H Asquith's three sons had served with distinction in the Royal Naval Division during the First World War, during which Arthur was wounded four times and received the Distinguished Service Order and two bars along with the French Croix de Guerre. The last wound Arthur Asquith received resulted in him having a leg amputated and his retirement from the Army, after which he took up an appointment in the Controller of Trench Warfare Department of the Ministry of Munitions.

Designed by Sir Edwin Lutyens   **Sculpted by** Eric Gill

Design Features:

The memorial is a Tuscan column made from Purbeck marble with a standing St George killing a dragon on top of the column. The column itself is on top of a tall narrow pillar of Portland stone. Stretching beyond the memorial is a yew hedge.

The Story behind The Memorial:

The wealthy Horner family, who owned land throughout Somerset, has been associated with Mells for many centuries, although the supposed connection between the children's rhyme of Little Jack Horner and the Horner family is a late Victorian invention with no basis in fact. The Horner's son, Edward, was killed at the battle of Cambray in November 1917, and is among those noted on the memorial.

Sir John and Lady Francis Horner had contacts with many well-known members of the artistic community including Lutyens, who carried out various works to their home, Mells Manor. Lutyens was also a friend of the Asquiths, through his collaborations with Gertrude Jekyll on country houses and gardens. The Horner's daughter, Katherine, was married to Raymond Asquith the eldest son of H. H. Asquith, who was killed during the Battle of the Somme, and this tragedy led to Lutyens being commissioned to design both the village memorial and to collaborate with Alfred Mannings in the design of a memorial specifically dedicated to Raymond inside the parish church.

The Inscription

The pillar bears the thought provoking inscription – WE DIED IN A STRANGE LAND FACING THE DARK CLOUD OF WAR AND THIS STONE IS RAISED TO US IN THE HOME OF OUR DELIGHT MCMXIV & MCMXIX above this inscription is incised a simple cross. On either side of the pillar are Portland stone panels which carry the names of those from the village killed during the First World War. Walls of random stone extend from both sides of these panels and in front of these two walls are stone benches.

The memorial bears the names of twenty-one men from the village who died in the First World War. Fixed to the stone walls above the benches are circular stone panels which have the dates of the Second World War along with the names of the eight men who were killed during that conflict

2. Churchyard Cross

All Saints Church, East Pennard, Mendip, Somerset BA4

Grade II*

It is not recorded who unveiled this memorial other than that it became a memorial in 1919. There are no records available as to who first built the cross, or who carried out the additional carving.

Design Features:

A three stepped base is surmounted by a square plinth from which rises a tapering shaft topped with a lantern cross. An image of the crucifixion is on the east face of the plinth and the west face of the plinth is blank.

The Story behind The Memorial:

This cross dates from the 15th Century, as does All Saints Church, and the only conversion carried out to make it into a war memorial is the addition of an inscription to the eleven men from the parish who were killed in the First World War, with a later inscription to remember the two men from the parish killed in the Second World War.

The adjoining All Saints Church, which also dates from the 15th Century, is Grade I listed.

The Inscription

There is a short inscription on the left side of the 6 o'clock face: THIS CROSS WAS RESTORED IN MEMORY OF THE MEN OF THIS PARISH WHO FELL 1914-1919 whilst on the right side of the same face: THIS STONE COMMEMORATES THE MEN OF THIS PARISH WHO FELL 1939-1945.

We were unable to locate an image of the Churchyard Cross. Mells War Memorial (below) previous page

3. Bridgewater War Memorial
King Square, Bridgewater, Somerset, TA6
Grade II*

cc-by-sa/2.0 - Kings Square and War... by Ken Grainger - geograph.org.uk/p/924033

Unveiled by Rudolph Lambart, the 10th Earl of Cavan in 1924. Cavan had been a career soldier after leaving Oxford University until he retired from the army in 1913. He was recalled at the start of the First World War and held a number of senior appointments, ending the war as Commander-in-Chief of British Forces on the Italian Front. He held a number of other positions before being appointed Chief of the Imperial General Staff in 1922 from which post he retired in 1926.

Designed and Sculpted by John Angel (1881-1960) who was born in Newton Abbot, Devon. He was apprenticed to a wood-carver at the age of 14, and received formal tuition at Exeter School of Art, Lambeth School of Art, and later at the Royal Academy School, where George Frampton became his mentor. He was elected to the Royal Society of Sculptors in 1919. Angel undertook his most notable work in the United States of America with his American-born wife in 1925. He also designed the Exeter War Memorial, which is featured on page 274.

Design Features:

The memorial comprises a large granite plinth with bronze plaques and a large bronze statue of a woman. The plinth is on a tree stepped base, with shallow raised crosses bearing plaques with the names of the fallen. The main figure is that of a woman representing Civilisation in long robes with her arms outstretched. In her right hand the woman holds a hollow globe with small figures standing on it. Kneeling on each side of the central figure are angels with open wings, their hands resting on the open book of law on the woman's knee. On the back of the memorial are three bronze panel which depict work, the family and learning under which a skeleton and figures representing Strife, Bloodshed, Corruption and Despair writhing in torment.

The Inscription

The third step on the base of includes the inscription – IN HONOUR OF THE MEN OF BRIDGEWATER WHO GAVE THEIR LIVES IN THE GREAT WAR 1914 – 1918.
Additional plaques have been added to the memorial to record the names of those killed in the Second World War, the Korean War, the Falklands Conflict and the Afghan conflict.
The memorial is sometimes referred to as the Angel of Bridgewater.

4. Bournemouth War Memorial

Pleasure Gardens, Bourne Avenue, Bournemouth, Dorset, BH2

Grade II*

Unveiled on 8th November 1922 by Major General J E B Seely, 1st Baron Mottistone. His biographical details are featured on page 250 with The Hampshire War Memorial. The dedication was carried out by the Suffragan Bishop of Southampton.

Designed by Albert Edward Shervey, Bournemouth's Deputy Borough Architect.

Design Features:

The memorial is constructed from Portland stone, adorned with bronze plaques and wreaths, and takes the form of a cenotaph comprising a 'Temple of Memory' set on a four-stepped base in the centre of a square gravelled area enclosed by a stone balustrade.

On the north side there are steps up to the gravelled area which are guarded by two lions, one asleep and one roaring, carved by local stone mason W.A. Hoare. This family firm still exists in Bournemouth and specialises in memorial masonry. Each side of the temple is decorated with a bronze wreath and garland and its four corners are supported by Doric columns topped by classic urns. The steps and balustrade are included in the listing.

The Story behind The Memorial:

The building of this memorial was planned to be part of a scheme that would give Bournemouth an improved civic area. The site of the memorial is the Pleasure Gardens which had been originally laid out in the mid-nineteenth century.

The Inscription

The principal inscription is on a bronze plaque with raised letters to the north side of the temple and reads: TO THE GLORIOUS MEMORY OF THE MEN AND WOMEN OF THE COUNTY BOROUGH OF BOURNEMOUTH WHO MADE THE SUPREME SACRIFICE IN THE GREAT WAR 1914-1918.
After the Second World War an additional plaque was added which, again, has raised letters: IN HONOURED MEMORY OF THE MEN AND WOMEN OF THE COUNTY BOROUGH OF BOURNEMOUTH WHO GAVE THEIR LIVES IN THE 1939-1945 WAR.

5. Briantspuddle War Memorial

Briantspuddle, Purbeck, Dorset, DT2

Grade II*

Unveiled on 12th November 1918. Whilst certainly not the earliest memorial to the dead of the First World War, there is a poignancy to the fact that this memorial was unveiled on the day after the armistice was signed. The dedication was by the Bishop of Salisbury.

Designed and Sculpted by Eric Gill.

Design Features:

A slender, tapering, Portland stone shaft, 24ft 6ins (7.5m) tall, and topped with a small square cross that stands on a pedestal and a four-stepped base. On the north side of the shaft is a sculpted figure of Christ, with a downward pointing sword in his left hand, and his right hand raised to show stigmata. Christ stands on a ledge under a small canopy.

On the south side, lower than the figure of Christ, is a seated figure of the Madonna suckling Christ: this figure too stands on a ledge and is under a canopy which has a relief carving of the Lamb of God, and is supported by small Purbeck columns. The inscriptions and names are within panels created by a triple colonnade of Romanesque arches on each face.

The Story behind The Memorial:

This memorial was commissioned by Sir Ernest Debenham, 1st Baronet, who had bought an estate in the area in 1914 with a view to living there following his retirement from his retail business. Debenham sought to expand the village using local materials and building in the local style under guidance from the architect and artist MacDonald Gill. As early as April 1915, Debenham commissioned MacDonald Gill's older brother, Eric, to design a war memorial for the village. Gill had produced drawings by the summer of 1915 and the memorial, which was paid for by Debenham, was built between February 1917 and August 1918.

There are similarities in the style of this memorial to that in Trumpington, Cambridgeshire and Harting in West Sussex, which were also designed by Gill.

In 2012 War Memorials Trust gave a grant for the restoration of the memorial.

The Inscription

The main inscription starts on the north face and continues to the south face, and reads: IT IS SOOTH THAT SIN IS CAUSE OF ALL THIS PAIN RIP – there are the names of the fallen on this face as well – BUT ALL SHALL BE WELL AND ALL MANNER OF THINGS SHALL BE WELL – this is a quotation from a mystic, Julian of Norwich, and dates from the Fifteenth Century. On the east face the inscription reads: TO THOSE WHO FELL IN THE GREAT WAR 1914 1919 together with more names – given that the memorial was unveiled in November 1918 these dates must have been added at a later date. There are seven names from the First World War and six further names were later added to the south face under the dates 1939 1945.

Briantspuddle War Memorial (left) previous page

Exter City War Memorial (right, and its Inscription (below) next page

The Inscription

Around the top of the plinth is engraved: IN PROUD AND GRATEFUL MEMORY OF THE MEN AND WOMEN OF EXETER AND DEVON WHO GAVE THEIR LIVES IN THE GREAT WAR 1914-1919 THEIR NAME LIVETH FOR EVERMORE. A bronze plaque was added after the Second World War which has the following inscription: THIS TABLET IS DEDICATED TO THOSDE WHO FELL IN THE SECOND WORLD WAR 1939-1945.

273

6. Exeter City War Memorial

Northenhay Gardens, Exeter, Devon, EX4

Grade II*

Unveiled on 24th July 1924 by Admiral David Beatty, 1st Earl Beatty, whose biographical details are featured on page 214 with the Reigate and Redhill War Memorial. The dedication was carried out by Robert Trefusis, the Bishop of Crediton. At the end of the service a trumpeter on Athelstan's Tower sounded The Last Post.

Designed by the local Exeter firm, Bennett and Greenslade.

Sculpted by John Angel whose biographical details are featured on page 256 with the Bridgewater War Memorial.

Design Features:

This is a substantial memorial reaching almost 31ft (9m) tall, with a cross-shaped plinth, 20ft (6m) tall, and is made from Devon granite with bronze statues. The intersections of the four arms of the plinth have a chamfered finish, and are topped by an octagonal column. On top of the column is a bronze statue of Nike, the Greek goddess of victory, who is holding aloft a laurel sprig by way of gratitude to Heaven. At her feet is a dead dragon to represent the destruction of tyranny and wrong.

There are superbly detailed life-sized, seated, figures on the each of the arms of the plinth. The four figures are – a soldier resting, a sailor who is astride the hull of a ship, which bears the coat of arms of the City of Exeter as a figurehead, and the words "semper fidelis" (ever faithful); a prisoner of war, inspired by the work carried out with prisoners in Germany by Lady Owen and a group from Exeter; and on the fourth platform, a nurse of the Voluntary Aid Detachment (V.A.D.), who is holding two bandages whilst, at her feet, are a sheaf of corn and an artillery shell to represent the work done by women during the war.

There is a cavity in the memorial, which holds a casket with the names of the 970 people from Exeter who died during the First World War: these names are also contained in a book held in the city archives.

The whole memorial is enclosed by low, inner and outer walls with small dome capped corner pillars which have a footpath between them.

The Story behind The Memorial:

Two major war memorials, which are both listed, were built in Exeter at the end of the First World War following a lack of communication between the Exeter City War Memorial Committee and the Devon County War Memorial Committee. They both blamed each other for failing to work on a joint memorial.

The figures of the soldier, nurse and seaman were cast at the Morris Art Foundry, who were responsible for 'justice' above the Central Criminal Court at the Old Bailey in London, while Nike and the prisoner were cast at A B Burton's Thames Ditton Foundry. Casts of all five figures were exhibited at the Royal Academy in 1922.

The total cost of the memorial was in excess of £6,000 which was raised by a public subscription.

274

7. Devon County War Memorial & Processional Way

Cathedral Green, Exeter, Devon, EX1
Grade II*

Unveiled by The Prince of Wales, the future King Edward VIII on 16th May 1921, whose brief biographical details can be found on page 67 in The Response. Sir Edwin Lutyens was present for the unveiling as was Hugh Fortesque, 4th Earl Fortesque, who had chaired the County War Memorial Committee.

Designed by Sir Edwin Lutyens.

Design Features:

Three stone steps lead up to a rectangular stone plinth above which is a three tiered rectangular base which changes, by spurs, into a lozenge shaped tapered shaft topped by a champhered cross. The memorial is 30ft (9m) high and the cross was carved out of a single piece of granite. The arms of the cross, which are no wider than the

base, are moulded close to the top of the shaft. The Processional Way which is part of the listing was not added until the 1970s and does not refer to the First World War.

The Story behind The Memorial:

There had been a proposal in December 1918 by the Dean of Exeter that the county's war dead be commemorated by the building of a cloister at Exeter Cathedral, although it was quickly realised that this would be too costly. Other proposals included the construction of a new wing at the Royal Devon and Exeter Hospital, while the chairman of the National Federation of Discharged and Demobilised Sailors and Soldiers said that any memorial was a waste of money and that the money would be better spent caring for veterans.

In the end, two memorials were built in Exeter: one for the City – as described on the previous page – and this one for the County, because the Devon County War Memorial Committee - headed by Hugh Fortesque - and the Exeter City War Memorial Committee, chaired by Sir James Owen, both sought to design the main memorial for Devon, with the other committee simply contributing funds. Both committees blamed the other for the lack of communication, but the   result is that Exeter now has two very fine, although very different, Grade II* listed War Memorials.

The Inscription

The central tier of the base bears the inscription: THE COUNTY OF DEVON TO HER GLORIOUS DEAD 1914-1919 TE DEUM LAUDEMAUS (Praise be to God) 1939-1945.

8. Plymouth Naval War Memorial

The Promenade, Plymouth, PL1   Grade I

Unveiled: The memorial was unveiled on 29th July 1924 by Prince George. In 1915 Prince George went to naval college, firstly at Osborne and later at Dartmouth, following which he served on HMS Iron Duke and HMS Nelson, and he remained as an officer in the Royal Navy until 1929.

Designed by Sir Robert Lorimer

Sculpted by Henry Poole

Design Features:

The memorial is situated in a prominent position on Plymouth Hoe. It is a large and impressive memorial consisting of a tall Portland stone obelisk topped with four ships prows and bronze figures to represent the four winds. It is surmounted by a copper sphere to represent the Earth. The inspiration for the memorial came from a naval "leading mark", a symbol which acts as a guide to navigation for ships entering the safety of a port. The obelisk sits on a square base with corner projections each of which has a lion couchant. Low down on each face of the obelisk is a naval badge of an anchor set within a laurel wreath, surmounted by a Navy crown.

Between the lions there are large bronze plaques. The plaque on the south, seaward, facing side carries the inscription, whilst the plaques on the other faces show low relief impressions of naval actions during the First World War. Around the base of the column are bronze plaques with the names of 7,251 naval personnel killed in the First World War. The names are arranged alphabetically within the year of the death and their role in the Navy, these roles themselves also being listed alphabetically. The names include personnel from Australia and South Africa, although other Empire/Commonwealth nations chose to make their own separate memorials.

The Story behind The Memorial:

The Royal Navy played a crucially important role during the First World War with some 50,000 men and women paying the ultimate sacrifice. As well as conventional naval warfare, the Royal Navy provided a division that fought as infantry on the Western Front.

After the end of the war the Imperial War Graves Commission were keen to find a suitable war to memorialise those of the Royal Navy who had no known grave and their solution was three identical memorials at Plymouth, Portsmouth and Chatham, these being the three principle manning ports.

The Inscription

The plaque on the south, seaward, face bears the following inscription: IN HONOUR OF THE NAVY AND TO THE ABIDING MEMORY OF THESE RANKS AND RATINGS OF THIS PORT WHO LAID DOWN THEIR LIVES IN THE DEFENCE OF THE EMPIRE AND HAVE NO OTHER GRAVE THAN THE SEA AND THEIR COMRADES OF AUSTRALIA SOUTH AFRICA NEWFOUNDLAND INDIA PAKISTAN CEYLON FIJI GOLD COAST HONG KONG KENYA MALAYA NIGERIA SIERRA LEONE AND BURMA WHOSE NAMES ARE HERE RECORDED.

WAR

(Hedd WYN. Died 31st July 1917. Age 30)

Why must I live in this grim age
When, to a far horizon, God
Has ebbed away, and man, with rage,
Now wields the sceptre and the rod?

Man raised his sword, once God had gone
To stay his brother, and the roar,
Of battlefields now casts upon,
Our homes the shadow of the man.

The harps to which we sang are hung,
On willow boughs, and their refrain
Drowned by the anguish of the years
Whose blood is mingled with the rain

9. Duke of Cornwall's Light Infantry War Memorial

Castle Canyke Road, Bodmin, Cornwall, PL13

Grade II*

Unveiled on 17th July 1924 by The Prince of Wales, Colonel in Chief of the Duke of Cornwall's Light Infantry, the future King Edward VIII, whose biographical details can be found on page 67 in The Response.

The dedication was carried out by Bishop Taylor Smith, Chaplin General to the Forces. Also present were J.C. Williams, Lord Lieutenant of the Cornwall, C.C. Morley High Sheriff of Cornwall, Vice Admiral Sir R.F. Phillimore Commander-in-Chief Plymouth, and Bishop Henry Southwell, Bishop of Lewes.

Designed and Sculpted by Leonard Stanford Merrifield (1880-1943), who was born in Gloucestershire and initially trained as a stone carver. He went on to study at Cheltenham School of Art, the City and Guilds of London School of Art, Kennington and, in 1904, the Royal Academy Schools.

Merrifield worked with Goscombe John prior to establishing his own studio in London, where he worked on a number of war memorials as well as private and institutional commissions. Merrifield became a Fellow of the Royal Society of British Sculpture in 1926 and was involved in running that body for many years.

Design Features:

The memorial comprises a bronze statue of an infantryman in full fighting order with helmet, and with a small box respirator in its case on his chest. The figure carries his rifle slung, but with bayonet fixed, and holds a Mills bomb (pin removed) in his right hand. The figure stands legs apart in a balanced, ready position, as if preparing to throw the grenade and is sculpted to appear as if he is stood in mud. The depiction of the soldier with his gas mask ready for use and holding a hand-grenade makes it very unusual. The statue is signed L. S. MERRIFIELD. Sc. 1922. A. B. BURTON. FOUNDER.

The statue stands on an octagonal moulded plinth of Cornish granite with a six stepped base. The North West front face carries a bronze cast of the coat of arms of the Duke of Cornwall surrounded by a laurel wreath, with the motto ONE AND ALL.

The memorial is flanked to the south and east by two coped granite kerbs inlaid with laurel wreaths, one for each battalion, and the regimental badges. These additions to honour the dead of the regiment in the Second World War were built in 1950 and were unveiled in a ceremony on 13th August 1950 by General Sir D Watson and Canon G.W. Harmon.

The Story behind The Memorial:

The memorial was paid for by the regiment to commemorate the 4,282 men of the regiment killed in the First World War. The regiment served in a number of theatres throughout the war, and suffered particularly heavy losses during the Third Battle of Ypres (the Battle of Passchendaele), with one battalion reduced to a fighting strength of 70 men by the 6th November 1917.

The regiment approached the artist Stanhope Forbes (of the Newlyn School) to produce a memorial, and he recommended Leonard Stanford Merrifield as sculptor. An ex-soldier, William Harvey Triggs, who Merrifield had previously used as a model, posed for the sculptor. The statue on the memorial was sculpted in 1922, but the memorial itself was not built until 1924.

The Inscription

The front face is inscribed ERECTED BY THE DCLI TO THEIR GLORIOUS DEAD 255 OFFICERS 4027 OTHER RANKS 1914-1919. The other faces all carry a bronze laurel wreath surrounding the number of a battalion. Clockwise from the front face they are inscribed: I FRANCE & FLANDERS 1914 – 1917 ITALY 1917 – 1918 FRANCE & FLANDERS 1918 – 1919 IV INDIA 1914 – 1916 SOUTHERN ARABIA (ADEN) 1916-1917 EGYPT AND PALESTINE 1917 – 1919 VI FRANCE & FLANDERS 1915 – 1918 VIII FRANCE & FLANDERS 1915 MACEDONIA 1915 – 1919 X FRANCE & FLANDERS 1916 – 1919 V FRANCE & FLANDERS 1916 – 1919 II FRANCE AND FLANDERS 1914 – 1915 MACEDONIA 1915 – 1919.

The terminal piers of the walls are inscribed IN PROUD MEMORY OF THEIR COMRADES WHO GAVE THEIR LIVES 1939-45 AND ALL MEMBERS OF THE REGIMENT WHO WERE SERVING WITH OTHER CORPS 1939-45. The wreaths contain the number of each battalion, with the associated battle honours inscribed alongside.

Architects

The most prolific designers and their memorials
that are featured in the book

Sir Herbert Baker (1862-1946)

Baker was the fourth of nine children who was born and died in the same house in Cobham, Kent. His love for architecture grew from wandering around ruins of old buildings in his youth, sketching them and seeing how they were built. He was educated at Tonbridge School, and at the age of 17 was articled to his cousin to start his architectural training, which involved three years at the Architectural Association School and Royal Academy Schools. In 1891 he became an Associate of the Royal Institute of British Architects and finished top of his class. The following year Baker went to South Africa to visit his brother and received a commission from the great colonialist, Cecil Rhodes to remodel his house. Rhodes paid for Baker to study in Greece, Italy and Egypt, after which he returned to South Africa where he lived for 20 years and was involved in the design of many major public and private projects, including the Honoured Dead Memorial to commemorate the Siege of Kimberley during the Second Boer War.

In 1912 Baker went to India to work with Lutyens, where he designed the Secretariat Building and Parliament House in New Delhi amongst other public buildings. His output was prodigious, with commissions throughout Africa and the United Kingdom including South Africa House, India House and one of the grandstands at Lord's Cricket Ground. It was Baker who presented the Marylebone Cricket Club with their famous "Old Father Time" weather vane. Not all of Baker's work was universally admired; when he rebuilt the Bank of England in Threadneedle Street London he demolished most of Sir John Soane's original structure, in what was referred to by Nikolaus Pevsner in his book 'Buildings of England' as "the greatest architectural crime, in the City of London, of the twentieth century."

Following the end of the First World War, Baker was one of the three architects appointed by the Imperial War Graves Commission to design and advise on the designs of war cemeteries and war memorials. He designed a total of 113 war grave cemeteries in France and Belgium, including Tyne Cot Cemetery, the largest British war cemetery in the world, together with 24 war memorials in England.

Baker was knighted in 1924 and in 1927 he was elected to the Royal Academy and received the Royal Institute of British Architects gold medal. He died in 1946 and is buried in Westminster Abbey.

Blackmoor War Memorial Cloister, Cross and Fountain   County of Kent Memorial Cross

The Hampshire, Isle of Wight and Winchester War Memorial   Hatfield War Memorial

Harrow School War Memorial Building   Overbury and Conderton War Memorial Lych-Gate

The Queen's Own Royal West Kent Regiment Cenotaph

The War Cloister, Winchester College   The Royal Berkshire Regiment Cenotaph

The Town and County War Memorial; Northampton

Sir Reginald Theodore Blomfield (1856-1942)

Blomfield was one of the three architects appointed by the Imperial War Graves Commission to design and advise on the design of war cemeteries and war memorials, both in the UK and abroad. He was born at Bow vicarage in Devon, where his father was the Curate: the family moved to Kent where his father became a Bishop.. Blomfield studied at Highgate School, Haileybury School in Hertfordshire and at Exeter College Oxford, where he received a First in Classics. In autumn 1881, he became an articled pupil at the architectural practice of Sir Arthur Blomfield, his maternal uncle, and at the same time, enrolled in the Royal Academy Schools, where he won the junior prize in 1882 and the senior prize a year later. By 1884 he had completed his training and set up his own practice in London.

Blomfield was involved in setting up the Art Workers Guild and was the first honorary secretary, where he worked mainly on individual houses, although he did take on a number of church, local authority and commercial designs.

Blomfield is best known for the Menin Gate at Ypres in Belgium, and the Cross of Sacrifice, also known as the 'War Cross' or 'Blomfield Cross', which is installed in almost every cemetery with 40 or more Commonwealth War Grave Commission graves. Across the world over 1,500 Blomfield Crosses have been erected, its design has been copied in many more places, and is considered one of the greatest pieces of war art.

Although none of Blomfield's work is included in this book, his importance as a designer of war cemeteries merits his inclusion in this section.

Blomfield was made an Associate of the Royal Academy in 1905 and elected to the Academy in 1914. From 1912 to 1914 Blomfield was President of the RIBA and he was knighted in 1919.

Sir Giles Gilbert Scott (1880-1960)

Both Giles Gilbert Scott's father and grandfather were architects, so perhaps it is not surprising that this was his chosen career. His grandfather had designed the Albert Memorial and the Midland Grand Hotel at St Pancras Station, London.

Scott went to the Jesuit school, Beaumont College, in Windsor principally because his father admired the buildings, which housed its preparatory school. At the age of 19 he became an articled pupil at the offices of Temple Moore, who had studied with his father. Scott had a free hand at the office because Moore preferred to work at home, with the management of the office being left to an office manager. In 1901 a competition was announced for the design of Liverpool Cathedral, which was only the third Anglican cathedral to be built in England since the Reformation.

Temple Moore's practice submitted a design, as did Scott in his own name, and with the encouragement of Moore, Scott's design was accepted by the judges in 1903, despite his being only 22 years old, a Roman Catholic and having never built a building.

In 1910 Scott decided that he was not happy with his initial design for Liverpool Cathedral and persuaded the committee to let start again from scratch with the design. The subsequent design lost a lot of the Gothic detail and replaced the original two towers with one large central one. Some idea of the original design can be perceived from the Lady Chapel. which was completed and consecrated before the second design was implemented. The Bishop of Liverpool in 1910 was Bishop Francis James Chavasse whose son, Noel, would go on to be the most decorated British soldier in the First World War, and was the only man to be awarded the Victoria Cross twice during that war, the second award being posthumously.

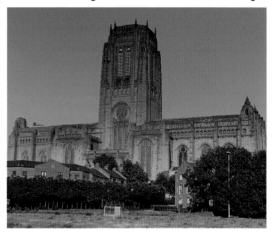

Scott's design for Liverpool Cathedral would ultimately see the creation of the largest church in the United Kingdom and the fifth largest in the world. Scott designed and built other churches whilst working on Liverpool Cathedral and his reputation increased. His frequent visits to Liverpool saw him staying at the Adelphi Hotel, where he met his wife who worked as a receptionist there; they had a long and happy marriage and had three sons.

During the First World War Scott served as a Major in the Royal Marines, where he was engaged in building and improving defences on the south coast of England.

If Liverpool Cathedral was important for its huge scale, one of Scott's other iconic designs was known for its more modest dimensions. The Kiosk no. 2 or K2 red telephone kiosk remains one of the best-known designs on the British street scene. There is a K2 phone box inside Liverpool Cathedral which puzzles some visitors! As if these two designs alone were not enough to ensure Scott's position as one of the most important British architects of the twentieth century, he also designed both Battersea Power Station and the current Waterloo Bridge in London. He was later also responsible for the reconstruction of the interior of the House of Commons after it was destroyed in an air raid in 1941.

Scott was responsible for the design and construction of 22 churches and 13 war memorials. He received many honours for his work – he was knighted in Liverpool by King George V in 1924 and a year later he received the Royal Institute of British Architect's (RIBA) Royal Gold Medal. RIBA appointed him as their President in 1933 which was their centenary year: in 1944 King George VI gave Scott the Order of Merit.

Scott is buried alongside his wife at Liverpool Cathedral, although their graves are outside the building, as burial inside was denied to him on account of his being a Roman Catholic.

Beaumont College

Clare College Memorial Court

Preston War Memorial

Wigan War Memorial

Sir Robert Stodart Lorimer (1864-1929)

Lorimer was the son of James Lorimer, Regius Professor of Public Law at Edinburgh University from 1862 to 1890. He was educated at Edinburgh Academy and Edinburgh University before beginning his architectural career. In 1885 he worked for Sir Robert Rowland Anderson in Edinburgh and later, in 1889, for George Frederick Bodley in London. In 1891 Lorimer returned to Edinburgh and started his own practice. Lorimer's work centred around the restoration of historic houses and castles as well as a number of both large and small new build houses. He was a committed exponent of the Arts and Crafts movement being elected to the Art Workers Guild in 1896.

In 1911 Lorimer designed a new chapel for the Knights of the Thistle in St Gile's Cathedral, Edinburgh. In 1919, he was commissioned to design the Scottish National War Memorial at Edinburgh Castle, which was opened by the Prince of Wales in 1927 and following which he was appointed KBE.

As well as the Scottish Nation War Memorial, Lorimer also designed the Dorian Memorial in Greece, the Chatham, Portsmouth and Plymouth Naval Memorials, with the last three being listed Grade I. In 1927 he designed St Andrews Garrison Church in Aldershot and Knightswood St Margaret's Parish Church in Glasgow, which was dedicated in 1932 after Lorimer's death.

Lorimer was President of the Incorporation of Architects in Scotland and a fellow of the North British Academy of Arts, he was knighted in 1911.

Lorimer died in 1929 following an operation for appendicitis.

Chatham Naval War Memorial

Plymouth Naval War Memorial

Portsmouth Naval War Memorial

Cumberland and Westmorland

Sir Edwin Landseer Lutyens (1869-1944)

It is surprising that, while most people in the country are familiar with the Cenotaph in Whitehall, very few will be aware of the name of its architect, Sir Edwin Lutyens, OM (1869-1944). Even those who are aware of him will know him primarily through the exquisite Arts and Crafts houses that he designed, often in collaboration with the garden designer Gertrude Jekyll, rather than through his work in connection with the First World War. And yet, more than any other architect, Lutyens was hugely influential in the way that we commemorate those who have died in conflict.

His attributes were recognised by Sir Fabian Ware, the Director General of the Imperial War Graves Commission and, in 1917, he was part of a working party that went out to the Western Front to advise Ware on the design of the war cemeteries. This led to him becoming one of the Commission's Principal Architects and being responsible for the design of 130 cemeteries on the Western Front as well as the brooding Memorial to the Missing of the Somme at Thiepval, the largest Commonwealth war memorial in the world, as well as memorials for the Commission in Sierra Leone and Zambia.

'Arts & Crafts'

However, it was throughout the villages, towns and cities of England that Lutyens had a particular role to play and he designed 52 war memorials for a rich variety of clients ranging from large cities to small villages as well as regiments, companies and public schools.

It was inevitable that many of his commissions would arise from people for whom he had built houses or were part of his social network however, the publicity surrounding the Cenotaph meant that Lutyens was seen as a natural choice and a safe pair of hands for the various war memorials committees that arose, many of whom would have had no experience of commissioning public work.

Not surprisingly, some of his clients wanted cenotaphs, either replicating the Whitehall original or with variations and, for some of the memorials he was also able to incorporate the painted stone flags that he had wanted to use in Whitehall because he felt that, incredibly though it may seem, the silk flags that the Government wanted would not be replaced when they became worn.

Some memorials also incorporated the Stone of Remembrance that Lutyens had designed for the war cemeteries and inscribed with the words chosen by Kipling – The Name Liveth For Evermore.

However, the memorials are only part of the overall picture and, equally important, are the stories behind their construction, many of which were straightforward but others which involved heated debates and arguments about locations and the form that the memorial should take.

New Delhi, India

In general the memorials have fared well over the years since they were built. Some have been moved, one is in storage but only two have been destroyed – one in a fire and one when a building in which the marble memorial lined the entrance lobby of a building that was demolished. Where severe damage has occurred – a German bomb, a car, lightning and a ram raid by thieves who wanted a bronze St George from atop one of the memorials – it has been repaired on each occasion.

The importance of Lutyens's memorials as a collection of national significance was recognised by Historic England in 2016 when, at the conclusion of a research project to look at the Listing of the memorials, they declared it to be a "legacy like that of Wren's churches or Nash's Regency terraces".

British Thomson-Houston Co Ltd War Memorial   Busbridge War Memorial

Devon County War Memorial   Holy Island War Memorial

Manchester War Memorial   Spalding War Memorial

Midland Railway War Memorial   North Eastern Railway War Memorial

Norwich Memorial and War Memorial Gdn Terrace   Rochdale Cenotaph

Southampton Cenotaph   Southend-on-Sea War Memorial

The Cenotaph, Whitehall, London   The Arch of Remembrance; Leicester

Civil Service Rifles War Memorial   York City War Memorial

The Mercantile Marine First World War Memorial   Mells War Memorial

War Memorial to the Lancashire Fusiliers; Bury   Royal Naval War Memorial

Sculptors
The most prolific sculptors and their memorials
that are featured in the book

Henry Charles Fehr (1867-1940)

Fehr was born in London to a family of Swiss origin, with one of his ancestors having been a former President of Switzerland. He studied at the City of London School and, from 1885, at the Royal Academy Schools, where he won medals and a scholarship, and first exhibited at the Royal Academy in 1887. From 1904 Fehr was one of the original members of the Royal British Society of Sculptors and was later elected as a Fellow. Working in both bas-relief and full sculpture Fehr completed a number of major public and commercial works principally in London.

Burton on Trent War Memorial   Colchester War Memorial   Keighley War Memorial

Eric Gill (1882-1940)

Eric Gill was one of twelve children born in Brighton to a minister of a small Protestant sect. The family moved to Chichester in 1897 and Gill was educated at Chichester Technical Art School, after which he began to train as an architect. He gave up architecture in 1903 and became a sculptor, typeface designer, stonecutter and printmaker; he was a member of the Arts and Crafts movement. Gill held strong Catholic views which were somewhat at odds with his erotic art work and his personal behaviour. His work can be found on Transport for London's offices in Broadway, Broadcasting House, the Midland Hotel in Morecambe and a number of listed war memorials. Gill also designed the first George VI definitive stamp series.

In the late 1930s Gill was made a Royal Designer for Industry by the Royal Society of Arts, which was the highest British award for designers. In 1938 he was a founder-member of the Faculty of Royal Designers for Industry.

Gill was a member of the Fabian Society for a time as a young man, although later in his life he had socialist leanings and was a pacifist. He died of lung cancer in 1940.

Bisham War Memorial   Briantspuddle War Memorial   Great Dunmow War Memorial

Harting War Memorial   Mells War Memorial   Stanway War Memorial

Trumpington War Memorial

Richard Reginald Goulden (1876-1932)

Goulden was educated at Dover College and at Dover School of Art, where he won a scholarship to the Royal College of Art in London. He initially studied architecture before changing to studying sculpture, winning prizes for both disciplines, together with a travelling scholarship for sculpture. After producing two panels for the Carnegie Trustees in Dunfermline, Goulden was invited to be their art advisor and he lived in Dunfermline for two years, during which time he designed the Andrew Carnegie statue in 1914 and the Carnegie Hero medal.

Goulden served with the Royal Engineers during the First World War, was mentioned in despatches, and injured to the extent that he was returned to England. After he recovered from his injuries, he became adjutant to the Australian Engineers in Brightlingsea, Essex, before moving to London to join the staff of the Chief Engineer of the Royal Engineers.

Goulden exhibited sixteen times at the Summer Exhibition of the Royal Academy between 1903 and 1932, was a member of the Royal Society of British Sculptors from 1906 to 1932, and a member of their council from 1919 to 1926. Goulden was a member of the prestigious Art Workers Guild from 1912 to 1932 and a committee member from 1928 to 1930.

Goulden designed eleven war memorials., and the following are featured in the book.

Crompton War Memorial   *Kingston-upon-Thames War Memorial*

Reigate & Redhill War Memorial   *The People of Dover War Memorial*

St Michael, Cornhill

Sir William Goscombe John (1860-1952)

John was born in Cardiff where his father, Thomas, was a wood carver and William assisted him before attending Cardiff School of Art. As a young man he adopted the first name, Goscombe, taken from a village in Gloucestershire, near where his mother was born. In 1882 he moved to London and studied, initially at the City and Guilds of London Art School, and later at the Academy schools, where he won the gold medal and travelling fellowship in 1887. John was made a Royal Academician in 1909 and was knighted in 1911. He designed and sculpted eighteen war memorials, of which three are featured in this book, as well as other memorials and sculptures for the facades of buildings.

Heroes of the Marine Engine Room, Liverpool   *Port Sunlight War Memorial*

The Response; Newcastle upon Tyne

Gilbert Ledward (1888-1960)

The third of four children, Ledward was born in Chelsea, London, the son of sculptor Richard Arthur Ledward. In 1905 he attended the Royal College of Art before moving to the Royal Academy Schools in 1910. In 1913 he won the British Prix de Rome scholarship for sculpture and the Royal Academy's travelling award and medal. In 1914 he was commissioned into the Royal Garrison Artillery, and in April 1918 he was seconded to the Ministry of Information as a war artist. In this role he produced a number of reliefs for the Imperial War Museum. Following the First World War, Ledward was in demand as a designer of war memorials, including the Guards Division and the Household Division, as well as two lions for the Memorial of the Missing at Ploegsteert.

From 1927 to 1929 Ledward was professor of sculpture at the Royal College of Art, and in 1934 he was elected a Royal Academician, having been an associate since 1932. He was President of the Royal Society of British Sculptors from 1954 to 1956, and awarded an OBE in 1956, the same year as he became a trustee of the Royal Academy.

Blackpool War Memorial   *Harrogate War Memorial*

Stockport War Memorial Art Gallery   *The Guards Memorial, London*

Henry Poole (1873-1928)

Henry Poole was born in Westminster, the son of Samuel Poole, who was also a sculptor. He studied at the South London Technical School of Art and then at the Royal Academy Schools from 1892 to 1897. Poole was a pupil of Henry Bates and George Frederick Watts and worked for E. A. Rickards. In 1921 he was appointed Professor of Sculpture at the Royal Academy Schools, a post which he held until his death.

Poole worked on many public buildings and carried out private commissions, including the lions for the Bund entrance of the HSBC offices in Shanghai. He provided the sculptures for the Portsmouth, Plymouth and Chatham Naval Memorials, all of which are listed Grade I, as well as the statue of Albert Ball VC in the grounds of Nottingham Castle.

Chatham Naval War Memorial   *Plymouth Naval War Memorial*

Portsmouth Naval War Memorial   *Statue of Albert Ball; Nottingham*

Louis Frederick Roslyn (1878-1940)

Louis Roslyn was born Louis Roselieb in Lambeth London, the son of a German sculptor. He studied at both the Westminster City & Guilds College and the Royal Academy. Roslyn worked at the Standard Plating works in Rosebury Avenue, London from 1906 to 1916, where his job title was 'sculptor and metallurgist'. In 1915 he enlisted in the Royal Flying Corps under his birth name of Roselieb. At the time of his enlistment he was described as "fit for service anywhere but not combative service", and there is an unexplained note on his record from Lord Derby, that Roslyn was not to be called up before 1st June 1917.

It is a matter of some debate as to when Roslyn changed his name from Roselieb, because his statue of Edward VII in 1911 was signed Roselieb, whereas in 1914 his work on Imperial Buildings was signed Roslyn. Although he enlisted under the name Roselieb in 1915, when he was discharged from the Royal Flying Corps in 1919 it was under the name Roslyn.

Following the First World War Roslyn designed twenty-six war memorials in the United Kingdom and one in Trinidad, West Indies. He became a member of Royal Society of British Sculptors in 1914 and was made a Fellow in 1923.

Darwen War Memorial   *Oswaldtwistle War Memorial*   *Rawtenstall Cenotaph*

Albert Toft (1862-1949)

Toft was born in Handsworth, Birmingham and his father was a modeller at Wedgwood Pottery, which is where Albert also started his career. He studied at art schools in Hanley and Newcastle upon Tyne and, in 1881 won a scholarship to study sculpture at the South Kensington Schools under Professor Edouard Lanteri. Whilst there, Toft won silver medals in his second and third years. From 1885 he exhibited at the Royal Academy, and in 1900 he received a bronze medal at the Universal Exhibition in Paris. Following the First World War, Toft provided sculptures for 15 war memorials; he was elected to the Art Workers Guild in 1891, and in 1938 he was elected a Fellow of the Royal Society of British Sculptors.

Hall of Memory, Birmingham   *Oldham War Memorial*   *Royal Fusiliers War Memorial*

George Herbert Tyson Smith (1883-1972)

George Herbert Tyson Smith was born in Liverpool, the son of an engraver and lithographic printer. He attended the Liverpool College of Art and was taught by Augustus John at the "Art Sheds". Tyson Smith was heavily influenced by the art of ancient Egypt and Greece, and after serving with the Royal Flying Corps during the First World War, he established a studio in Liverpool's Bluecoat Studios.

Tyson-Smith's output was prodigious, working on 27 war memorials and 16 other major projects, predominately in the Liverpool and Merseyside area.

He was the brother-in-law of the sculptor Edward Carter Preston, who designed the memorial plaque or "Dead Man's Penny" (rght), which was presented after the First World War to the next-of-kin of service personnel killed in the war.

Birkenhead War Memorial   Liverpool Cenotaph   Accrington War Memorial

Southport War Memorial Obelisk, Colonnades, Pools of Remembrance and Memorial Gardens

Casting bronze figures and bas-reliefs

Many of the memorials in this book include one or more figures, some of them extremely detailed. The bronze figures are very impressive, but the process which takes them from the sculptor's sketch pad to final completion is both long and complicated, requiring considerable skill on the part of both the sculptor and the founder.

Bronze itself is a mixture of copper and tin in various combinations although, for the sake of round figures, 90% copper to 10% tin is a common mixture. The large copper component explains why when bronze is exposed to the weather a blue coloured deposit can be seen leaching into surrounding stonework.

The figure or other detail on a war memorial will have started life as a sketch or series of sketches by the sculptor from life. In the case of the Guards Memorial, see page 184, and the image below, the models for the figures are guardsmen from the five Foot Guards Regiments whilst the figures on the West Derby memorial were drawn and subsequently sculpted using the brother and the widow of the officer portrayed as models.

The bronzes on the memorials in this book will all have been made using the lost-wax casting technique, which starts with the sculptor making a small study model of their work. In many cases these models would have been used in the event of a competition to find a sculptor or for approval by a war memorial committee.

Once everyone concerned is happy with the basic design and composition, a larger plaster or clay model is then made using wood, wire and even cardboard or paper as a frame. This model allows the sculptor to perfect the fine details and, once these are added, a mould is made from plaster or rubber. A wax model with a solid plaster core held in place by  copper pins, assuming that the figure is going to hollow, is then made from this mould and one or more wax sprues are added, both to help the molten metal to all parts of the mould and to allow the escape of gasses.

The wax model is then surrounded by a further mould, or shell of clay or ceramics which is heated in a kiln until all the wax runs out, and to ensure that there is no moisture of any sort inside the mould. The shell will be inverted for this part of the process. Whilst the shell is still hot the bronze, heated to 1,200 degrees centigrade, is then added slowly from the base. Bronze has a property which means that just before it sets it expands slightly, which means that it fills even fine details of the mould and them when it cools, it shrinks again which means that the removal of the mould or shell is facilitated. Once the metal has cooled, the pins and sprues are removed as is the plaster core, to reduce the possibility of corrosion from within.

The majority of the sculptures on the memorials featured in this book would have been cast in one, although the more complex groups would have been made by casting the figures separately and welding them together. Once the surface of the piece has been polished, a corrosive material is added to give the surface a patina, which will allow black paint to be applied which will inhibit the formation of Verdigris on the metal.

Portland Stone

Many war memorials are made from Portland stone, perhaps most notably The Cenotaph in Whitehall, London. Portland stone is, essentially, a white-grey limestone and is quarried specifically on the Isle of Portland, Dorset.

It was the Romans who first quarried stone on Portland, as early as the 14th century it was being carried, by ship, to London. By the 17th century, quarrying was sufficient large scale for Inigo Jones' Banqueting House and Christopher Wren's St Paul's Cathedral (right) to be built from the stone. Transport of Portland stone was made dramatically easier when the Isle of Portland was connected to the mainland by railway in 1865. The stone for the various war memorials in this book may have come from any of a number of quarries that had been active producers of stone since the middle of the 19th century.

The stone was extracted by a combination of blasting and a method called 'plug and feather'. Blasting was, and indeed still is, done using gunpowder which produces a "heave", which dislodges the rock rather than fragmenting it. The system of 'plug and feather' or 'plugs and wedges', involves drilling a line of holes, into which two metal plugs or feathers are inserted. These pieces are wider at the bottom than the top and both are tapered and curved at the top. A tapered plug is then inserted between the feathers and these are tapped in turn until a crack appears in the stone. Variations on this method of stone cutting have been used since ancient Egyptian times.

The iconic Imperial (later Commonwealth) War Graves Commission grave stones in the many First World War cemeteries were made from Portland stone, as were those of the Second World War and subsequent conflicts.

Acknowledgements

I should like to thank Helen for her patience in listening to all the stories my research revealed, Buster the Spaniel who sat with me faithfully as I typed every word, and Dr. Mike Benbough-Jackson at Liverpool John Moores University for his inspiration during my undergraduate degree.

The information about Lady Denman in the Women in the First World War piece was kindly supplied by the WI's archivist and historian Anne Stamper.

Thanks to Anna Wilson, Senior Development Officer (War Memorials) for the Civic Voice piece, and to Tim Skelton who contributed Lutyens' biographical details.

Many photographs of the memorial were taken by, and remain the property of the editorial team.

With other photgraphs that are not the copyright of Elgar Estates Publishing, these are predominantly used under the Creative Commons License.

We are pleased to attribute the following photgraphs:

(Originators and page numbers)

Adrian S Pye- 149; Alexander P Kapp- 26, 29; Barrie Tobias- 81; Barry Shimmon- 259; calflier001- 108; Chris Downer- 271; David Dixon – 40, 53, 76, 94, 164; Ethan Doyle White – 225; Historic England - 98, 156; HJ Mitchell – 133; Ian Capper- 215; Ivan Hall- 273; John Yeadon – 78; Jonathan Billinger- 113; Kevin Gordon- 232 (bottom); Michael Westley – 91; N. Chadwick- 196; Pam Fray – 230; Paul Gillett- 263; Peter Facey- 264; Peter Trimming- 265; Philip Halling – 114,115, 208; Richard Croft – 125, 133; Rod Allday- 277; Rose and Trev Clough- 229; Robin Sones – 84; Stephen Craven – 84; Tim Skelton– 166, 217, 243; Tom Oates – 269; Tristan Forward- 232 (top); William Metcalfe - 163; The Imperial War Museum London - Front Cover.

If any photographs have not been attributed, the publishers would be glad to make good in future, please email us at the address below

Special thanks to Mike Short, who has now worked with the Editor on two books and still retained his enthusiasm, energy and good humour!

Comments on the guide's content, and any feedback are more than welcome. Don't hesitate to contact us at info@commemorativeplaques.co.uk